A PHILOSOPHY OF CHRISTIAN MATERIALISM

INTENSITIES: CONTEMPORARY CONTINENTAL PHILOSOPHY OF RELIGION

Series Editors:
Patrice Haynes and Steven Shakespeare,
both at Liverpool Hope University, UK

This series sits at the forefront of contemporary developments in Continental philosophy of religion, engaging particularly with radical reinterpretations and applications of the Continental canon from Kant to Derrida and beyond but also with significant departures from that tradition. A key area of focus is the emergence of new realist and materialist schools of thought whose potential contribution to philosophy of religion is at an early stage. Rooted in a vibrant tradition of thinking about religion, whilst positioning itself at the cutting edge of emerging agendas, this series has a clear focus on Continental and post-Continental philosophy of religion and complements Ashgate's British Society for Philosophy of Religion series with its more analytic approach.

Other titles in the series:

Praying to a French God
The Theology of Jean-Yves Lacoste
Kenneth Jason Wardley

Heidegger on Death
A Critical Theological Essay
George Pattison

Intensities
Philosophy, Religion and the Affirmation of Life
Edited by Katharine Sarah Moody and Steven Shakespeare

Re-visioning Gender in Philosophy of Religion
Reason, Love and Epistemic Locatedness
Pamela Sue Anderson

A Philosophy of
Christian Materialism

Entangled Fidelities and the Public Good

CHRISTOPHER BAKER

William Temple Foundation and University of Chester, UK

THOMAS A. JAMES

Covenant Presbyterian Church, Southfield, MI, USA

JOHN READER

Ironstone Benefice, Diocese of Oxford and William Temple Foundation, UK

ASHGATE

Published by
Ashgate Publishing Limited
Wey Court East
Union Road
Farnham
Surrey, GU9 7PT
England

Ashgate Publishing Company
110 Cherry Street
Suite 3-1
Burlington, VT 05401-3818
USA

www.ashgate.com

British Library Cataloguing in Publication Data
A catalogue record for this book is available from the British Library.

The Library of Congress has cataloged the printed edition as follows:
Baker, Christopher Richard, 1961-
 A philosophy of Christian materialism : entangled fidelities and the public good / by Christopher Baker, Thomas A. James, John Reader.
   pages cm. -- (Intensities : contemporary continental philosophy of religion)
 Includes bibliographical references and index.
  ISBN 978-1-4724-2732-8 (hardcover) -- ISBN 978-1-4724-2733-5 (ebook) -- ISBN 978-1-4724-2737-3 (epub) 1. Wealth--Religious aspects--Christianity. 2. Materialism--Religious aspects--Christianity. I. Title.
 BR115.W4B34 2015
 261.8--dc23

2014039114

ISBN 9781472427328 (hbk)
ISBN 9781472427335 (ebk – PDF)
ISBN 9781472427373 (ebk – ePUB)

Printed in the United Kingdom by Henry Ling Limited, at the Dorset Press, Dorchester, DT1 1HD

Contents

About the Authors

Revd Dr John Reader has been both a parish priest and theological author and educator over the past 30 years. Recent books include: *Blurred Encounters*; *Reconstructing Practical Theology*; *Entering the New Theological Space* co-edited with Christopher R. Baker; *Christianity and the New Social Order* with John Atherton and Chris Baker; *Theological Reflection for Human Flourishing* written with Helen Cameron, Victoria Slater and with Chris Rowland; *Heterotopia* written with Caroline Baillie and Jens Kabo.

Thomas A. James is pastor of Covenant Presbyterian Church in Southfield, Michigan. He holds a PhD from Union Presbyterian Seminary, and is author of *In Face of Reality: The Constructive Theology of Gordon D. Kaufman*, and several articles in *Political Theology*, *Zygon*, *The American Journal of Theology and Philosophy*, and *The Bulletin of the North American Paul Tillich Society*. He served as Assistant Professor of Theology at Union Presbyterian Seminary from 2008 through 2012.

Professor Chris Baker is William Temple Professor of Religion and Public Life at the University of Chester and Director of Research for the William Temple Foundation. He has written and co-edited eight books and 30 book chapters and journal articles exploring the relationship between religion and urbanisation, the role of religion in public policy and social welfare and the role of religion in civil society and the reshaping of church within the urban environment. Publications include: *The Hybrid Church in the City*, *Postsecular Cities* edited with Justin Beaumont, and *Christianity and the New Social Order* written with John Atherton and John Reader.

Acknowledgements

The authors would like to acknowledge the following sources of inspiration and development in the completion of this volume. First, we would like to acknowledge the role the Arts and Humanities Research Council (AHRC) who funded a research network proposal entitled *Philosophy and Religious Practices*. The network ran for two years (2012–14) and involved the direct contribution of both Professor Chris Baker (as co-investigator) and Revd Dr John Reader as a major contributor and advisory group member. The aim of the network was to strengthen the ties between philosophers of religion, other researchers on religion (such as practical theologians) and stakeholders in religious communities. It consisted of a four-way collaboration between the Department of Philosophy at the University of Liverpool, the Department of Theology and Religious Studies at the University of Chester, the Department of Philosophy, Theology and Religious Studies at Liverpool Hope University and faith communities in the North-West. The network itself emerged and was funded as a direct result of an innovative conference held at the University of Chester in 2011 which brought together, for the first time, practical and public theologians and philosophers of religion to discuss the topic of 'Speculative Philosophies and Religious Practices – New Directions in the Philosophy of Religion and Postsecular Practical Theology'. Out of that discussion a special edition of the journal *Political Theology* emerged on the theme of Speculative Philosophies and Religious Practices (2012). The network held four conferences, including a final international conference on the theme of Philosophy, Religion and Public Policy held in April 2014. A dialectical process of engagement between philosophies of religion, practices of religion and empirical research on religion and the impact of this renewed interest and engagement with philosophical and religious ideas on public policy and public life has been modelled by the Chester conference and subsequent AHRC network. This has profoundly influenced the structure, methodology and content of this volume, especially where the volume explores the engagement between environmentalism and philosophical and theological materialism.

Second, the authors wish to thank Professor Dawn DeVries of Union Presbyterian Seminary in Richmond, Virginia, USA, and Professor Hollis Phelps of The University of Mount Olive in North Carolina, USA, for their incisive comments on the theological chapters of this volume. Any remaining inadequacies in what is written are of course our responsibility alone. Finally, our thanks to Russell Reader from Lancaster who prepared the final draft text using IT skills beyond the capacity of the individual authors.

Introduction

A Philosophy of Christian Materialism – Entangled Fidelities and the Public Good

The impetus for this book emerged from a groundbreaking conference held at the University of Chester in June 2011 which brought together, for the first time, practical and public theologians and philosophers of religion to discuss the topic of 'Speculative Philosophies and Religious Practices – New Directions in the Philosophy of Religion and Postsecular Practical Theology'. Out of that discussion a special edition of the journal *Political Theology* emerged on the theme of Speculative Philosophies and Religious Practices.[1] It contained a number of papers exploring the interface between key developments in continental philosophy concerning the re-emergence of the Real as an ontological and material category, the de-privatisation of religion in the public sphere and the implications of these shifts for philosophy of religion and practical and public theology. Philosophy of religion was characterised in this collection as in the process of re-establishing its credentials in the face of an assertive post-liberal Christian theology which has claimed, in close collaboration with postmodern critiques of philosophical idealism and anti-realism, to restore theology as the Queen of Sciences. There was also a strong feeling expressed at the conference, that philosophy of religion had, in its current more analytical forms, disconnected itself from the material practices of religion and thus from engagement with the non-academic public sphere.

It is in addressing the conundrum presented by this conference that we anticipate this volume has an important contribution to make to the excellent *Intensities* series, commissioned to explore the recent 'realist' and materialist turns within modern continental philosophy, and their implications for philosophy of religion. In this volume, we attempt the ambitious task of constructing a philosophy of Christian materialism fit for purpose for the twenty-first century and that engages with its existential and structural complexities. In doing this we

[1]   Chris Baker, John Reader and Daniel Whistler, 'Speculative Philosophies and Religious Practices – New Directions in the Philosophy of Religion and Post-secular Practical Theology', *Political Theology* 13.2 (2012): 141–55.

hope to make an important contribution to philosophy of religion and the way it views religious practice and engagement in the actual world. However, we are confident that in addressing this primary task, we also enrich the disciplines of practical and public theology with vitalising conceptual frameworks emerging from the re-engagement of philosophy with the Real. Integral to this process is the reassembling of Christian theology and the institutional church in new and hyper-connective ways with the public sphere in which it is currently engaged. This deeper connection to the complex materiality of the actual world we are proposing to call an ethics and ontology of entangled fidelities; aka a new relational Christian realism.

We undertake the explication of this new philosophy of Christian materialism by way of a multi-layered hermeneutical process. This involves the history of theological and philosophical ideas; reflections on human and non-human material situatedness and their multiple entanglements; critical analysis of contemporary ideas and themes within continental philosophy; a synthetic reformulation of key theological ideas and motifs into a coherent account of relational Christian realism; and a strategic representation of these elements in the service of a transformative progressive agenda for public and political change.

The volume lays the foundation for this enterprise by identifying the current state of play between philosophy of religion and theology. The shift towards speculative realism in modern continental philosophy, exemplified by such writers as Messailloux, Brassier, Harman and Hamilton Grant, following in the tradition of the likes of Deleuze, Badiou and Latour has, to some extent, wrong-footed and surprised both philosophy of religion and theology. The rejection of a privileged and idealised human subject-object correlation lies at the heart of these shifts. What is being reclaimed is a proper respect for the mystery of the Other (as one object of singular intensity among a growing multitude of other objects) and the deep interconnectedness of all material objects, not within a transcendent/immanent dualism, but within a single immanent plane. The challenge for both philosophy of religion and theology is to rediscover their own capacity for interconnectedness in an increasingly interdependent but atomised public space, where responses and solutions to deeply complex and constantly novel assemblages of events require a deep faithfulness to material processes and an eschewing of simplistic and/or knee-jerk responses.

The present dominance of the post-liberal and Radical Orthodoxy tradition, with its onto-theological stance towards the material world, is sophisticated and eloquent in its critique of the relativism of postmodernity, but tends to be as hubristic, arbitrary and internalised in its neo-Christendom worldview as the secularism it seeks to annul. In this view, the Church also operates as its own autonomous and alternative polity. The transliteration of this detached view of the Church into the public space tends to produce an either over-optimistic and/or nostalgic view of religion as the one-stop shop for all the ills of the world. Such a religious perspective is likely to be ill-equipped to deal with the current complexities and superdiversity that not only characterises the public space, but increasingly characterises individual postmodern sensibilities and a desire not to be essentialised or pigeon-holed.[2]

A better connected philosophical approach we propose is to return (but critically return) to the realist tradition in Christian theology, which was the mainstream theological position of most Protestant churches in the 1940s, '50s and '60s. Thus the likes of Dietrich Bonhoeffer, the Niebuhr brothers, Paul Tillich, William Temple and, from a Catholic tradition, Karl Rahner have much to contribute to the new turn towards speculative realism within philosophy. We outline these points of similarity: that Christian realism engages non-theological sources of insight; and therefore any claims about God's relation to the world are claims about 'empirical states of affairs that can be measured by broad features of human experience';[3] and that faith is a practice tied up with other practices that are characterised as secular. But the work of these authors is only a launching pad for a radically reformulated version of Christian realism. We are not advocating a simplistic and nostalgic return to a previous golden age. We are clear that these guides and mentors can only take us so far into the new terrain and we firmly identify the dead ends that need to be circumnavigated. For example, traditional Christian realism is still too narrowly correlational (that is, still caught up in a radical distinction between human 'subjects' and non-human 'objects') and thus over-anthropocentric. Niebuhr's conceptual relational framework in terms of I–Thou encounters fails to account for 'the force of non-human agents that the revisionary thrust of realism demands'.[4]

The next chapter maps those current theoretical debates and shifts that we feel are most relevant in their analysis of the current twenty-first-century zeitgeist. It begins with establishing, via the work of sociologists and anthropologists, the complex materiality of the world including that of religion. All religious material culture, according to the likes of Vasquez, Gibson and Ingold is embedded,

---

[2]   See for example Charles Taylor and his reference to the post-Durkheimian dispensation of expressive individualism whereby the sacred and the spiritual are no longer intrinsically related to society, but rather to the new individual consumer culture released by postwar affluence. Charles Taylor, *A Secular Age* (Cambridge, MA: Harvard University Press, 2007).

[3]   See p. 14 of this volume.

[4]   See p. 19 of this volume.

relational and interactive. Thus we, as embodied beings (or objects), 'intra-act' and engage with each other, 'not as independent entities but as agents within a single material matrix of becoming'.[5] This suggests an understanding of reality as a non-anthropocentric, networked, flexible and immanentist materialism, which affects our religious practice as much as any other forms of human activity. This engagement with sociology and anthropology provides the foundations for a detailed engagement with Gilles Deleuze's rhizomatic categories of thought. Central to the concerns of a relational Christian realism are Deleuze's categories of immanence, difference and repetition. Out of these classifications flow more specific debates on the categories of becoming, ethics and politics which are of direct significance for the construction of a relational Christian realism.

Meanwhile, Bruno Latour's philosophy of the social opens up new spaces of creative ethical and material engagement with its rejection of the objective ontologies of both religion and modernism which, he suggests, are there to merely allay human fears of disorder and mob rule. Instead he proposes a more inclusive form of 'realism' in which all material objects, both human and non-human, are accorded a history and complexity. All events therefore are unique assemblages of 'things'. Thus a full analysis of what goes into creating an event entails understanding the role of all the actants (both human and non-human) that contribute to the production of that event. This view of reality leads Latour to develop ideas associated with the importance of circulating references, actor network theory and an ethics based on 'matters of concern' rather than 'matters of fact'. There are clear and direct crossovers into environmental ethics and politics that we can derive from Latour's sociological realism.[6] But as we will show, these materialistic ethics based on democratic notions of assemblaging and commonwealth have profound implications for a materialist Christian philosophy.

The final key voice from continental philosophy that actively stimulates the development of a philosophy of Christian materialism is that of Alain Badiou. Badiou bemoans the turn from political idealism to political managerialism at the end of the last century. The destructive and Nietzschean-anticipated violence that begat the 'new man' (sic) of a godless humanity in 1917, freed from the impositions of a God-dominated horizon, has since the 1980s reverted to a safe managerialism that suppresses the radical and the new. Like Deleuze and Latour, Badiou is keen to speculate on the source and impact of the new, and so he develops ideas concerning the discontinuous and unexpected power of the Event. But unlike Latour and Deleuze, Badiou also wants to generate a more active expression of human subjectivity; hence his idea that the Event calls us into faithfulness and action in order to follow the ethical impetus of that event. However, this fidelity is contingent on the Event, not the other way round, so that human subjectivity is still enmeshed or entangled within the materiality of the other objects with which it interacts. It is this faithful subjectivity that brings about political change within the global system, thus negating the deadening hand of managerialism and consensus. Badiou and other post-Marxist philosophers such as Žižek, Hardt and Negri and Eagleton[7] are exploring Christian ideas and discourses as counter-narratives to the managerial and post-political era in which we now allegedly live. It is this managerialism which stops references circulating and thus contributes to a culture of hopelessness, inertia and disconnectedness.

These tropes from continental philosophy are then refracted into a philosophy of Christian materialism via a series of theologemes (namely building blocks of ideas or myths that contain theological content). These theologemes correlate directly to existing categories of systematic and dogmatic theology, but in these processes of correlation they are deterritorialised and then reassembled. This process of deterritorialisation, we suggest, ensures that the inner (or virtual) meaning of these categories is broken open in order to engage with the challenges and demands of constructing a public good fit for the twenty-first century.

These theologemes revolve around the traditional Christian theological categories of God, Creation, the Human, Sin (the Fall) and Redemption and Christology. These theologemes are elaborated in chapters 3 and 4, but a brief indicative account of how one of them is reassembled will indicate the kinds of processes involved. The theologeme that shapes all the others is clearly that which denotes God.

Humankind, in Gordon Kaufman's terms (elaborating on Tillich), needs a motivational concept of the event of God by which we can imaginatively draw together the many dimensions of our knowledge and experience in order to engage coherently and thus fruitfully for the common good. 'We human beings need to construct some kind of unified, though revisable, framework by which

---

7   Slavoj Žižek, *The Monstrosity of Christ – Paradox or Dialectic?* (Cambridge, MA: MIT Press, 2009), *Paul's New Moment: Continental Philosophy and the Future of Christian Theology* (Grand Rapids, MI; Brazos Press 2010); Michael Hardt and Antonio Negri, *Empire* (Cambridge, MA: Harvard University Press, 2001); Terry Eagleton, *Reason, Faith and Revolution: Reflections on the God Debate* (New Haven, CT: Yale University Press, 2009), *Culture and the Death of God* (New Haven, CT: Yale University Press, 2014).

to engage the ungrounded multiplicity which is the world.'[8] To this end we propose that ideas of God are deterritorialised and then reterritorialised in the following ways.

First is the idea that God is the constant ungrounding of any tendency, within human and nonhuman systems, that seeks to reify the actual in the world. These processes of reification create what Deleuze calls 'striated' or gridded space in which creativity and newness is suppressed. Understandings of what is meant in continental philosophy by the terms 'actual' and 'virtual' are vital for understanding the premises upon which a relational Christian realism is based and these are discussed fully later on.

Put in broad terms, there are two dimensions to the Real which are not separated by different ontological planes, but are symbiotic modalities of a single plane of immanence. These two dimensions are the actual and the virtual. The actual expresses, but does not exhaust reality; actual states of affairs are contingent and merely express deeper laws or tendencies within ecologies of being. These laws tend to express processes or scenarios of either entropy or evolution. These laws or tendencies are driven by the virtual – that is to say the hidden power within all objects that is not reduced to the ways that these powers get actualised. Actual events are therefore real as they occur, but these actual events do not exhaust the Real since these powers always withdraw at the point of their actualisation.

So if we want to associate the theologeme of God with the power of the virtual, we are suggesting that God does not operate in an additional realm that transcends the material (or actual) world. The ontological content of God has to be filled out within a radical plane of material immanence. This is the ontological basis for the deep, but also messy relationality that underpins the ethics of entangled fidelities. It offers the possibilities of new and hitherto unexplored vistas of engagement and orientation within a deep solidarity with the rest of the created order.

The downside to this radically contingent view of divinity is that we can't project or rely on anything other than our own maturity and resourcefulness to manage and nurture the constant fragility of the commonwealth of objects that humans are enmeshed in. We have to constantly be alert to, and confront, accretions of domination and hierarchy within the commonwealth. To refer to the idea of God as virtual is not to deny that God is real. Rather, God is the immanent milieu of the actual; 'the unmitigated pluralism of circulating pre-

---

[8]   See p. 77 of this volume.

political forces that are constantly astir ... within actual states of affairs'[9] and therefore never allows things to settle. In this view, God is 'the movement of deterritorialisation' or ungrounding. As we conclude later, this suggests a theology of hope that ultimately must counterbalance and 'overcome' a theology of fear or despair:

> ... not [hope] in the traditional closed off sense as an ultimate point in historical time against which all other realities are deeply contingent – but created by the fact that the constant menacing of the actual world by contingency is what creates the possibility for radical and systematic change ... a theology of hope ... is generated from within a radically open system of multiple possibilities, rather than a foreclosed single trajectory of linear progression.[10]

The second motif associated with the theologeme of God is that which is aligned to fidelity (as understood as loyalty and trust). Badiou, as we have already briefly seen, construes fidelity as a 'kind of subjectivity evoked by a decisive event'.[11] The multiplicity and chaos of the actual is not generally sufficient to motivate us into acts of love and commitment because there is no object to focus on. But the unanticipated and discontinuous Event that erupts (as it were) from the vast ungrounded virtual Real that churns within the actual concretises and particularises the idea of God, thus making possible 'a stance of subjective commitment to the God beyond objects'.[12]

Finally, there is within the idea of God the affirmation of what Paul Tillich called a 'spiritual presence'. At this point the gathered people of God (the *ekklesia*) unite their commitment to the Event to the sense of awe and imagination engendered by that selfsame commitment. This combination of imagination, awe and commitment allows them to see within the multiplicity of objects (or the commonwealth of the Kingdom), the possibility of bringing into being, 'new possibilities, new structures and new orientations'.[13] In other words it harnesses the power of the virtual towards intentional forms of transformation that characterise the form of God. These new possibilities and structures are integrated places and spaces of the Christ Event (*Gestalten Christi*) for those 'who see the world through faith'.

---

[9] See p. 82 of this volume.
[10] See p. 189 of this volume.
[11] See p. 99 of this volume.
[12] See p. 99 of this volume.
[13] See p. 100 of this volume.

These three motifs of ungrounding, fidelity to the Event and *Gestalten Christi* constitute a form of Trinitarian engagement between the virtual and the actual. This reflects in turn

> ... a relational Christian account of God [that] supports the acknowledgement of an entanglement of multiple fidelities on the basis ... that God is expressed in multiple communal and social trajectories and thus produces multiple subjectivities which are present in the commonwealth in which we participate, and thus that circulate as well in us as persons.[14]

It is then, in the spirit of that naming and discerning the *Gestalten Christi* within the multiple fidelities created by the Latourian commonwealth that we move from the abstract to the concrete. In the final section of the book we attempt to walk the talk we have set ourselves by applying the principles of relational Christian realism to situations of everyday engagement: urban community empowerment (or localism); education; and the environment. We apply these principles both in terms of analysis of the multiplicity of objects that frame our three case studies, but also in terms of the levels of impact or change that these enacted principles induce in those objects in which they are located.

---

[14]   See p. 100 of this volume.

Chapter 1

Relational Christian Realism – The What and the Why

The theological turn in the continental philosophy of religion appeared to be a boon for religion. Theologemes long treasured in religious traditions began to appear more frequently in philosophical literature, as religiously inclined philosophers were emboldened by the collapse of enlightenment rationalism and its critique of mere belief. Now, under a postmodern regime, philosophical opinion was ranged against various forms of 'foundationalism' which would require of religion the articulation of its rational warrants. Since all perspectives are, in the end, arbitrary, philosophical repudiations of faith as irrational were seen as doubly so.

One spectacular symptom of this phenomenon has been the wide hearing achieved by a highly particularist, hierarchical and authoritiarian theological perspective within the philosophy of religion. In some ways, the Radical Orthodoxy of John Milbank, Graham Ward, Catherine Pickstock, and others represents a jujitsu-like inversion of the secular: exploiting the unrelenting relativism of postmodernism, which had been pursued in the name of a secularising pluralism which prevents the establishment of any perspective on the ultimate, Milbank and his colleagues are able to effect a radical questioning of the secular itself. Since all strictures against non-founded perspectives are now arbitrary because the strictures themselves are just as reliant upon an ultimately unjustified perspective, there is no reason to rule out a perspective that claims privileged access to truth, and thus that such a perspective can legitimately arbitrate all others. From the flux of relativism emerges all of the dogmatic machinery of the Church.

There is more to Radical Orthodoxy than simply a clever inversion, of course. Milbank's central claim in *Theology and Social Theory: Beyond Secular Reason* and subsequent works is that the secular, both as the idea of a realm of human life that is disentangled from religion and as the actualisation of that idea in corporations, governments and other institutions, is a contingent construction of modernity. Further, it embodies a view of the world that is, from a Christian theological perspective, manifestly false. Its falsehood, for Milbank, consists in its ontologising projection of agonism. Against Christian (Augustinian) claims that violence and evil are parasitic distortions of the peace and social harmony that flows from the goodness of God, and are thus deprived of ontological status, the secular views contingent human situations of struggle as characteristic of reality at its deepest level. Under the regime of the secular, people are seen as inherently in opposition to each other, and scarcity and violence become the twin themes of economy and the political. Milbank urges that political and economic liberalism are entangled in this error, as are racist fascisms and, above all, global capitalism and the nihilism that is its inevitable result.

This interpretation of the secular gives Milbank critical leverage against modern social theory and also prevailing forms of postmodernism. Put as simply as possible, Milbank finds a single strand of thought running through the political economy of Ricardo and Smith, the sociologies of Durkheim, Weber and Marx and the postmodernism of Derrida and Deleuze, a thinking which is based on a heretical distortion of the Christian inheritance of the West. In Smith, for example, human life is seen as driven by competition over scarce resources. In Weber, sustainable ways of life have to be bureaucratised, on the assumption of inevitable conflict. In Deleuze, following Nietzsche, persons are constituted by plays of pre-personal force that are in perpetual struggle for supremacy. It is this purportedly basic reality of struggle that is not accounted for by Christian accounts of love and that therefore warrants a sphere of human life that is autonomous, independent of theological claims and convictions. This autonomy, as Milbank sees it, is insidious. By severing the structures that govern our corporate lives from their theologically articulate purposes, and thus from substantive accounts of the human good, we are left simply with a permanent battle between arbitrary powers. Milbank's constructive point, warranted by this deconstruction of secularity, is that the ontological agonism that is at the root of the secular is contingent. It is possible to organise life much differently, even on the largest human scale. It is possible to structure human life in concert with the way of love. But this is precisely to reject the secular, and to embrace the Church.

Yet, as we have already pointed out, Milbank's argument relies upon its own type of arbitrariness, implied in postmodernism itself. Since there is no perspective-neutral reason, for Milbank, reason doesn't dictate which perspective to adopt. Ultimately, the choice between nihilism and catholic Christianity with which Milbank confronts us is arbitrary in terms of reason: it is simply a matter of 'taste'. This rationally non-coercive appeal to aesthetic preference makes it seem as if Radical Orthodoxy's radical claims to intellectual dominance – its claim that theology is the Queen of the Sciences which arbitrates over social theories, for example – are innocent, just because the choice of perspectives is merely persuasive rather than forced by compelling argument.

However, a question here is whether this appeal to 'taste' with respect to such a momentous choice doesn't in the end impose a kind of arbitrariness that is just as agonistic as the arbitrariness of power in ancient paganism, modern liberalism and nihilistic postmodernism. It is important to note here that Milbank is not trying to get Christians to form sectarian enclaves – rather, he is arguing for a renewal of Christendom. But, if theology is really going to rule, then we can ask about whether appeals to 'taste' are as innocent as they first appear.

The problem is not simply Radical Orthodoxy's, even though the ambitions of the latter dramatically sharpen some of the issues at stake, but is rather that of the postmodernity on which it relies – specifically, upon its account of knowledge and truth. What we have in various kinds of post-liberal theology as well as philosophical turns to religion in phenomenological traditions is a kind of internalism about sources of insight that rules out all appeals to evidence and reasons not already framed by the favoured perspective. Though Milbank eschews fideism, Radical Orthodoxy would seem to rely upon it.

Milbank certainly understands the problem, though he would forcefully reject the way we are characterising it. In *The Future of Love*, he urges that the choice between a Christian ontology of peace and the agonistic ontology of secularism is actually far from arbitrary. To choose the former, he argues, is to opt for reason – to believe that reason goes 'all the way down' to the fundamental nature of reality. To opt for ontological agonism, on the other hand, is to hold that reason, ultimately, is illusory, a mere cover for power. The pointed question Milbank asks is whether, in the end, one can really opt for a position that holds to its own illusory character?[1]

But this is an unconvincing argument. It seems to confuse the question of whether reasons can be given for holding a belief to be true with that of whether reality as a whole is rational or grounded in some principle of reason. Is it not possible to hold non-aporetically to the absolute truth of unreason? As we will see shortly, one of the more powerful new philosophical positions today, Quentin Meillassoux's speculative materialism, holds to just such a view. For Meillassoux, truth is not illusory in the least. On the contrary, there are truths about external reality (what he calls 'the great outdoors') that are absolute and perfectly transparent to human reason. The content of these truths is precisely

---

[1]   John Milbank, *The Future of Love: Essays in Political Theology* (Eugene, OR: Cascade Books, 2009), 219.

the absence of a principle of reason at the heart of reality. The ultimate nature of things, according to Meillassoux, is chaos (or, 'hyper-chaos'). So, what you get here is a rational ontology of the absolute truth of unreason. We will have much to say about this view later, but at the moment it only needs to be emphasised that there is nothing contradictory about this strategy.

The philosophical alternative articulated in this book, however, shares with Radical Orthodoxy a definite inspiration by theological themes. Our rejection of Radical Orthodoxy is not a rejection of the theology so much as it is a rejection of the malicious combination of fideism and authoritarianism that has characterised much theology in recent years. By contrast, a theology which embraces the challenges and opportunities of a philosophical realism may offer useful material for reflection in a new realist and materialist mode.

And, in our view, it does. In some ways, the approach to the philosophy of religion we are seeking to develop in this volume is a redeployment or reconfiguration of an earlier theological discourse that had become marginalised in the great twentieth-century rush toward postmodernism, and in the various returns to orthodoxy that the latter has underwritten until quite recently. 'Postmodernism' here is shorthand for the ways in which what Quentin Meillassoux calls 'correlationism'[2] was radicalised in the last third of the previous century. According to Meillassoux, Kant's correlation of subject and object famously made the object 'in itself' unknowable, and his postmodern heirs pushed this scepticism to the point where objects independent of human involvement became unthinkable, as they can purportedly only be thought in terms of historically and culturally particular conventions of language.[3]

For Meillassoux, the connection between postmodernism and the 'return to religion' in philosophy as well as broader culture becomes apparent at this point. In the context of such deep scepticism about the real, threats to religious beliefs based on empirical knowledge can be bracketed by a relativising 'for us' (or perhaps, 'for them').[4] Even the most widely attested scientific theories are always only 'theories', and competing viewpoints are protected from scrutiny on the grounds that they inhabit different and incommensurable linguistic worlds. Perhaps unfairly, Meillassoux accuses postmoderns of a capitulation to religious dogmatism that is effectively a form of 'creationism', since for both scientific creationists and postmoderns, scientific data about the origins of the

---

[2]　　Quentin Meillassoux, *After Finitude: An Essay on the Necessity of Contingency*, trans. Ray Brassier (London, UK: Continuum, 2008), 5–10.

[3]　　Ibid., 7.

[4]　　Ibid., 112–19.

universe are ignored and their philosophical implications are muted.[5] If a lack of cosmological reflection upon well-established theories in Derrida, for example, is insufficient to label him a creationist, Meillassoux's more substantial point is that the failure to think that which predates human articulation in language is a failure to engage with what he calls 'the great outdoors' which is indifferent to its relation to human beings.[6] It is for this reason that, for Meillassoux, the critical force of the real in postmodernism is effectively dissolved, and therefore so is any intellectual resistance to fantasy, utopia or (for that matter) reaction.

Our purpose here is not to engage in direct defence of the 'return to the real' in more recent philosophical reflection, but to offer a philosophical re-engagment with the tradition of Christian realism in theology that achieves some degree of consonance with it. What is clear at the outset is that such a return raises for theologians once again the kinds of questions that have been systematically suppressed in the recent past: questions about how theological insight relates to and is warranted (or not) by non-theological discourses. In each case what we call here 'the return to the real' means a renewed confidence that there is a 'pushing back' of things in the world upon subjects who know them. There is an insistence that language is not self-authenticating, but needs to be adjudicated and revised according to a broad range of experience and knowledge.

And it was this responsiveness to the real that in fact defined the methods of earlier generations of Christian realists. Many of them were not theological empiricists *per se*: they did not build their doctrinal claims, for example, on supposed foundations of human experience or upon other kinds of empirical data.[7] But for them, the ability to account for such things was crucial in warranting theological claims and convictions. Reinhold Niebuhr's famous critiques of neo-liberalism in politics and economics, and of early forms of what we now call 'neo-conservative' foreign policies, were driven by the claim that

---

[5]   Ibid., 47.

[6]   Ibid., 7.

[7]   A more forthrightly empirical theologian who nevertheless had much in common with the Christian realist tradition is Bernard Meland. See, for example, *Fallible Forms and Symbols: Discourses on Method in a Theology of Culture* (Philadelphia, PA: Fortress Press, 1976), vii, where Meland writes that his purpose is to 'pursue the ultimacy within experience as an efficacy of the lived event'. Later, he claims participation in a 'line of protest and inquiry, extending from Barth, Tillich, and Niebuhr to Whitehead and Wieman in the nineteen twenties [which] formed a new frontier of realism, breaking free of the enclosure of mentalism which had engulfed philosophical thinking in the West for more than three hundred years and which had shaped the imagery of theological liberalism since the time of Kant' (Meland, 5).

they cannot do justice to history, and thus to human experience.[8] And so, any 'return to religion' of the sort we saw prior to the rise of the new materialism, based on scepticism about knowing things 'in themselves', would have seemed to these thinkers a cheap and intellectually lazy evasion of the task of theology to interpret real life in the world.

Any number of theologians may be drawn upon as precursors for a relational Christian realism, including a host of thinkers who wrote just before the rise of postmodernism such as John Bennett,[9] and Reinhold and H. Richard Niebuhr.[10] In this first chapter we will focus on the latter as a telling though imperfect example of what we are after, since he provides a theological framework which is already both realist and explicitly relational. It should be noted here that this choice indicates already a broader conception of 'Christian realism' in this book than one which merely focuses on the necessities of power politics and the use of force. While H. Richard Niebuhr was unwilling to rule out resort to coercive measures by states under duress, what makes him a 'realist' is rather his insistence that Christian faith engages non-theological sources of insight and his confidence that claims about God's relation to the world are claims about empirical states of affairs that can be measured by broad features of human experience. In other words, Niebuhr understood that human fidelities are necessarily entangled, in large measure because each fidelity is an attempt to engage the real. The resulting interpretation of religion, for Niebuhr, is that there is not a self-sufficient realm of pure religion: rather, it is always a practice which is tied up with other practices that we ordinarily deem 'secular'. In his preface to a central methodological text, he endorses Paul Tillich's 'belief-ful realism', which both claims that the theology is an intellectual enterprise that seeks to give a credible account of the real and acknowledges that no such accounts are perspective-neutral but are in fact enabled by involvement in a tradition or a community of inquiry.[11]

---

[8]   Examples of this kind of argument in Niebuhr would number in the hundreds. In one that is somewhat arbitrarily chosen by the authors, Niebuhr writes that 'the tragic irony of this refutation by contemporary history of modern man's conception of history [i.e., the myth of progress] embodies the spiritual crisis of our age'. Reinhold Niebuhr, *Faith and History: A Comparison of Christian and Modern Views of History* (New York, NY: Scribners, 1951), 8.

[9]   See, for example, John C. Bennett, *Christian Realism* (London, UK: Student Christian Movement Press, 1941).

[10]   Examples of Niebuhr's espousal of a realist perspective are multiple. Two classic sources are his *Gifford Lectures, The Nature and Destiny of Man: A Christian Interpretation, Vols I and II* (New York, NY: Scribners, 1941, 1943), and *Faith and History: A Comparison of Christian and Modern Views of History* (New York, NY: Scribners, 1951).

[11]   Niebuhr, *The Meaning of Revelation*, ix.

Niebuhr was influenced by the radical empiricism of William James and Josiah Royce, and its sociological inflection in the thought of George Herbert Mead, and his basic appeal to religious experience as direct warrant for theological construction reflected Jamesian and Schleiermacherian influences:

> As we regard this I-Thou relationship of persons who know each other as knowers but acknowledge each other as covenanting, promise-making free selves, we become aware of the fact that the community of faith, like the community of knowledge, is not a simple dyad. As in the community of the knowing I and the knowing Thou a third reality, the common object, is present, so in the community of faith a third reality besides I and Thou comes into view. We may for the present, with Josiah Royce, call this third reality a cause and note its presence in all the common covenant relations of men.[12]

Both faith and empirical knowledge, here, are socially embedded and articulated, but in both cases there is an independent object to which the knowing/believing parties are accountable and which impinges upon them. So we see Niebuhr in this text and in others going beyond the Kantian subjectivism of the Schleiermacher tradition. Theology is not the science of the religious subject, but is attuned above all to objects with which communities of subjects engage.

In another seminal text, we find him regarding what he calls 'external history' (a non-confessional, scientific explanations of events) as crucial to faithfully realistic theological construction:

> In the first place, beginning with internal knowledge of the destiny of self and community, we have found it necessary in the Christian church to accept the external views of ourselves which others have set forth and to make theses external histories events of spiritual significance ... This is necessary because the God who is found in inner history, or rather who reveals himself there, is not the spiritual life but universal God, the creator of not only of the events through which he discloses himself but also of all other happenings.[13]

This attention to non-confessional perspectives is warranted, ironically, by a confessional allegiance. But it is also required by it, so that that which is

---

[12]   H. Richard Niebuhr, *Faith on Earth: An Inquiry into the Structure of Human Faith*, ed. Richard R. Niebuhr (New Haven, CT: Yale University Press, 1989), 50–51.

[13]   Niebuhr, *The Meaning of Revelation* (New York, NY: Macmillan, 1941), 62, 63.

established most securely by the community of knowers (historians in particular, here) impinges directly upon perspectives developed within faith communities. What is thus implicit and sometimes explicit in Niebuhr's own version of theological realism is a strong doctrine of creation which warrants serious engagement with empirical knowledge and broader human experience. Martin L. Cook once characterised Niebuhr's method as one of 'open confessionalism' because it begins with a commitment to a distinctive revelatory locus which gives perspective and yet is perpetually open to revision and expansion on the basis of experience.[14] If God is an active power and presence within all dimensions of the created order, it makes sense that what we know and are learning about the world should have an impact on what we believe about God. It is the openness of Niebuhr's approach which renders it both realistic and (unlike Barth) open to revision under the pressure of the empirical.

In this same preface to *The Meaning of Revelation*, Niebuhr framed his project as the result of a confluence of Karl Barth's objectivism and Ernst Troeltsch's historicism.[15] Niebuhr's Barthian trajectory played out in a theology which insists on the irreducibility of God not only to any subjectivity or feature of human experience but also to any privileged locus of revelation or any communal ritual or language.[16] We may note that Niebuhr's realism radicalised the objectivist trajectory in Barth, turning it against the exclusively revelational stance of Barth himself. God is 'bigger' than Scripture, and cannot be domesticated to its stories.

But realism is only one side of the story. The historicist trajectory in Niebuhr leads to an emphasis upon the many relations between knowers and objects that Bruno Latour uncovers in the context of science studies.[17] For Niebuhr, human experience is always wrought in shifting contexts of concrete, historically particular 'confidences' and 'loyalties'.[18] This means that even the experiences connected to religious faith cannot be abstracted from a variety of social interactions in which we are embedded. We know and encounter God only in terms of concrete relations that mediate the power and presence of God to us. Building on the social theory of Ernst Troeltsch, Niebuhr held that modern

---

[14]   Martin L. Cook, *The Open Circle: Confessional Method in Theology* (Minneapolis, MN: Fortress Press, 1991).

[15]   Ibid., ix–xi.

[16]   Thomas A. James, 'Responsibility Ethics and Postliberalism: Rereading H. Richard Niebuhr's *The Meaning of Revelation*', *Political Theology* 13.1 (2012): 40–49.

[17]   Bruno Latour, *Reassembling the Social: An introduction to Actor-Network Theory* (Oxford University Press, 2007).

[18]   Niebuhr, *Radical Monotheism and Western Culture* (Louisville, KY: Westminster/ John Knox Press, 1960), 16–23.

forms of life are characterised by a rational differentiation of spheres, and we may participate in several of them. Thus, in Niebuhr's view we know God in terms of multiple entanglements. These are not subjective states: they are real relations between actors – reflecting their dependencies and their capacities, but always in relation to a crowd of others.

It is important for our purposes to note that these 'relational' and 'realist' trajectories are not at odds in Niebuhr, but are in fact mutually reinforcing. Relations are always relations between selves and others and a 'third' thing to which the self-other relation itself refers.[19] Thus, I am confident in my friend because she and I are both confident in our nation, or our community or church and so on. In other words, I–Thou relations are never self-sustaining, but always refer to a wider network of trust.

The entanglement of fidelities within a vast, dynamic network requires orientation, some ultimate referent in terms of which a coherent perspective on the collective with which we interact can be maintained, even if always under revision. Human agency thus conceived seems to call for some kind of faith or devotion which can adequately hold it together. Niebuhr talked about this in terms of a 'centre of value'[20] which for Christians and many others is God. It is the centre of value, and its capacity to orient a vast assemblage of things and relations, that powers a distinctively theological relational realism.

This Niebuhrian trajectory suggests an account of redemption which, though profoundly Christian, is radically different from many recent proposals which do not or cannot take the empirical into account. Redemption, for Niebuhr, is 'permanent revolution'.[21] For him, there is no stopping point to transformation, but rather a capacity to go on with the project of building communities in a way which honours the contributions of various actors and mitigates the harshness of the clashes between them. As such, redemption is never achieved ultimately, but is always on the way. In Niebuhr, Christological affirmations suggest patterns for God's redemptive involvement in the world, and these patterns are distinctive Christian 'lenses' because they indicate surprising reversals (for example, power being made perfect in weakness) which faithfully and compellingly interpret experience in the world.[22]

---

[19]　Ibid., 47.

[20]　Niebuhr, 'The Center of Value', in *Radical Monotheism and Western Culture*, 100–113.

[21]　Niebuhr, *The Meaning of Revelation*, 133.

[22]　A prime example of these reversals is a section of *The Meaning of Revelation* in which Niebuhr reconfigures classical meanings of power, unity and goodness. See ibid., 134–9.

But they do not: in contrast to radical orthodoxies, eschatological theologies such as those of Moltmann[23] and Pannenberg,[24] and various forms of post-liberalism, warrant a 'completed' picture of salvation. By 'completed' we do not mean a form of realised eschatology. For Moltmann, and Pannenberg, quite the opposite is the case – they construct accounts of the world as fundamentally open precisely because God's salvific engagement with it is not yet complete. Nevertheless, the vision of redemption these theologians give is of a redemption that has reached a conclusion – or, more properly speaking, that will reach a definite conclusion in a determinate future.

Radical Orthodoxy is closer to a realised eschatology, of course, since it views redemption in terms of the existence of a true church. Salvation, within this scenario, must mean 'liberation' from cosmic, political, economic and psychic dominium, and therefore from all structures belonging to the saeculum, or temporal interval between the Fall and the final return of Christ. This salvation takes the form of a different inauguration of a different kind of community.[25] Here we therefore have a clearer example of a 'completed' salvation, one that points to something within history as the final disclosure of history's possibilities. A relational Christian realism, by contrast, is always indeterminately open, both in terms of its epistemology and its eschatology. The perspective of faith does not give us information about the possibilities and limits that may be realised in the future. And, this uncertainty is ontologised, as it were: the future is not just unknown, it is open.

The problem with completed views, from a Christian realist perspective, is that they always run up against the resistance of the real – the real church as an institution in time and space or real history as that which is not fully absorbed into the perfection of the divine life. In a corollary fashion, they tend therefore to run afoul of human experience, asking us to challenge or qualify what we know from experience on the basis of a prescribed faith that is taken on authority. Again, faithlessness is not the only alternative – a relational Christian realism acknowledges a faith that frames its reception and interpretation of human experience, but it is a faith which is constantly renegotiated in light of the latter.

Despite the good beginning, we believe that, going forward, a return to the real that is rigorously deployed demands a more radical critique and

---

[23] See, for example, Jürgen Moltmann, *The Coming of God: Christian Eschatology*, trans. Margaret Kohl (Minneapolis, MN: Fortress Press, 1996), 261–7.

[24] Wolfhart Pannenberg, *Systematic Theology*, Vol. 3, trans. Geoffrey Bromiley (Grand Rapids, MI: Eerdmans, 1997), 580–607.

[25] John Milbank, *Theology and Social Theory: Beyond Secular Reason*, 2nd ed. (Oxford, UK: Blackwell, 2006), 394.

reconstruction of Christian doctrine than evidenced by Niebuhr's writing, and that the resources that we engage throughout the rest of this book can aid in such an effort. Niebuhr's theology, from the perspective of relational Christian realism, is still too narrowly correlational (that is, still caught up in a radical distinction between human 'subjects' and non-human 'objects') and thus stubbornly anthropocentric. Also his tendency to frame networks of relations in terms of I–Thou encounters fails to account for the force of non-human agents than the revisionary thrust of realism demands. Still, his 'open confessionalism' is quite pliable in the face of empirical realities without succumbing to a thorough secularisation of Christian belief, and can thus support a nimble and still faithful approach to contemporary problems. Additionally, Niebuhr's Augustinian account of the existential human predicament, modified by his emphasis upon the centrality of relations to selfhood, is suggestive of both the relationism and the realism that we will develop in this volume. In order to make a fresh beginning, however, we will need to raise basic philosophical questions, taking up a new realist discourse in contemporary philosophy.

Chapter 2
Philosophy and Material Practice: Deleuze, Latour, Badiou

Having established that an alternative philosophical approach would be of benefit to the study of Philosophy of Religion generally, it is necessary to illustrate why this is also of importance for the analysis and examination of material religious practice. What is now so different about religious practice and our understanding of it that it requires a change of terminology and a different conceptual framework? In due course we will address this through academic discussion, but it will help to offer practical examples of one of the ways in which religious practice itself has been undergoing a metamorphosis.

A few years ago one of the authors was invited by a then parishioner to a 'Buddhist Christmas Party'. There can be no more obvious example of the crossing of boundaries and mixing of traditions that is becoming a commonplace in religious practice. The experience was a strange one in that it comprised a meditation led by a Buddhist monk who had travelled some distance expressly to conduct this part of the gathering and which lasted about 20 minutes, and was followed by a typical 'bring and share' Christmas buffet which could have been taking place in any church hall in the country. The venue for this was actually a school hall. As one looked around and listened to the conversations one began to wonder how many of the other people present were in fact also practicing churchgoers. The person who had issued the invitation had been brought up as a member of the Church of England, had been a Sunday school teacher in her teenage years, did still attend church on occasions, but was now delving for herself into other religious traditions, particularly Buddhism and Hinduism. One suspected that some of the other attendees could equally as well have been churchgoers, but that they found something of value from both the meditation and the fellowship in this particular group. In which case there could be doubt that they would tell their parish priest about this other sphere of religious activity for fear of being considered 'outside the fold'. The questions this raises are about how people now view religion – is it a cultural or spiritual resource of some kind – and how this has changed their understanding of authority within specific religious traditions. Both are characteristic of recent developments in religious practice.

Another similar encounter had occurred a few years before whilst the same author was running a training day on 'New Age and Postmodernity'. One of the attendees had come along out of curiosity to see what the established church was saying about what was then being termed 'New Age spirituality' as he himself was now involved in what would have been seen from the outside as part of this movement, and was in fact holding informal teaching sessions of his own on various religious traditions in his own front room. After some interesting exchanges at the original session there was a meeting at his home to learn more about what he was doing and why. Perhaps because I was open to his approach and non-judgemental about what he was trying to do, the conversations developed over time. He had also been brought up within a strong Christian household, but had become disillusioned with the church as an institution and its failure to address issues which were of importance to him and his family. As a result he had turned his back on formal Christianity and begun his own personal search – something that is very easy these days given access to material through the internet. To cut a long story short, in due course he returned to the institutional church, went forward for ordination, and was, at one stage, chaplain to the suffragan bishop in the Diocese, also acting as an official link to the alternative religious movements across the area – a unique appointment as far as one knows. His ministry included coming round to established church groups and teaching elements of the Christian spiritual tradition, most of which were entirely unfamiliar to regular congregations. This raises the question of why this is the case and the extent to which the churches have lost touch with this part of their own tradition.

In time, however, the frustrations of dealing with the Church of England as an institution once again emerged, and this particular person withdrew in order to further develop his own teaching and spiritual guidance ministry. He has since published a number of books and produced material that can be accessed on the Web. Once again, one could argue that this account is characteristic of recent developments in religious practice and highlights the need for a new discourse and understanding of what is happening beyond the boundaries of formal religious institutions.

So what exactly is happening and how is it to be interpreted? An early attempt to describe and identify these changes was made though what became known as the Kendal Project, carried out by academics and researchers from the

University of Lancaster and headed by Linda Woodhead and Paul Heelas.[1] Their argument was that what was being encountered was a 'turn to the subjective'. Some of this material was used in a subsequent book, but whilst being critical on what appeared to be a simplistic explanation of a more nuanced and complex process.[2] Although this now seems a little dated, it was the beginning of an important study from within the sociology of religion that has still not been taken seriously enough within the established churches.

What are the issues which emerge from this work? First, that people now have the confidence and capacity to pursue their own faith journey independently of established traditions. This then challenges the supposed authority of church teachers and leaders who are no longer the trusted professionals and experts who tell others what to believe or how to practice. One might call this a 'democratisation' of religion. Those who choose to follow their own path either remain on the fringes of the established churches, but do so uncomfortably and quietly, or else simply walk away from them altogether. The fact that all of this is seen as a matter of choice is itself one of the most important aspects of the change in religious practice. Once one makes a choice, it is clear that other choices were always possible, and that one might search for criteria as to how to make such a choice in the first place. Where do such criteria come from and are they not, in some sense, then external to the traditions that one is selecting from? These are not perhaps 'lifestyle choices' in the normal sense, but they do represent a different attitude towards authority as previously exercised within most religious traditions. They are an exercise of individual freedom or autonomy, perhaps on the grounds of 'what seems good for me'. If even those who remain within the traditions now view their faith in this way – and this is increasingly likely – then the leaders and 'professionals' within those traditions may be operating with what I called 'zombie categories' if they continue to believe that they still possess much real authority.[3]

What is now to be encountered across a range of religious practices and beliefs is a much greater flexibility, freedom and willingness to both select and subsequently abandon whatever appears to be helpful and credible at a particular time. There is a fluidity, a process of change and flow and a much greater propensity to make up one's own mind irrespective of what any faith establishment might teach and promote. The other side of this is that some

---

[1]   Paul Heelas and Linda Woodhead, *The Spiritual Revolution: Why Religion is Giving Way to Spirituality* (Oxford, UK: Blackwell, 2005).

[2]   John Reader, *Reconstructing Practical Theology: The Impact of Globalization* (Aldershot, UK: Ashgate, 2008), 63–6.

[3]   Ibid., 4.

people find such a prospect overwhelming and confusing and therefore choose not to choose, but to place themselves within an authority structure that takes those choices away from them. But the fact remains that they have still exercised an original decision to take this particular path, hence a 'taken-for-granted' authority has still been undermined. This is perhaps one of the explanations for the apparent disjunction between what the research shows is the difference between the 'official' views of religious leaders on certain issues, such as gay marriage and assisted dying, and those of many people 'in the pews', the latter being more open and liberal than the official Church line on these matters (see the YouGov polls in the UK used by the Westminster Faith Debates in the Religion and Society Project).[4]

An equally significant piece of work from within the international field of Religious Studies is that of Manuel A. Vasquez.[5] Once again, a brief survey of this will highlight the urgency of developing new frameworks of interpretation and the possible links with the philosophical ideas which we will pursue in this book. From a more global perspective, Vasquez draws out the constant crossing of boundaries and increased complexity of material religious practice as it is now to be encountered. He sets himself the following tasks:

> ... the need to develop new perspectives that explore the transnational production, circulation and consumption of religious goods, the fashioning and control of religious bodies, the constrained creativity involved in the emergence of hybrid religious identities, the relations of domination and resistance that mediate the formation of orthodoxy and heterodoxy, the practices that make possible the creation of spaces of livelihood, which often dovetail with sacred landscapes, the ways in which religion enters physical and virtual flows and networks, including the global mass media and the Internet, and the close interplay between popular culture, popular religion, and consumer capitalism.[6]

Rather than approaching religion as a set of beliefs, and restricting its study to that of religious texts and authority structures, Vasquez sets out to utilise other disciplines such as cultural and ethnic studies, feminist theory, anthropology and neuroscience in order to examine the actual material practices which

---

[4]   The recent research has been published in Linda Woodhead (ed.) and Rebecca Catto, *Religion and Change in Modern Britain* (Abingdon, UK: Routledge, 2012) which contains some of the material that has emerged from the Religion and Society Project.

[5]   Manuel A. Vasquez, *A Materialist Theory of Religion* (Oxford, UK: Oxford University Press, 2011).

[6]   Ibid., 3.

constitute the reality of religion in contemporary societies. Very much what we are describing in the context of the Christian tradition as a relational realism. Rather than looking to straightforward, causal and linear interpretations of what is happening, this is to take seriously the complex, inter-connected, emerging and often indeterminate nature of the ways in which religion is being practiced by embodied individuals and developing communities.

One of the ways in which religious practice has changed is that it is now much less tied to specific places, buildings or locations. There is a transnational circulation of religious goods through polycentric networks, such as the distribution of audiotaped sermons, the teachings of charismatic pastors or missionaries, sacred music or relics. All of this challenges the congregational understanding of religious life as circumscribed by a territorial space and contained within a religious building. Global religious movements such as Pentecostalism find their outlets across a diverse range of locations and adapt accordingly whilst retaining an internal integrity. It is interesting to note that in the UK the most significant area of Church growth is amongst the Black, Asian and minority ethnic communities and in the new churches formed in the last 100 years.[7] One also notes that it is the influx of Roman Catholics from places such as Poland that has led in turn to the welcoming of Polish Catholic priests to boost the numbers and support those growing congregations. So there is constant movement, fluidity and cross-fertilisation of practices and ideas even within denominations, simply because this is the pattern within the wider culture and society.

Vasquez argues therefore that the existing models of Church life developed from the modernist tools of the social sciences are no longer adequate to cope with this scale and nature of change. Ideas of centre and periphery, for instance, are no longer adequate to describe this complexity, and Vasquez advocates utilising the language of Deleuze and Guattari of deterritorialising and reterritorialising to portray this rapid movement of ideas and practices.[8] We will develop this discourse ourselves in due course. Taking a lead from the discourse developed by Appadurai which talks about 'ethnoscapes', 'technoscapes', 'financescapes', 'mediascapes' and 'ideoscapes', Vasquez proposes that we now talk about 'religioscapes' or 'sacroscapes' to help us acknowledge the flow and flux, the trails and lines of flight that better describe the movement through space and time that characterise contemporary religious practice:

---

[7]   David Goodhew (ed.), *Church Growth in Britain: 1980 to the Present* (Farnham, UK: Ashgate, 2012), 253.

[8]   Vasquez, *A Materialist Theory of Religion*, 282.

The task of the religion scholar is to map out the operation of religion in each scale, elucidating the connections, tensions, and cross- fertilizations among scales. Rather than a frozen abstraction, a particular sacred space is a relatively stable but contested moment at the intersection of multiple power-laden social relations.[9]

Examples of this from within supposedly stable and normal parish life would be the changing nature of weddings, where even the Church of England has now relaxed its residence qualifications to regularise what has been happening increasingly in any case, to allow the most tenuous of family connections to be enough to hold a wedding in a particular (chosen) church. Parish boundaries are still of importance, but in a different and more fluid way, and one finds eclectic and unexpected influences emerging in the actual liturgy that couples request, often derived from the media, but sometimes from their own wider or global experience.

The alternative model proposed by Vasquez draws upon the work of James Gibson and Tim Ingold – the first a psychologist and the second an anthropologist – and, in particular, their stress upon embeddedness, relationality and interactivity, while still holding onto the role of emplaced and embodied practice. Gibson talks about an ecology of perception and an approach which transcends the subject-object split in which perception is a cooperative and interactive process. Things have what he terms 'affordances', spatial and spatiotemporal properties that they furnish to their observers. Whilst these are real, they are also always relational. This links to the ideas of Karen Barad who argues that the self and his/her surroundings 'intra-act' and engage with each other not as independent entities but as agents within a single material matrix of becoming.[10] Ingold develops this further by talking about knowing as a set of inscriptive practices on both the body and the environment, or a 'wayfaring' or tracing of routes in which individuals adjust and fine-tune themselves in response to the environment in which they find themselves. This, in turn, transforms those surroundings through a process of co-determination. Thus a relationship with space and place is what shapes and determines material religious practice, rather than some pre-existing and predetermined set of beliefs or means of exercising one's faith. By using this rather unfamiliar terminology, Vasquez highlights the non-anthropocentric, networked, flexible and immanentist materialism that he advocates as an understanding of religious practice. In this way he hopes to have overcome the disabling dichotomies that are prevalent in religious studies, that

---

9   Ibid., 284.
10   Ibid., 315.

have privileged belief over rituals, the private over the public, text and symbol over practice and mind and soul over the body. His objective is not to reverse these but to give a full account of material religious practice. Other authors on whose work he draws in the process are Deleuze and Guattari, Spinoza, Nietzsche and Harraway as well as Gibson and Ingold.[11]

In due course, this book will pursue the development of an alternative discourse utilising some of the same sources, but also drawing upon Bruno Latour and Alain Badiou in proposing the notion of entangled fidelities, but it is important to note that similar ideas and sources are being drawn upon within the field of religious studies. As a preparation for this though it will be suggested that one specific concept from the work of Deleuze and Guattari might be of benefit when examining aspects of contemporary religious practice. This is their notion of the rhizome.[12] One might suggest that one now encounters 'rhizomatic religious practice' and then offer a practical example.

Following the definition of a rhizome as given by Bonta and Protevi,[13] one can begin to see how this assists in the process of developing an appropriate discourse for material religious practice. A rhizome contains six principles: connection (all points are immediately connectible); heterogeneity (rhizomes mingle signs and bodies); multiplicity (the rhizome is 'flat' or immanent); asignifying rupture (the line of flight is a primary component which enables emergence or consistency; cartography (maps of emergence are required); and decalcomania (the rhizome is not a model like a tree, but an 'immanent process'). The value of this concept is that it evokes the hidden network quality of interlinked forces that have adapted to resist the forces of an external environment which could include official institutions and structures. Rhizomes have the capacity to by-pass hierarchies and the barriers they sometimes construct to emergence and development. They are also difficult to eradicate as they move from one manifestation to another and can easily re-establish themselves elsewhere. The internet, for instance, is the classic example of a rhizome, both escaping formal, external control whilst impinging upon the existence of all its users, but also constantly being the subject of concerns about monitoring and inappropriate usage. Connectedness is surely its key characteristic as well as its tendency to elude all authoritarian and hierarchical

---

[11]　Ibid., 324.

[12]　Deleuze and Guattari, *A Thousand Plateaus* (London, UK: Continuum, 2008), Chapter 1, 3–28.

[13]　Mark Bonta and John Protevi, *Deleuze and Geophilosophy: A Guide and Glossary* (Edinburgh, UK: Edinburgh University Press Ltd, 2006), 136–7.

control. We also note that the internet is itself a democratised resource for religious ideas and practices.

Does this complex discourse and source of unfamiliar ideas help in understanding how religious practice is now developing? Let us take the example of what has become known in the UK (and beyond) as 'Messy Church'. For those not familiar with this, Messy Church has grown from nothing a few years ago as a sort of global brand for informal worship and activity sessions for young families. There are now a series of publications, website resources and other training available under this particular banner. The basic notion is that of an activity session related to a teaching theme, probably followed by a very short and informal act of worship using that theme, and then a time for play and social interaction. In many ways it is a contemporary equivalent of what used to be called 'Sunday schools', but repackaged and rebranded to make it more acceptable and 'user-friendly' for a much more demanding and interactive culture. In what ways does this look like rhizomatic religious practice?

Connectivity is central. Although this is a 'global brand' it can and invariably is adapted to local circumstances rather than offering a prescriptive format that must be followed. One can access the resources through the internet and take as much or as little of what is provided as seems appropriate. So there is no central control or hierarchy determining how it is to be used. There is a network model of operation here. Signs and bodies are certainly mixed in the process as the patterns contain both practical activity, music and creative play as well as straightforward religious content and stories. The structure is also flat or immanent as sessions are run by groups of parents and church leaders as appropriate and are tailored to the context. Other aspects of the process that might be encountered are a crossing of boundaries between different denominations – the group that one of the authors is involved in has members from the Methodist Church, a Baptist congregation, as well as Roman Catholics and Anglicans – as well as a crossing of parish boundaries with families coming together as an interest group rather than as a congregation. As well as using internet resources, the main means of communication between the members is actually by texting. The links outward to other related groups include a local preschool, two local mother and toddler groups, as well as at least two local primary schools. The existence of this group has also fostered other church-related activity such as a music festival and services for special occasions such as Christmas and Mothering Sunday, church fêtes and of course baptisms from within the group and beyond. In other words, this does not follow the old pattern of congregational life based upon strict boundaries and a formal hierarchy. Although still traditional in that it claims a heritage and uses content from the Christian tradition, it has a 'life of its own' with connections and 'lines of flight' moving off in many different directions. Thus, one might argue, here is an example of rhizomatic religious practice, a deterritorialising and reterritorialising of work with families and young children.

One simple example, therefore, but a pointer to the need to develop a new and different discourse which recognises that an embedded and interactive religious culture requires the resources that contemporary philosophy and related disciplines can now offer.

Deleuze and Religious Practice

In the previous section reference was made to the work of the anthropologist Tim Ingold who has utilised philosophical ideas to work across boundaries in addressing issues from within his own discipline. This is useful now for two reasons. Firstly, it sets the tone for the project of this book which itself commends interdisciplinary operations as essential to developing a relational Christian realism. It also however offers an excellent practical example of how the writing of Deleuze (and to a lesser extent his sometime collaborator Guattari) is of relevance to our concern with religious practice. Before delving more deeply into the work of Deleuze himself, a chapter by Ingold will now be briefly examined in order to show the importance of this.

In a recent book[14] Ingold poses the question of where we are to place human culture in the nexus of human environmental relations. Where do the requirements of such culture emerge from if not from the environment itself? Ingold then goes on to turn this question around and to ask instead about the sources of environmental meaning for non-human animals as the wider context within which cultural meanings can then be located.[15] To cut directly to his conclusion, he states that 'to perceive the environment is not to look back on the things to be found in it, or to discern their congealed shapes and layouts, but to join with them in the material flows contributing to their – and our – ongoing formation'.[16]

What is of direct interest to us is not just his conclusion but the journey he makes to reach this destination, and, in particular, his use of Deleuze along the way (he also draws on Latour as we will also do). In case one might argue that this

---

[14]   Tim Ingold, *Being Alive: Essays on Movement, Knowledge and Description* (Abingdon, UK: Routledge, 2011), Chapter 6, 76–88 entitled 'Point, Line, Counterpoint: From Environment to Fluid Space'.

[15]   Ibid., 77.

[16]   Ibid., 88.

has nothing to do with religious practice, it needs to be pointed out that the last 30 years has seen an increasing involvement of religious groups in environmental matters as will be described in greater detail in a later chapter. One of the blocks in this, one might suggest, certainly from within the Christian tradition, is that the doctrinal conceptual frameworks regarding the nature of God, Creation and Salvation seem inadequate and inappropriate to engage the understandings of the relationship between the human and the non-human now required. Once again, this will be described more fully in the next chapter. For the moment we work on the assumption that this is an important area of religious practice and therefore of concern to a relational Christian realism.

So how does Ingold use Deleuze? Clearly, one of his objectives is to find different ways of describing the relationship between the human and the non-human, and therefore to set the former in the wider context of a more holistic view of the world. Having already referred to the work of thinkers such as Gibson and Heidegger, Ingold turns to Deleuze who offers an alternative to the latter in laying out the relationship between an ecology of the real and a phenomenology of experience:

> A more radical alternative, however, would be to reverse Heidegger's priorities, that is, to celebrate the openness inherent in the animal's very captivation by its environment. This is the openness of a life that will not be contained, that overflows any boundaries that might be thrown around it, threading its way like the roots and runners of a rhizome through whatever clefts and fissures leave room for growth and movement.[17]

The value of Deleuze's language and indeed his ontology is that life is not lived within perimeters but along lines. Rather than boundaries and the restrictions that they describe, it is about 'lines of flight' or 'lines of becoming'. Life is open-ended, and its impulse is not to reach some destination but to keep on going:

> Thus in life as in music or painting, in the movement of becoming – the growth of the organism, the unfolding of the melody, the motion of the brush and its trace – points are not joined so much as swept aside and rendered indiscernible by the current as it flows through. So it is that the line does not link the spider and the fly, or the wasp and the orchid, but passes between them, carrying them away in a shared proximity, in which the discernibility of points disappears.[18]

---

[17] Ibid., 83.
[18] Ibid., 83.

In other words, one encounters what we describe in this book as entanglements, entwinings or meshworks which cannot be disentangled or separated out and presented in a linear fashion. This is the texture of the world, and it is within this that humans also find themselves and develop their interrelationships with each other and with non-human nature. 'In this tapestry, there are no insides and outsides, no enclosures or disclosures, only openings and ways through.'[19] Ingold reminds us that Darwin himself gives an account of standing before 'the plants and bushes clothing an entangled bank' in his *The Origin of the Species*, therefore offering an image of the world as he encountered it. The challenge now is to see how humans also participate and engage with the world in the same way, rather than standing apart from it and controlling or determining what happens. In order to do this though one needs a new and different ontology, as the one that we work with, certainly in the Christian tradition, is that of hierarchy and causality.

Deleuze on Immanence, Difference and Repetition

This is undoubtedly one of the most difficult and challenging sections of the book so far and demands both patience and close attention. Before we enter into this particular entanglement, we must offer some account of Deleuze himself as interest in his work has only just begun to surface in recent years, although there is a growing body of scholarly work within philosophy and also in theology. Deleuze is probably best known for his collaborative writing with Guattari but was also a significant philosopher in his own right and wrote a significant number of solo books.[20] There are those who now argue that his first major solo book is a great work of philosophy, and will be seen in due course alongside Descartes' *Discourse on Method*, Kant's *Critique of Pure Reason* and Heidegger's *Being and Time*, as each introduces novel and groundbreaking methods into philosophical practice.[21] The challenge of this is the sheer difficulty of the language and concepts that Deleuze employs, but in order to show how he offers

---

[19]   Ibid., 84.

[20]   Deleuze and Guattari, *A Thousand Plateaus: Capitalism and Schizophrenia* (London, UK: Continuum, 2008) is probably the best known of the joint writings, but these also include the earlier volume of this, *Anti-Oedipus* (London, UK: Continuum, 2006) and *What is Philosophy?* (New York, NY:Columbia University Press, 1994).

[21]   Essay by James Williams, Difference and Repetition, in Daniel W. Smith and Henry Somers-Hall (eds), *The Cambridge Companion to Deleuze* (Cambridge, UK: Cambridge University Press, 2012), Chapter 2, 34.

the alternative conceptual framework as used by Ingold and relevant to religious practice there is no choice but to enter this unfamiliar world.[22]

To assist in coming to terms with this opening encounter with Deleuze, I will draw on another chapter in the Cambridge Companion.[23] As the title of the chapter suggests, Deleuze can be interpreted as reversing a central tenet of Platonism, a task previously attempted by Nietzsche. Platonism is not to be reduced to the distinction between the world of essences and the world of appearances, or the intelligible and the sensible, rather the fundamental distinction which Plato makes is that between icons and phantasms, or images and simulacra. Plato also talks about the difference between the copy and the model. Whereas a copy is defined in relation to the original, which it resembles more or less, the simulacrum is that which seems to conform to the original, but in reality unfolds outside the relation between the original and the copy. It is the nature of each of these differences which is at the heart of the debate which Deleuze then pursues.

Why is this of any importance? The reason Plato introduces these ideas is an attempt to construct the basis for judgements and thus to control, politically as well as philosophically, the danger that anything can lay claim to anything, that anything can be taken to mean anything, unless it is clear what is 'of the essence' and what is a mere copy or imitation. Unless such distinctions can be made, then the threat to Athenian democracy was that rhetoric could carry the day as people were unable to judge between what was being said and the reality that was to be experienced. This sounds like a very contemporary problem when we have to somehow work out what is 'spin' or propaganda as it used to be called, and what is the empirical base, if any, of what is presented to us by politicians and the media on a daily basis. So one can see that what both Plato and Deleuze are struggling with is a vital issue for human society.

Deleuze's argument, however, is that by attempting to address the issue in the way that he does, Plato, in this effort to establish a definitive authority by which such judgements can be made, introduces the concept of transcendence into both philosophy and politics. In basic terms, there is now the concept of something (or someone) beyond, by reference to which one can discern what is true, and what is only a pale reflection or distortion of the truth. This then has a clear link to Christianity to the extent to which it understands God as just such a transcendent force or being. According to Deleuze, transcendence should

   [22]   Gilles Deleuze, *Difference and Repetition* (London, UK: Continuum, the Athlone Press, 1994).

   [23]   Essay by Miguel De Beistegui, 'The Deleuzian Reversal of Platonism', Chapter 3, 55–81 in *The Cambridge Companion to Deleuze*, eds Smith, D.W. and Somers-Hall, H.

have no place in philosophy, as it is a means of exercising the religious, moral and political distribution of power. This is then also reflected in the discourse of representation, which is derived from the same project of political order and control. Plato's ontology is one of hierarchy, power and control, as the very notion of transcendence always offers a source which can 'trump' or outweigh whatever is deemed to happening 'at a lower level'.

The other concept which Plato introduces to further enforce this approach is that of the Idea. Ideas designate beings in their truth, whereas semblances are nothing real. The Idea is the principle of selection that allows one to distinguish between images, and especially between likenesses and semblances. It is the philosopher who is, of course, the best judge of all this, which is why, for Plato, the philosopher makes the best ruler. The Idea is the origin of all appearance, as it is not itself an image, but the model after which all images are formed. For Deleuze, the development of Platonism turns philosophy into a police operation, a way of guarding against the threat of that which is not original, essential or even true in its being.

How does Deleuze construct an alternative to this system and what are its implications for theology and religious practice as well as for philosophy?

> In place of the system of representation, dominated by the paradigm of imitation, resemblance, and participation, and the systematic exclusion of simulacra, Deleuze construes a system of difference, insisting all along that such a system is the only reality, and that the world of representation is itself an illusion. Were it not for the connection between difference and repetition, however, the reversal of Platonism would remain incomplete.[24]

Within the Platonic system, it is the repetition of the same in the other, the imitation of the original, that determines the view, but this obviously sees repetition as a form of degradation. What is repeated is a lesser version of what happens in the first instance. Deleuze wants to break this cycle by arguing that what returns is not the self-identity or self-presence of the original in some lesser form, but difference itself. 'All that returns, and returns always, and always differently, is difference.'[25] If this were not the case, then there would be no possibility of anything new emerging in the world, no possibility of creation or evolution. Instead of repetition there is re-production as the world is produced as a result of a principle of difference that never ceases to return.

---

[24] Ibid., 74.
[25] Ibid., 75.

None of this is easy to understand as it opposes what is a fundamental grounding for the way in which philosophy, and indeed much theology and politics operates. If Deleuze is onto something important here, as we will argue that he is, then it challenges some of the most basic understandings of the way that we have become accustomed to think about God, creation and our relationships within and between both. Firstly, it challenges the very concept of transcendence and points instead to a concept of immanence – one which underlies the thought of Ingold in the previous section – an entanglement of humans and non-humans where there is no hierarchy of beings and no definitive human determination of what happens in the world. Secondly, this undermines any interpretation of God or the divine as a form of transcendence – that which is above and beyond the world and human life – and becomes the criterion against which to judge the 'here and now'. Thirdly, it also brings to an end the concept of a linear causality, the idea that things come into being as a result of the movement directly from some identifiable origin towards something else, so from x to y to z, in a straightforward fashion. If there is only difference and re-production, then the very nature of becoming and change is much less clear and traceable, as we will see shortly. Each of these is indeed a massive intervention and potential overturning in the conceptual frameworks which we probably take for granted, and requires an intellectual reconfiguring of significant proportions. And this is just a beginning! What must happen next is the investigation of how this impacts upon understandings of change, development and becoming, as these also are critical for religious practice.

Deleuze and Becoming

Just to re-emphasise that what Deleuze is arguing for is a paradigm shift, or a completely different way of seeing the world and the place of humans within it, here is a passage from his book that lays this out explicitly:

> Repetition in the eternal return never means continuation, perpetuation or prolongation, nor even the discontinuous return of something which would at least be able to be prolonged in a partial cycle (an identity, an I a Self) but, on the contrary, the reprise of pre-individual singularities which, in order that it can be grasped as repetition, presupposes the dissolution of all prior identities. Every origin is a singularity and every singularity a commencement on the horizontal line, the line of ordinary points on which it is prolonged like so many reproductions or copies which form the moments of a bare repetition ... If

"being" is above all difference and commencement, Being is itself repetition, the recommencement of being.[26]

Rather than A leading to B and then to C through some sort of causal mechanism and deriving from an original or first cause, each instance or event is of and in itself, is a singularity, and not a repeat or pale reflection of an original being, itself then only a copy or lesser version of that original. In which case, all that we encounter is indeed difference, that which is not to be compared with some other identity from which it differs, but being as it is in its own right. So all that is exists on the same level of being in so far as it does not come into existence as the result of some greater or higher transcendent force, but then one is still left with the question of how to explain or describe how that which is new or different does emerge or come into being. Simply to say that there is A, and then B, and then C and so on indefinitely does not seem to satisfy the need for further explanation. This is where Deleuze begins to develop further his terminology (sometimes with Guattari), and how his – and their – work is of interest to other disciplines and therefore also to the study of religious practice.

Each of the terms that is developed relates to other terms that also require explanation, so wherever one begins in this process it is impossible to avoid other complex concepts. What is required is patience to stay with the ideas, using examples, until it begins to become clear what is being said. So one might begin with what Deleuze says (and Guattari in this case) about becoming to see where it leads. Becoming is the production of a new assemblage.[27] One then needs to give an example of what is meant by this. A prime example of an assemblage is what they call the wasp-orchid.[28] In this new configuration or assemblage, the orchid becomes necessary to the wasp and vice versa and what is created is what D&G call the wasp-orchid machine. This new becoming does not have a subject separate from itself. So it is not that the wasp stays the same and simply adds a new property to those that already define it, nor that there is some goal or finish distinct from the block of becoming as the orchid is also changed in the process. In complexity theory terms, the new assemblage or symbiosis is marked by emergent properties above and beyond the sum of the parts. Another term that D&G use in this context is 'reterritorialising', as it describes a process where the old territory is not returned to, even though the same components are involved. Deterritorialising is the process by which bodies leave an assemblage following

---

[26]   Gilles Deleuze, *Difference and Repetition*, 201–2.

[27]   Gilles Deleuze and Félix Guattari, *A Thousand Plateaus: Capitalism and Schizophrenia* (London, UK: Continuum, 2008), 237–8.

[28]   Ibid., 11.

the lines of flight that are constitutive of that assemblage but then reform themselves into new configurations. A line of flight is the threshold between assemblages or the actual path of deterritorialisation, a move that triggers the splitting of what exists, what are called bifurcators of attractors which are strong enough to create some new configuration. Lines of flight require the crossing of boundaries, but they are never pure as a result. Examples would be when one converts from one religion to another, or one profession to another, as it is unlikely that one can completely release oneself from the influence of the one and move seamlessly into the other.

This way of understanding has something to offer to the analysis of the movement between religious practices and traditions that was referred to in the earlier examples in this chapter. There is unlikely to be a clear-cut boundary within a new personal faith assemblage even when one supposedly 'converts' from one tradition to another – say from Christianity to Islam – as certain components of the earlier assemblage remain part of one's identity even though something new is being formed. In the cases where people move backwards and forwards between traditions, however, it is even more complex and fluid, and we encounter individuals who adopt certain aspects of a tradition but retain elements of their original faith. Although the sociology of religion has talked about diversity as a characteristic of current religious practice, it is now moving to articulate the concept of superdiversity, which is a recognition that individuals carry within themselves elements of different traditions at the same time. Hence the complexity, blurring of boundaries and faith entanglements that make the picture so difficult to describe with any accuracy. This is also relevant, of course, to the encounters between faith and non-faith or between theology and non-theological disciplines. What the terminology of Deleuze helps us to see is that the idea of some pure or original faith content is probably a misunderstanding of the way things are or ever were. The only approach is to examine each assemblage in individual and proper detail – a key aspect of relational Christian realism.

So what we learn about the process of becoming and emergence from the concepts which Deleuze introduces is that this is always complex, messy and entangled, and that each new assemblage or machine has to be looked at in its own right. Without the idea of causality to fall back on, it will not do to say that if certain external conditions are fulfilled, then such a course of action is likely to follow. This is a challenge to much public discourse and the way in which the media often present matters in order to shape public opinion. Assumptions that a particular state of affairs, for instance the levels of asylum seeking in the country, will automatically lead to certain social or welfare consequences have to be questioned and examined in proper detail. Even to suggest that x causes y in each particular case must be challenged as this represents a conceptual mistake according to this new framework. In the case of the Global Financial Crisis, to give another example, there have been multiple attempts to discover or provide an explanation for the events that occurred and then to offer solutions which will avoid a repeat. These now seem too simplistic and merely a linear description of the new assemblages which have come into being and which are not the direct result of any determining human courses of action. As we look to respond to the events that often overtake us unawares, the terminology of Deleuze can help us to realise that we have a limited control of and understanding of how and why things happen, let alone our own role in shaping these events. To return to the original example from Ingold, we are part of the various material flows which shape our environment and are therefore subject to factors beyond our control, while ourselves being part of the assemblages and machines that are formed, and are thus an influence upon the lines of flight that develop.

Deleuze and Ethics

One obvious concern and potential criticism of this new approach is that it lends itself to a form of moral relativism. So if there are no criteria or transcendent groundings of the judgements we have to make, then 'anything goes' and what is deemed ethical is no more than what a particular group of people or community deem to be so at the time. If all is simply difference and repetition or re-production then does it make any difference if we behave in one way or another? If this were the case then Deleuze's work would be of questionable use for religious practice which certainly wants to address the issue of how we are to conduct our relationships with each other and the non-human creation.

A vital challenge to this comes from the feminist interpreter of Deleuze, Rosi Braidotti, and it is important to see how she launches this.[29] She argues that Deleuze's engagement with ethics is at the heart of his philosophy. His ethics of freedom and affirmation show clearly that he is not going down the line of a relativist approach based on the so-called de-centred subject. The idea that only a steady identity resting on the firm grounds of rational and moral universalism can guarantee human decency, moral agency and ethical probity is challenged by Deleuze's concept of the nomadic subject. He also offers a more affirmative

---

[29]   Rosi Braidotti, Nomadic Ethics, in *The Cambridge Companion to Deleuze*, eds Smith, D.W. and Somers-Hall, H. (Cambridge, UK: Cambridge University Press, 2012), Chapter 8, 170–97. Also her *Nomadic Theory: The Portable Rosi Braidotti* (New York: Columbia University Press 2010).

view of what it is to be and become human than many of his contemporaries as well as taking a distinctive line from the Levinas-Derrida interpretation of the relationship between the subject and otherness. By contrast he sees otherness as the expression of a productive limit, or generative threshold, which calls for an always already compromised set of negotiations – in other words, he acknowledges the entanglements of real ethical engagement:

> Nomadic theory prefers to look for the ways in which Otherness prompts, mobilizes, and allows for flows of affirmation of values and forces which are not yet sustained by the current conditions. Insofar as the conditions need to be brought about or actualized by collective efforts to induce qualitative transformations in our interactions, it requires the praxis of affirmative ethics.[30]

So this is an ethics of affirmation, but also one which takes the cruel, messy outside-ness of life as a whole into account, as life is immanent to and coincides with its multiple material actualisations. There is an emphasis upon generation, creativity and the vital forces which are essential to Deleuze's overall philosophy. The proper object of ethical enquiry is thus not the universal or individual core of the lone subject, so much as the effects of truth and power that his/her actions are likely to have upon others in the world. Hence, this is a kind of ethical pragmatism, linked perhaps to a possible relational Christian realism, which examines the impacts we have rather than the motives from which we might operate. We are embodied beings in relationship with others and the non-human world and there is therefore a connection once again with environmental concerns. Rather than a hierarchical understanding of the nature of these relationships, Deleuze builds upon the concept of immanent relations of mutual constitution through a transversal, collective rhizomatic web of relations. None of this is to deny the existence of vulnerability, pain or other negative aspects of life, but to aim to transform them through positive cooperation and shared action. The subject is an affective entity, both shaping and shaped by the encounters with others in the widest sense. This requires a proper acknowledgement of the bodily part of human nature and resists reducing ethical considerations to a purely intellectual level.

This links back strongly to Deleuze's concepts of becoming and illustrates the extent of the affirmative dimension of his approach:

---

[30]　Smith and Somers-Hall, *The Cambridge Companion*, 172.

This turning of the tide of negativity is the transformative process of achieving freedom of understanding, through the awareness of our limits, of our bondage. This results in the freedom to affirm one's essence as joy, through encounters and mingling with other bodies, entities, beings and forces. Ethics means faithfulness to this potentia, or the desire to become. Becoming is an intransitive process: it's not about becoming anything in particular, only what one is capable of and attracted to and capable of becoming. It's life on the edge, but not over it.[31]

Therefore this is a positive vision of the subject as a radically immanent and intensive body; an assemblage of forces or flows, intensities and passions that solidify in space and consolidate in time. It implies a commitment to duration and this faithfulness that is also a key term for our relational Christian realism, but it does not depend upon the difficult if not impossible requirement of mutual recognition in the manner of a Levinas or Derrida. It also extends our relationships beyond the immediately human which is more difficult to argue from within a Levinasian ethics:

As we have seen, for Braidotti, Deleuze provides an ethical approach which is about affirmation, transformation, faithfulness, endurance and sustainability, each based upon the entangled and embodied relationships that are the result of his ontology. Affectivity, intensity and a commitment to be aware of the impact one has upon others are each central to this vision of what it is to become human. There will be limits to this and thresholds through which we cannot pass, and this is where an understanding of the problems advanced capitalism is creating in terms of our relationships with the planet come into play. As Braidotti says: "this makes the question of negotiation of thresholds of sustainability all the more urgent".[32] She concludes that a nomadic, Deleuzian ethics prioritizes relation, praxis, and complexity as its key components and thus promotes a triple shift: Firstly, it continues to emphasize a radical ethics of transformation in opposition to the moral protocols of Kantian universalism. Secondly it shifts the focus from a unitary and rationality-driven consciousness to ontology of process, that is to say, a vision of subjectivity that is propelled by affects and relations. Thirdly, it disengages the emergence of the subject from the logic of negation and attaches subjectivity to affirmative Otherness – reciprocity as creation, not as negation of Sameness.[33]

---

[31] Ibid., 179.
[32] Ibid., 194.
[33] Ibid., 194.

Deleuze then offers an ethics of materialism in that it is firmly grounded in the here and now as well as the reality of bodily existence with all its entanglements and complexity. It is pragmatic yet with a vision which is open-ended rather than prescriptive. As such it is far from being an example of moral relativism and thus both builds upon its alternative philosophical ontology and also points towards specific political concepts and interventions, which are what we now need to examine.

Deleuze and Politics

Just as there are questions regarding the ethical dimensions or implications of Deleuze's work, so there are also similar issues surrounding his writing (and that with Guattari) when it comes to politics. This is important for material religious practice as this attempts to address the structural and institutional levels of human life. So, for instance, in the UK, there is much debate about the extent to which churches should become involved in welfare provision as the austerity measures of the current government include the withdrawal of funding from both the statutory and voluntary sectors. Should churches allow themselves to be drawn further into this on the grounds that this is part of Christian service to the wider community, and, if they do so, how can this be combined with a critical perspective on government policies and practices? Then there is a wider issue of how people of faith might understand or become engaged with the new political movements that are emerging such as Occupy. We have already mentioned environmental concerns as another area of interest for religious practice. Does Deleuze's work have anything to contribute to this process of political engagement?

Before we examine some interpreters who have reservations on this matter, it makes sense to look at one of the sections of D&G's work that appears to offer explicit political commentary.[34] The central issue here seems to be that of what level politics operate on, that of the macropolitical or micropolitical. Their answer is clear:

> Every society, and every individual are thus plied by both segmentarities simultaneously: one molar, the other molecular. If they are distinct, it is because

---

[34]   Gilles Deleuze and Félix Guattari, *A Thousand Plateaus: Capitalism and Schizophrenia* (London, UK: Continuum, 2008), Chapter 9, 1933: Micropolitics and Segmentarity, 229–55.

they do not have the same terms or the same relations, or the same nature or even the same type of multiplicity. If they are inseparable, it is because they coexist and cross over into each other ... In short, everything is political, but every politics is simultaneously a macropolitics and a micropolitics.[35]

This begins to sound like another acknowledgement of the essential entanglements of human life in this sphere of activity, but it does not tell us very much about the actual relationships between the macro and the micro. One would need to examine individual instances in proper detail, which is what D&G then continue to do over the next few pages, looking at fascism, totalitarianism and bureaucracy. Does this however address the question of how to make judgements about political practice or how best to become engaged in order to pursue the ethical concerns as articulated in our previous section? It does seem as though D&G focus their attention on micropolitics as the inescapable dimension which impinges upon and shapes all others:

> ... the stronger the molar organization is, the more it induces a molecularization
> of its own elements, relations and elementary apparatuses. When the machine
> becomes planetary or cosmic, there is an increasing tendency for assemblages to
> minituarize, to become micro-assemblages.[36]

I think there is a need to be cautious in how this is interpreted. It would seem that what D&G are saying is descriptive rather than prescriptive – this is, their reflection on how things tend to work rather than being a recipe for political action itself, but it would be easy to assume that they are recommending that politics is most effectively pursued at the micro level. They do then go on to talk about the movements of global capital and finance as a quantum flow, but they are careful not to restrict responses to this to any one level but rather to encourage engagement at all dimensions, concluding that 'something always escapes'.[37] Perhaps this is their way of acknowledging the Deleuzian theme of excess and overflowing which is characteristic of his understanding of ethical responses. In the entanglements one can never finally pin down or contain the various lines of flight that emerge beyond human control or imagining.

Hence one can conclude that for D&G politics is indeed a 'both-and' and not an 'either-or':

---

35   Ibid., 235.
36   Ibid., 237.
37   Ibid., 240.

> Politics operates by macrodecisions and binary choices, binarized interests; but the realm of the decidable remains very slim. Political decision making necessarily descends into a world of microdeterminations, attractions and desires, which it must sound out or evaluate in a different fashion.[38]

Politics and its judgements are always molar, or made at the macro level, but it is the molecular or micro that makes or breaks it when it comes to practice and implementation. This is surely simply a matter of observation.

There are, however, commentators who read more into this; these include a recent publication on politics after Deleuze.[39] Widder draws from Deleuze's work the conclusion that 'molecular desire has an ontological primacy in so far as it constitutes the forms that seem to arrest, divide and control it'.[40] Having taken this position Widder proposes that the danger of operating at the macro level is that events and activity at the micro level will somehow 'slip through the net' and in fact determine what will occur, so he wants a third kind of politics, that of creative becoming, that which moves beyond both the micro and macro. He also states that Deleuze and Guattari offer no firm normative rules to distinguish creative or positive changes from those that are dangerous and destructive.[41] It appears from this that he sides with those who would dispute that Deleuze (and Guattari) offer any criteria by which one can judge either ethical or political practice. I think we have already seen from the work of Braidotti that this is not the complete picture; hence one might question Widder's interpretations. This is of real importance for religious practice as the issue of whether simply to engage at the local and micro level is a constant controversy, and there is a real tendency, or temptation, to restrict activity to what is local and easily accessible and to avoid getting drawn into the level of national policy-making and detailed planning. This is an issue that has been addressed elsewhere in the field of public policy so I will not go further with this now.[42]

Another approach which it is worth mentioning is that of Clayton Crockett, who recommends that one take seriously the ideas of Deleuze on limits and thresholds and suggests that D&G are intent upon pushing capitalism to its outer limits in order to bring about radical change and the point where it

---

[38] Ibid., 244.

[39] Nathan Widder, *Political Theory after Deleuze* (London, Continuum, 2012).

[40] Ibid., 132.

[41] Ibid., 135.

[42] John Atherton, Christopher Baker and John Reader, *Christianity and the New Social Order: A Manifesto for a Fairer Future* (London, UK: SPCK, 2011).

breaks down and frays apart.[43] Without going into the details of this as it will return when it comes to considering the environmental and political aspects of a relational Christian realism later in the book, this is perhaps another attempt to push Deleuze's thinking beyond what he actually writes, but seems to me a more creative one than that of Widder.

There is however another strand of interpretation of Deleuze's work coming from a more explicitly Marxist or post-Marxist position that does require attention. The political philosophers and activists who are acknowledged to have been most influenced by him are Michael Hardt and Toni Negri.[44] In each of these major texts they draw upon the notion that what will bring about changes in the 'full spectrum dominance' of global capitalism are the lines of flight which are already present within the system. In other words, one is in the midst of the classic political debate about whether change will come about through evolution or revolution. This is a crude way of putting it, but does get to the heart of the issue and highlights potential differences with other post-Marxist commentators such as Badiou, whom we will draw upon later in this chapter. If there is indeed such a 'flat ontology' as Deleuze appears to propose, with difference and repetition rather than causality as the basis of emergence and development, then it will not be possible for some unforeseen and external event to intervene in the course of history. Much of this centres on the various responses to the events of May 1968 in France and the reactions of those who had been optimistic for the prospects of real change and the start of some sort of Marxist uprising. There are those who then became disillusioned and thus revised their political stance and hopes in what others termed a compromise with capitalism, having abandoned or scaled down their claims for radical change. Badiou is perhaps the major figure who still stands for the latter – along with more recent work of Žižek – and believes that there can and will be events which break into the system from the outside, thus challenging the views of Hardt and Negri that the seeds of change are already within the system.

In one way, this is still the debate between transcendence and immanence which also has strong theological overtones. Deleuze, as we have seen, is in favour of immanence and his whole work reflects this. Hardt and Negri agree with him and this shapes their political philosophy. It is the Marxist scholar and political philosopher Alex Callinicos who describes this debate most fully and challenges

---

[43]   Clayton Crockett, *Deleuze beyond Badiou: Ontology, Multiplicity and Event* (New York: Columbia University Press, 2013), 171.

[44]   Hardt and Negri, *Empire* (London, UK: Harvard University Press, 2000); *Multitude* (London, UK: Penguin Books, 2004); *Commonwealth* (London, UK: Harvard University Press, 2009).

Hardt and Negri on the grounds that this is inadequate to address the real political issues. If 'all is grace', which is a good theological way of expressing this approach, then how can one discriminate between those aspects of the current system that will lead to change for the better, and those that will perpetuate current injustices?[45]

Once again, this is surely another key debate for religious practice. Does one work within the existing system, hoping for change despite all the evidence to the contrary, but keeping one's aspirations and motivation alive by building upon the local, small-scale and incremental improvements that are in evidence? Or does one eschew such political involvement and keep a distance from current politics completely, either operating within an enclave which claims to practice alternative values, or else waiting for some sort of apocalypse when God will intervene and overturn the course of events? Where does a relational Christian realism stand on this question?

Just before we draw this section to a close, it would help to review one further contribution which utilises Deleuze in a direct and positive way for political ends. Again from within a broadly Marxist position, Franco 'Bifo' Berardi, in a recent response to the Global Financial Crisis, shows how the work of D&G can be put to creative use in interpreting these events.[46] D&G draw a distinction in their early work between desire and need. Berardi argues that when money takes the lead in the psychic investment of society, as it has done leading up to the crisis, then desire takes a paradoxical turn and starts to produce need, scarcity and misery: 'the effect of financial abstraction is the constant deterritorialization of desire.'[47] Desire should instead be an enhancer of vision, or a spur to creative activity, but it has instead been turned into something destructive and undermining of relationships and political action. One can also see that the result of the financialisation of the global economy has been to push societies towards the limits of their physical capacity as environmental problems as well as social ones begin to dominate. So here are two dimensions of Deleuze's work that begin to help us interpret current events and to offer a critique, despite the concerns of some commentators that his ideas fail to engage critically enough with practical politics.

One can conclude then that there is much in the Deleuzian corpus – and we have not even begun to do more than scratch the surface of this – that has a

---

[45] Alex Callinicos, *The Resources of Critique* (Cambridge, UK: Polity Press, 2006), 105–7.

[46] Franco 'Bifo' Berardi, *The Uprising: On Poetry and Finance* (Los Angeles, CA: Semiotext(e), 2012), 109–14.

[47] Berardi, *The Uprising*, 109.

positive and challenging contribution to make to the study of material religious practice. His ontology, his theories of becoming and emergence, as well as thoughts on ethics and politics, all provide evidence that a relational Christian realism and its emphasis upon entangled fidelity has much to learn from his overall philosophy.

Latour and Religious Practice

Latour and Realism

The second of the major figures with whom relational Christian realism will engage is Bruno Latour, best known perhaps as one of the founders of what has been called Science and Technology Studies[48] and also of what has become known as Actor Network Theory.[49] Latour is an anthropologist but now writes also in the fields of philosophy and has delved into the subject matter of religion and theology. An edition of the journal *Political Theology* focused on the interface between theology and Speculative Realism contains two chapters which build upon Latour's ideas,[50] plus there is a chapter in an earlier book which is possibly one of the first to bring Latour's thought into this particular debate.[51] This book will now take some of these ideas further in illustrating how Latour's work is of relevance to the study of religious practice, in this section concentrating specifically on the following themes: Latour's understanding of realism; his notion of truth as circulating reference; his reconfiguration of the relationship between the human and the non-human; his concept of reassembling and attention to detail plus his questioning of the traditional distinction between fact and value and the need to realise that values are always already entangled in

---

[48] See for instance, Sergio Sismondo, *An Introduction to Science and Technology Studies* (Oxford, UK: Wiley-Blackwell, second edition, 2010), Chapter 8 on Actor Network Theory.

[49] See for instance, John Law and John Hassard, *Actor Network Theory and After* (Oxford, UK: Blackwell Publishing, 2005).

[50] Chapters by John Reader, Speculative Realism and Public Theology: Explorations; and also by Anna Strhan, Latour, Prepositions and the Instauration of Secularism, both in *Political Theology, Volume 13, No 2,* 2012 published by Equinox. Both were developed from papers given at a conference at the University of Chester in June 2011.

[51] Chapter 12 by John Reader, Truth in Science and Theology: Latour, Žižek and the Theory of Circulating Reference in *Entering the New Theological Space: Blurred Encounters of Faith, Politics and Community,* eds Baker, C.R. and Reader, J. (Farnham, UK: Ashgate Publishing Ltd, 2009).

many so-called neutral political decisions; and then finally the implications of his ideas for our understanding of human subjectivity.

As one of our aims is to establish a relational form of Christian realism, Latour's interpretation of realism seems the appropriate place to begin. In his book of 1999 Latour sets off a train of thought which, in some ways, contains echoes of Deleuze's concerns about ontology.[52] He questions why we have developed the idea of an outside world looked at through a gaze from the very uncomfortable observation post of a 'mind in a vat'. Rather than taking this position for granted, Latour sets himself the task of retracing our steps to see if an alternative understanding can be revealed.[53] He says that it is in order to avoid the unruly crowd and the threat of mob rule that we have come to rely on an inhuman resource, the objective object untouched by human hands. So we search for something that has no human origin, no trace of humanity and which is 'coldly outside of the City'.[54] Although Latour is talking specifically at this point about science, there are clear parallels with what Deleuze argued about Plato and the development of the concept of transcendence. It is in order to guard against the notion that 'anything goes', or that the uneducated and untrustworthy views of the many might determine what is true or acceptable, that there is this appeal to something beyond the human and which provide criteria for truth. The problem with this notion of the mind in the vat is that it so detaches humans from the actual operation of the scientific method and the world of which we are always already a part, that it creates a series of misconceptions which then hamper a more accurate understanding of the reality of scientific practice. Hence Latour is striving towards a form of realism:

> When we say there is no outside world, this does not mean that we deny its existence, but, on the contrary, that we refuse to grant it the ahistorical, isolated, inhuman, cold, objective existence that it was given only to combat the crowd. When we say that science is social, the word social for us does not bear the stigma of the "human debris" of the "unruly mob" that Socrates and Callicles were so quick to invoke in order to justify the search for a force strong enough to reverse the power of "ten thousand fools".[55]

---

52   Bruno Latour, *Pandora's Hope:Essays on the Reality of Science Studies* (Cambridge, MA: Harvard University Press, 1999).

53   Ibid., 12.

54   Ibid., 13.

55   Ibid., 15.

So what Latour aims to bring to the surface is the reality, or actual practice of science, and to show how humans in fact operate in relationship with all the other components of the process of discovery and experimentation. He argues that realism will emerge when, instead of talking about objects and objectivity, we begin to speak of non-humans that have been socialised through the laboratory and with which scientists and engineers begin to swap properties. Non-humans also have to be granted a history, and allowed the multiplicity of interpretations, the flexibility and the complexity that have so far been reserved for humans. Instead of the three poles – a reality 'out there', a mind 'in there' and a mob 'down there' – we arrive at what Latour calls a 'collective'. At a later stage he will use the term 'assemblage' with which we are already familiar from the work of Deleuze, the general intention being the same, of arguing that there are always very particular configurations of components, both human and non-human, which come together for specific reasons and in order to perform particular functions. We can see then that we live in a hybrid world, made up of people, stars, electrons, nuclear plants and markets (amongst many other things), and that we need to examine in detail in each individual instance, how these various elements are being combined in a collective or assemblage. This is a form of realism, but, as one commentator says, this is a relational realism, one which in denying any notion of essentialism bears some resemblance to Whitehead's holistic network-ontology and process philosophy.[56] Having introduced this central theme we now need to press further into Latour's work to examine the implications of these ideas and how they might relate to religious practice. One obvious possibility is this reconfigured relationship between the human and the non-human which we have already encountered in both Ingold and Deleuze.

Latour and Truth as Circulating Reference

As those familiar with contemporary philosophy will know, arguments about the theory of truth are well-trodden and somewhat stale paths to follow. The correspondence theory of truth which argues that the words we use somehow correspond to the reality of the external world and the objects being referred to is probably the best established, but this is exactly the 'mind in the vat' solution that Latour brings into question. If we start from this assumption of a split between fact and language, how do we effectively overcome it? It is difficult to see how words can directly 'correspond' to what is out there in the world. Latour

---

[56] See Graham Harman, *Towards Speculative Realism: Essays and Lectures* (Alresford, UK: Zero Books, 2009), 81.

suggests that what scientists do in practice is to blur the distinction between language and states of affairs. By examining in detail specific examples of scientific field work, he shows that the real question we should be asking is that of how the world can be progressively packed into discourse through successive transformations so that a stable flow of reference might ensue in both directions. Taking the example of a sampling of soil in the Amazon forest for which he was present as an anthropologist, Latour says:

> The plants find themselves detached, separated, preserved, classified and tagged. They are then reassembled, reunited, redistributed according to entirely new principles that depend on the researcher, on the discipline of botany, which has been standardized for centuries and on the institution which shelters them, but they no longer grow as they did in the great forest. The botanist learns new things, and she is transformed accordingly, but the plants are transformed also.[57]

He concludes from this practice that there is indeed both truth and reality, but that this is not a matter of correspondence between words and things, but a matter of movement, of process, of transformations that take place as the hard work of research plays itself out, and that therefore what we are dealing with is a chain of changing relationships. Truth value is something that circulates rather like electricity through a wire, and the challenge is to keep this circulation going. The truth of what scientists say does not come from their breaking away from society or its conventions, mediations or connections, but from the safety provided by the circulating references that cascade through a great number of transformations and translations, and over which nobody has any durable control. So the more connected a science is, the more it can keep the references circulating and the more accurate it will become.

How might this notion of truth as circulating references be of relevance to the study of religious practice? In the first place it tells us something important about the actual process of study and the ways in which the varied and different components of what is involved need to be looked at in detail through their interconnections and interrelationships. Isolating very specific practices or activities as if they were not connected to wider webs of beliefs or relationships is to decontextualise them and disconnect them from the reality in which they occur. One might argue, therefore, that the approach of Radical Orthodoxy with its idealistic view of the Church, and indeed theology, as the only legitimate sphere of operation for those of faith simply fails to take into account

---

[57]   Latour, *Pandora's Hope*, 39.

the current realities of church life. When proposing that the Church – and this often just means the Church of England in a UK context in the case of Radical Orthodoxy – should become deeply involved in the work of welfare provision as the state increasingly withdraws and throws it back to voluntary associations, is there any real consideration of the resource implications of this? Then there is also the matter of how truth is to be understood within the field of religion. If Latour's ideas are to be taken seriously, as we argue in this book, then one could argue that problems of fundamentalism and a dogmatic approach occur precisely when particular groups or individuals try to stop the references circulating by proclaiming that they possess the truth and that one needs to look no further. Rather than pre-empting the process of discovery and debate it would be better to work to 'keep the references circulating' and to keep feeding in new ideas and experiences. This would indeed be perceived as a threat to the established religious authorities who prefer to claim clear access to truth for themselves, but then, as we have seen with the argument of Deleuze regarding Plato, is this not a matter of retaining power and control and therefore keeping the masses at bay in case they should come up with the unorthodox or unacceptable? One of the significant features of religious practice is precisely this challenge to authority that is emerging from people exercising their own autonomy when it comes to matters of faith and practice. So, in reality, the references are now circulating much more readily as people attempt to work things out for themselves, no longer trusting in the 'powers that be', very often discredited by practices that contradict the principles for which they claim to stand.

The Human and the Non-human

As we have already seen in the ideas of Ingold and Deleuze, there is a growing movement to redefine or describe the relationship between humans and non-humans, and which has significant implications for our understanding of environmental concerns. It is in a later book that Latour turns his attention to this matter in greater detail, but the seeds of the debate have already been sown.[58] As somewhat with the discussion about theories of truth where we see that a strict division between external reality and supposed internal perception only serves to obfuscate what is actually taking place, the division between subject and object also does not help in understanding what happens in the practice

---

[58]   Bruno Latour, *Politics of Nature. How to bring the Sciences into Democracy* (Cambridge, MA: Harvard University Press, 2004).

of science. Latour likens this to a tennis match where each side is determined simply to return the ball to the other side. As a result:

> ... we can say nothing about subjects that does not entail humiliating objects; we can say nothing about objects that does not entail shaming subjects ... subjects and objects do not belong to the pluriverse whose experimental metaphysics we need to reconstruct: "subject" and "object" are the names given to forms of representative assemblies, so that they can never bring themselves together in the same space and proceed together to take the same solemn oath.[59]

As with the pair of terms, human and non-human, this challenge by Latour does not refer to a distribution of the beings of the pluriverse, but to an uncertainty, a profound doubt about the nature of action, and to a variety of positions regarding the difficulties of describing what it means to be an actor within this process. So, according to traditional interpretations, it is only humans who can be correctly described as actors, which turns everything non-human into a mute object which only behaves or responds. Latour goes on to argue that both of the pairs of terms, subject and object, and human and non-human create a problem for the Political Ecology which he is examining in this book. Instead then of being content with these pairs, he wants to look again at how what have been described as non-humans and objects also participate in the activities we hope to study, and are indeed actors, or what he now calls 'actants', and how indeed the humans and subjects participate in concert and association with these actants through what we must understand as a different form of agency. This requires that we abandon talk of subjects and objects altogether:

> ... objects and subjects can never associate with one another; humans and non-humans can. As soon as we stop talking about non-humans as objects, as soon as we allow them to enter the collective in the form of new entities that hesitate, quake, and induce perplexity, it is not hard to see that we can grant them the designation of actors. And, if we take the term "association" literally, there is no reason, either, not to grant them the designation of social actors.[60]

Latour's objective here is to find out what equipment has to be available to populations in order for them to assemble into a viable collective, instead of separating into two illicit assemblies that render each other mutually powerless

---

59   Ibid., 72.
60   Ibid., 76.

and prohibit the exercise of public life. Perhaps a good example of this from the study of religious practice would be the impact of technology upon how ideas and practices now circulate more freely as, for instance, already referred to in the work of Vasquez. The technology itself can be seen as a significant actor or actant in the ways in which religious practice has recently developed. Access to the internet as a source of religious ideas which people can then process for themselves, plus the creation of 'virtual churches' or the use of video streaming to bring groups together despite physical distance, are both obvious examples of this. Then there is the interpretation of religious institutions as portrayed by the media which is a major influence upon the opinions of those who have not themselves encountered faith and practice in any other way and which can appear to determine how faith is viewed in the wider society.[61] It is difficult to describe the role of the supposedly external factors such as these unless we change the language as Latour proposes to talk about the human and the non-human.

Another arena of application is the environmental and Latour has also made interventions in this. In an article published in 2009[62] he argues that any convincing ecological spirituality will also have to adopt this language of the human and the non-human. The limitation of traditional Christian approaches to the subject has been its own understanding of nature and the separation of what is human from what is deemed to be natural:

> If all "progress in spiritual life" has been accomplished by removing ourselves from "the world" (or alternatively in converting back from a spiritual dream to a "strictly naturalistic" vision of life on earth) we will always have to abandon non-humans in order to reach the spirit (or what we have to take as a merely material res extensa to protect us from the irrationality of religion.[63]

We have to go beyond the view that non-humans have just been emerging for centuries in order to be so many props to show the mastery, intelligence or design capacities of humans. They have their own intelligence, their own cunning and their own design and thus exist in and for themselves and in their own right. If it is always a matter of religion encountering nature, then one of them has to go, that often being religion. If religion flees from any involvement with non-humans or with science, it will become irrelevant and will be condemned with

---

61 See for instance, Elaine Graham, *Between a Rock and a Hard Place: Public Theology in a Post-Secular Age* (London, UK: SCM Press, 2013), 90–92.

62 Bruno Latour, 'Will Non-Humans be saved? An argument in ecotheology', *Journal of the Royal Anthropological Institute*, 15 (2009), 459–75.

63 Latour, *Will Non-Humans*, 471.

having forfeited the world to save only the souls of humans and incarnation will have been in vain. Instead then it needs to re-engage with both and to reinterpret its understanding of the relationship between the human and non-human that will come about through a change of terminology and the conceptuality that accompanies it. Without going into this in further detail at the moment, it will be seen how this impacts upon more traditional doctrinal understandings in later chapters of the book.

Matters of Fact and Matters of Concern

Having moved away from the notion of Actor Network Theory, at one point Latour then returns to the concept in order to offer another explanation of what it was designed to achieve.[64] He explains that what lay behind this development was simply a realisation that something unusual had happened in the history and sociology of scientific hard facts which required a rethinking of the language including the redefinition of the human and the non-human. What happened was the connections between non-social objects such as microbes and reefs insisted on being associated with the more normal social entities:

> Either they were rejected out of social theory because they did not look social enough, or they were welcomed into it. But then the very concept of social had to be deeply altered. This second solution was the defining moment of what was later called ANT.[65]

So, for instance, Latour says fishermen, oceanographers, satellites and scallops might have some relations with each other, relations that might make others do unexpected things. Adding the term 'social' to this adds nothing to the explanation though, so the social dimension of this vanishes. On the other hand, is there anything that the non-social adds to the equation? It would appear not, therefore the social then returns as a movement of circulation, as the process of connection with non-social things. Hence the social is back as association or assemblage. What exists are 'translations between mediators that may generate traceable associations'.[66] Actor Network Theory was devised in order to address this awareness of the different types of relationships that exist in practice between the human and the non-human. One needs to move ever closer to the detailed

---

[64]   Bruno Latour, *Reassembling the Social: An Introduction to Actor Network Theory* (Oxford, UK: Oxford University Press, 2007).

[65]   Ibid., 106.

[66]   Ibid., 108.

reality of how these relationships operate and to describe them in appropriate detail rather than attempting to detach oneself from the process as some sort of objective observer.

Why is this important for religious practice? If one were to take any specific example of a faith-based intervention in public life or matters of policy commitment, one would discover that religious leaders and commentators tend to make rather sweeping statements that do not give adequate attention to the details of the debate. One approach has been to argue that this level of detail should be left to the 'experts' and that the Christian perspective is only to state matters of broad principle.[67] That, however, is to remove the level of relationships from the debate in a way that a relational Christian realism finds inadequate. What is required instead is proper research which must include the insights and contributions of other disciplines rather than assuming the theologically imperialistic stance of Radical Orthodoxy. Hard work this may be, but this is surely the better mode of engagement with such issues. One of the concerns with this might well be that those of faith do not possess the skills or the knowledge to enter this level of discussion, that they are 'out of their depth' when it comes to dealing with matters of fact. Once again though Latour has an answer to this as well as he prefers to talk about 'matters of concern' rather than 'matters of fact':[68]

> The discussion shifts for good when one introduces not matters of fact, but what I now call matters of concern. While highly uncertain and loudly disputed, these real, objective, atypical and above all, interesting agencies are taken not exactly as object but rather as gatherings.[69]

What is gained by this? Matters of fact are only partial and often political renderings of matters of concern. Specifically they may exclude not only the depth reality of the involvement of non-human components of states of affairs, but also the dimension of value judgements that are always already entangled in the way that they are presented. In which case, talking about a matter of concern would be a means of acknowledging that those other than 'experts' have

---

[67]   See for instance William Temple's interpretation in his 'Christianity and Social Order' as commented on in John Atherton, Christopher R. Baker and John Reader, *Christianity and the New Social Order* (London, UK: SPCK, 2011), 1 and the chapter following pp. 1–21 which questions the limitations of this approach.

[68]   Bruno Latour, 'Why has critique run out of steam? From Matters of fact to Matters of concern', *Critical Inquiry*, 30, (Winter 2004), 225–48.

[69]   Bruno Latour, *Reassembling the Social*, 114.

a legitimate voice in the ensuing debate, and that part of their role might be to draw to the surface the value-laden discourse employed by those experts but which purports to be value-free.

An example of this would be the discourse surrounding management and marketing now prevalent in our global business culture which likes to present itself as being value-free, whilst actually embodying a very specific set of values:

> Far from being a neutral vessel directed at maximising rationality and efficiency, management promotes an array of values in tune with neoliberal/consumer age capitalism; self-realisation, enrichment, liberty autonomy, entrepreneurialism, pragmatism, flexibility, mobility, adaptability ... etc.[70]

To be able to talk about matters of concern offers the opportunity to highlight these embedded values and thus to introduce alternative ones from the very start of the process of debate. This process is part of what Latour is referring to when he talks about 'reassembling'. It requires going back to the beginning of what is being discussed and then working slowly and deliberately through the detail in order to acknowledge the various components that are involved in any particular assemblage, including any values that may be part of this as well as all human and non-human gatherings. We get closer rather than being further away. We are aware of the complexity of what is a particular matter of concern and we allow the references to keep circulating. These are essential aspects of a relational realism.

Human Subjectivity

As one might expect from our review of the ideas already mentioned, there are implications here for our understanding of human subjectivity. If we are talking about a different set of relationships between the human and the non-human then it is inevitable that how the human operates within that whole will now have to be reconsidered. The crucial issue is that of the limits of what we understand by autonomy. How much control do humans actually exercise in these relationships when we are arguing that the non-human components also act as agents to some degree? As with previous sections we can do no more than introduce and touch upon the arguments which will be further developed later in the book.

---

[70] Francois Gauthier and Tuomas Martikainen (eds), *Religion in Consumer Society* (Farnham, UK: Ashgate, 2013), the introduction by the editors and Linda Woodhead, p. 21.

In a chapter written in 2008, Latour articulates his position in the context of a discussion about environmental concerns.[71] The question he is addressing is that of why it is that such concerns fail to make a breakthrough in terms of political discourse and action despite contemporary popular movements. His suggestion is that the presentations have yet to make connections with the level of feelings and emotion and have remained too intellectually focused. Thus they could learn something from the ways in which religious discourse operates. One of the problems, as we have seen already, is that science tends to try to create a distance between the human and the non-human by talking about matters of fact and objectivity, whereas what is required is a recovery of connectivity and an awareness of the entangled and complex nature of human and non-human relationships. We need to recognise the greater levels of attachment between things and people.

In response to this, Latour goes on to consider the strange connections between mastery, technology and theology. Using the Frankenstein myth, he concludes that the moral of the tale is not that of the error of creating this strange creature, but rather the results of the Creator abandoning the creature to himself. It is this failure to follow through, or to keep faith with one's creation, that needs to be brought into question. So it is not the technology itself which causes the problem, but the absence of love for or commitment to that which is created – 'as if we had decided that we were unable to follow through with the education of our own children'.[72] What we should be working towards, therefore, is a politics of things in which humans are entangled, involved, implicated and, to use theological terminology, incarnated. This requires a reassembling of our understanding of what it means to be or become human which acknowledges the different levels of human subjectivity, what one might call the pre-autonomous as well as the autonomous.[73] There are also clear theological connections here as one might interpret the Christian position as one where God as Creator is deeply folded into, implicated and incarnated into creation rather than distanced and remote from it. So we begin to catch glimpses of where Latour stands on the issue of human subjectivity.

There is, however, a further example from his work that makes his position more explicit.[74] Latour takes the image of the puppet and the puppeteer to help

---

[71] Bruno Latour, 'Its development stupid' or 'How to Modernize Modernization' in *Postenvironmentalism*, ed. Proctor, J. (Cambridge, MA: MIT Press 2008), 1–13.

[72] Latour, *Its Development Stupid*, 11.

[73] John Reader, *Blurred Encounters: A Reasoned Practice of Faith* (Glamorgan, UK: Aureus Publishing, 2005), 135.

[74] Latour, *Reassembling the Social*, 216.

us understand better the relationship between human agents and social forces. It is common to encounter the interpretation that outside forces or influences are like the hands of the puppeteer pulling the strings of humans as puppets. Latour suggests that the relationship is more complex and interesting than this and that we need to view it as a process of circulation in which no one factor completely determines another, but that they might simply have the power to make another react in a different way. So there is not an outside made up of social forces which then determines the human that is inside as if they were a puppet on a string and not in any control. One has to be able to impute some degree of creativity and control to the human through intentional or moral action, even though this is always through the relationships with the non-human involved. By contrast, Latour argues that:

> The only way to liberate the puppets is for the puppeteer to be a good puppeteer. Similarly, for us, it is not the number of connections that we have to diminish in order to reach at last the sanctuary of the self. On the contrary, as William James so magnificently demonstrated, it is by multiplying the connections with the outside that there is some chance to grasp how the inside is being furnished. You need to subscribe to a lot of subjectifiers to become a subject and you need to download a lot of individualizers to become an individual.[75]

One of the key problems with the old model is that it operates with a linear model of causality, a theme that we encountered in the work of Deleuze. What we encounter instead is the mediating of the relationships in that one component or actant is capable of creating a response in another, and that the variety of connections is always substantial and to an extent unpredictable in its activity. One needs to question the interpretation of action as always beginning from or being deliberately initiated by a human actor. So what we have instead is an understanding that the blurring, entangling, bundling up and interconnecting of the elements, both human and non-human, through attachment and proximity, is a more accurate description of how things relate and change. Hence the notion of human autonomy, an independent and unrelated process of causality originating from a human decision and intended course of action, is itself a limited and unhelpful way of viewing how the world operates. This also requires though that reassembling of the different levels of what it means to be human that we often fail to take into account when we see ourselves as simply autonomous individuals. We are always already more complex than that as

---

[75]   Ibid., 216.

different factors within ourselves play their part in how we respond to situations and the decisions that we then make. Human subjectivity is itself entangled, folded and complex.

Overall then we can see that Latour offers a different interpretation of human subjectivity, related to his other insights into a form of realism, the need to understand the relationships between the human and the non-human and his suggestion that we distinguish between matters of fact and matters of concern. Each of these points towards a new and different discourse, very much as does the work of Deleuze, and therefore a challenge to established ways of viewing the world which offers insights into contemporary religious practice. Whether this in itself though is enough to satisfy a relational Christian realism we now go on to question through an examination of some of the work of Badiou.

Badiou and Religious Practice

In this section we will investigate how Badiou's philosophy adds to the notion that the examination of religious practice will benefit from contemporary philosophy. This will be done under three headings. First, the differences between and links with the work of Deleuze will be discussed using particularly the latter's concept of disjunctive synthesis. Second, a major focus will be on Badiou's understanding of human subjectivity, a theme that occurs in the work of both Deleuze and Latour. Finally we will track a recent text of Badiou to see how his work has developed in the light of later events and how this contributes to the discussion about religious practice.

Disjunctive Synthesis

One of the intriguing aspects of religious practice is the apparent human capacity to hold a particular set of beliefs and then to contradict these through actual implementation. Is this more than hypocrisy, and does it mean that the critics of those of faith have a strong argument in suggesting that the results of such commitment inevitably lead to violence or conflict? An example of this might be the activity of many environmental campaigners who decry the practice of multiplying carbon emissions and yet continue to stack up air miles by flying to the numerous international conferences to discuss this very issue. Is this more than a case of 'do what I say and not what I do'?

Evidence from within educational research shows that students can hold several conceptions of the same phenomenon simultaneously and that within threshold concept theory there is a notion of students oscillating between different liminal states.[76] In other words, it is possible to see how there are concepts that might help analyse and understand how different and conflicting ideas are held in tension and how this can be part of a creative process.

Hence we should be interested in the evidence that the early Christians appear to have believed both that the Kingdom of God had arrived and that the world as it is shows no obvious signs of this. So there are almost parallel worlds existing in the same space/time. There is also the tension between espoused and operant theology identified in the field of Theological Action Research (the difference between what believers claim is their source of authority and motivation for action, and what is clearly the case in practice).[77] Is this again a contradiction or perhaps what Deleuze has called a disjunctive synthesis? One might also comment on the capacity of politicians (and maybe also the electorate) to hold contradictory interpretations simultaneously, for instance, that one can both make massive cuts in public spending and still expect an increase in employment, even when all the evidence suggests otherwise.

So to the concept of disjunctive synthesis as developed by Deleuze and then employed by Badiou. This is as described by a Deleuze commentator:

> A disjunctive synthesis is not a reduction through abstraction but a transforming addition that connects by creating differences. Events are such disjunctive syntheses. The second condition then adds that the syntheses take place on two irreducible sides of reality: on sense and expression; virtual and actual; surface and depth. So any process, or disjunctive synthesis, is dual: parallel but asymmetrical syntheses spread out on either side for any event and for any series.[78]

Badiou, in a book published in 2007, then uses the concept in the following way.[79] Reflecting upon the history of the twentieth century he says that the century thought about itself simultaneously as end, exhaustion, decadence and as absolute commencement. Part of the century's problem is the conjunction of these two convictions. It appears to act according to one of two maxims: the one

---

[76] Caroline Baillie, Jens Kabo and John Reader, *Heterotopia, Alternative Pathways to Social Justice* (Alresford, Hants, UK: Zero Books, 2013), 27.

[77] Helen Cameron, John Reader, Victoria Slater with Chris Rowland, *Theological Reflection for Human Flourishing:Pastoral Practice and Public Theology* (London, UK: SCM Press, 2012), Chapter 1.

[78] James Williams, *Gilles Deleuze's Logic of Sense: A Critical Introduction and Guide* (Edinburgh, UK: Edinburgh University Press, 2008), 27.

[79] Alain Badiou, *The Century* (Cambridge, UK: Polity Press, 2007), 31.

calls for renunciation, resignation, the lesser evil, together with moderation, the end of humanity as a spiritual force and the critique of grand narratives. The other, which dominated between 1917 and the 1980s, inherits from Nietzsche the will to break the history of the world in two, and seeks a radical commencement that would bear within it the foundation of a reconciled humanity. The relationship between these two is not a dialectical correlation, but an entanglement, one between necessity and will. This is a disjunctive synthesis. Violence takes place at the point of this disjunction. Violence is legitimated by the creation of the new man, this now being a godless humanity within the horizon of the 'death of God'. 'A godless humanity must be recreated, so as to replace the humanity that was subject to the gods. In this sense, the new man is what holds together the fragments of the disjunctive synthesis.'[80] The twentieth century tried to turn into reality (because of its 'passion for the real'), the promises of a new humanity espoused by the nineteenth century. The result has been huge loss of life and destruction, so politics has now abandoned this and returned to managerial efficiencies rather than political ideals. This will be significant for how Badiou now views politics as we will see in due course.

This highlights one of the key differences between Badiou and Deleuze, which is how they understand ontology and whether 'the new' is created out of what already exists (Deleuze) or whether it is radically discontinuous with what has gone before which is Badiou's interpretation. There are clear echoes of the theological tension between two different worlds and whether or not it is possible or desirable to turn a utopian vision into a present reality, and what happens when one does make that attempt. How can one be both a realist and a utopian at the same time? There is the major disjunctive synthesis perhaps (for believers anyway), and one could argue that it is within this tension and liminal space that we must live and attempt to be creative. It is clear though that one cannot begin to understand Badiou's work without some grasp of his ontology and how it relates to that of Deleuze, as their differences have both political and theological implications. It is to this that we now turn.

The way in which Badiou and Deleuze conceive 'the multiple' (Badiou) or 'multiplicities' (Deleuze) is sharply opposed, with Badiou upholding a mathematised paradigm in the tradition of Plato and Descartes, and Deleuze an organicist or vital paradigm, derived directly from Bergson. For Badiou, Deleuze's doctrine of the world and being as a continuous totality renders it impossible to account for an event as the singularity of a rupture and also reintroduces transcendence. For Deleuze, Badiou's paradigm remains truncated,

---

[80] Ibid., 32.

as for there to be multiplicity there must be at least two multiplicities. This may sound obscure, but this difference is central to their respective ontologies and how either might relate to a more traditional faith-based metaphysics.[81]

Badiou sets out to destroy the popular interpretation of Deleuze as the champion of desire, free flux and anarchic experimentation – some of which stems from his collaboration with Guattari. So it is Deleuze as a metaphysical thinker who is of interest to Badiou, with his thesis of the univocity of being as essential to this. Deleuze proceeds by producing pairs of concepts; the virtual and the actual; chance and the eternal return; the fold and the outside. Hence, for Badiou, Deleuze still draws on a form of transcendence through using 'the virtual' as a level which is a foundational level beneath 'the real' or the actual. Deleuze himself would have challenged this description and claimed that Badiou failed to recognise the true nature and purpose of his distinctions.

There was, over a period of time, a correspondence between Deleuze and Badiou, which the former brought to an end without a meeting, but this remained in the latter's hands when Deleuze died. From these it is clear that Deleuze's texts operate within a 'vital' or 'animal' paradigm of open multiplicities (pace Bergson), whereas Badiou operates from within a mathematical paradigm. Deleuze apparently accuses Badiou of confusing 'multiple' and 'number' whereas Badiou says it is inconsistent to uphold the virtual Totality or what Deleuze calls 'chaosmos', because, with regard to sets, there can be neither a universal set, nor All, nor One.

Assuming that there is this choice of paradigms between the organicist and the mathematical, where would theology stand? A process theology or philosophy would appear more in tune with Deleuze who emphasises continuity and emergence from within, but one could argue that an approach which requires discontinuity, thresholds or a concept of conversion would be more in tune with Badiou and his notion of the event, which, as will see, also links to his notion of faithful subjectivity. The event is something which occurs unannounced and unexpectedly and cannot be read out of existing conditions. Linking to the possible turn to the subjective and an interest in personal or spiritual development, Deleuze appears superficially the more attractive, but once one examines his concept of human agency, this becomes less so, and Badiou's concept of human subjectivity as the location where change happens becomes of more interest. So there is a tension here between a Deleuzian approach which emphasises continuity and development from within, and a Badiou

---

[81] See Alain Badiou, *Deleuze: The Clamor of Being* (London, UK: University of Minnesota Press, 2000).

approach which talks instead about radical change, rupture, discontinuity and an intervention from the outside.

Badiou argues that the thesis of the univocity of Being guides Deleuze's entire relation to the history of philosophy, in that his key references are to others who maintain that Being has a single voice (Duns Scotus, the Stoics, Spinoza, Nietzsche, Bergson).The thesis says that univocity does not signify that being is numerically one, which is an empty assertion. The power of the One is much rather that beings are multiple and different, they are always produced by a disjunctive synthesis and they themselves are always disjointed and divergent. Nor does univocity mean that thought is tautological (the One is the One). Rather, it is fully compatible with the existence of multiple forms of Being. It is in a single and same sense that Being is said of all its forms.

The price one must pay for inflexibly maintaining the thesis of univocity is clear according to Badiou. Given that the multiple (of beings, of significations) is arrayed in the universe by way of a numerical difference that is purely formal as regards the form of being to which it refers, and purely modal as regards its individuation, it follows that, ultimately, this multiple can only be of the order of simulacra – and if every difference without a real status is classed as a simulacrum, then the world of beings is the theatre of the simulacra of Being.

This would make Deleuzianism a Platonism with a different accentuation. But it is the disjunctive synthesis that is opposed to Plato: beings are merely disjointed, divergent simulacra that lack any internal relation between themselves or with any transcendent Idea whatever. Difference is all there is. Then Deleuze is left with the thorny question of the names of Being. What could be the appropriate name for that which is univocal? Is the nomination of the univocal itself univocal? And if Being is said in a single sense, how is the sense of the 'single sense' to be determined?

In the various experiments which Deleuze carries out to answer these questions, it is clear that a single name is never sufficient, but that two are required. This is because Being needs to be said in a single sense both from the viewpoint of the unity of its power and from the viewpoint of the multiplicity of the divergent simulacra that this power actualises in itself. In order to say that there is a single sense, two names are necessary. So Deleuze provides a multiplicity of names of Being, which is itself correlative with the unprecedented determination with which he upholds the ontological thesis of univocity and the fictive character of the multiple. Here Badiou is referring to Deleuze's principle doublets of the virtual and the actual; time and truth; chance and the eternal return; the fold and the outside.

'Virtual' is the principle name of Being in Deleuze's work, or rather virtual/actual is the pair together, as two names are required for the One in order to test that the ontological univocity designated by the nominal pair proceeds from a single one of these names. But Deleuze goes along with the current belief that this is not a matter of positing a ground or foundation of any sort. So beings as simulacra are not degraded copies of Being as they are fortuitous modalities of the univocal and can only be thought in their anarchic coexistence through disjunctive synthesis. The simulacrum denies the original and the copy, the model and the reproduction, as we have already seen in the section on Deleuze's ontology.

Where Badiou says this doctrine falls down is dealing with the question of parts rather than the whole. How can we speak simultaneously of both complete determination and only a part of the object? Deleuze's answer is that every object is double without it being the case that the two halves resemble each other, one being a virtual image and the other an actual image. Badiou challenges this and, to avoid this predicament, poses the univocity of the actual as a pure multiple, sacrificing both the One and the images, which is what the virtual would have to be according to Deleuze. Now obscure as this is, it could be that this is potentially important for theology – can it not more easily accommodate Deleuze's theory of the double as, for instance, a disjunctive synthesis between the world as it is, and the world as it is in the Kingdom?

Badiou, at this stage, sums up his difference from Deleuze as that between the All and Grace (or the event) with Badiou going for the latter and Deleuze the former. The question for religious practice is how this might illuminate the tension between the world as it is, and the world as it should be according to various visions of faith. How can the divisions between the utopian interpretations of the outcome of right practice and the reality of human behaviour be reconciled? Does there have to be a concept of an external intervention in order for change to occur? If Badiou offers a secularised version of grace then Deleuze provides a view of creation which is based on development and continuity from within. As we shall now see, this is central to understanding what further insights Badiou can now contribute to the study of religious practice.

Badiou's Theory of the Subject

If the previous section seems too complex and philosophically oriented, the reason one needs to be aware of this part of Badiou's work is because what follows can best be understood from within this approach to ontology and with a firm grasp of the questions Badiou sets out to address. On one level, his main question is deceptively simple – how can what is new come into the world? We have seen that his answer to this is radically different from that of Deleuze, and that this will have implications for their respective understandings of both ethics and politics. Badiou's is a theory of the event, of that which cannot be anticipated occurring, of moments of truth which are a principled break with the way things are. It is not surprising then that there are echoes here of a religious nature as this sounds as if it could be talking about revelation or even resurrection. Even more so then we have to encounter his notion of human subjectivity and the way in which this builds upon his ontology in order to be aware of the danger of reading into this a strictly religious interpretation.

We have seen that both Deleuze and Latour move away from a notion of the autonomy of the lone individual, controlling their lives through deliberate choice without reference to the non-human let alone other humans. Both share an idea of the human as interacting with the non-human, and both shaping and being shaped by the specific assemblages, collectives or associations in which they happen to become entangled. Whilst this is attractive and helpful when it comes to thinking about our relationships with creation – to use a theological term – the weakness of this approach is that it tells us little about the notion of human agency, and, in particular, what motivates or moves people to engage in collective ethical or political action. One might argue that some understanding of commitment which explains how and why people act in one way rather than another might also be required. So although there are possible criteria to be derived from both Deleuze and Latour – for instance, adhering to that which is life enhancing and creative rather than life denying or destructive, or a decision to 'keep the references circulating' – how do these help when decisions have to be made and stands taken on particular issues? There will often come a point when the talking and deliberating has to stop. What happens then?

This is the point at which Badiou's ideas on subjectivity come into play. But, like the truth and the event which Badiou is so keen to advocate as being apart from the existing structures or conditions of life, the subject only comes into being at the point at which a commitment, or fidelity to a cause comes into action. Once again, this is less a matter of individual autonomy and more of an external point of activity in which one finds oneself engaged and embroiled. There is no subject as such until or unless that point of faithfulness arises, nor is it the case that this is an individual matter but rather being part of something greater than oneself. Both the truth and indeed the human subject are exceptional, moments of intervention that cannot be explained in terms of other external conditions.

Recent theological interest has centred on this, particularly as Badiou has written a book on Saint Paul, using him as a possible example of the fidelity that he is attempting to describe.[82] One must beware of reading too much into this as Paul is just an example and does not represent any sort of Christian commitment by Badiou. So why is Paul of interest to him? It is his faithfulness to that which he believes to be universal which is of importance:

> ... since truth is evental, or of the order of what occurs, it is singular. It is neither structural, nor axiomatic, nor legal. No available generality can account for it, nor structure the subject who claims to follow in its wake.[83]

So the Christian subject does not pre-exist the event which he declares – in this case of course, the resurrection. The truth that he declares is entirely subjective (it is of the order of a declaration that testifies to a conviction relative to the event). It cannot be assumed or described under any existing law. Fidelity to the event is crucial, for truth is a process and not an illumination – this sounds more like Latour than it does a formal acknowledgement of any sort of revelation. Then a truth is indifferent to the state of the situation – in the case of St Paul, the Roman State – so this has nothing to do with existing opinions let alone political structures. There is no subject as such until the point of commitment takes over.

This refers back to an earlier book by Badiou[84] and it is worth noting some of his descriptions from this text also. One should not interpret this process as being a positive or creative one as far as the individual is concerned: 'I call subjectivization the interruption of the vacillation by the excess. It is a destruction.'[85] The subjective process owes its unity to the twoness of justice and the superego. A subject is nowhere given to knowledge, it must be found. One can only arrive at the subject, it cannot be plotted or determined in advance or by deliberate design. Thus we can see that there is yet another attack upon the notion of individual autonomy, but one that does not emerge from what is already in existence as with Deleuze and Latour, but comes from what is unexpected and beyond any human control or shaping. Faithfulness or fidelity is a matter of remaining in the zone of what is taking place, possibly in spite of oneself or what is in one's own personal interests. So a subject is not an individual or a person as we would normally think of them, but more like the location of change in the world, and this is as likely to be collective as it is personal. St Paul is of interest

---

[82]   Alain Badiou, *St Paul: The Foundation of Universalism* (California, CA: Stanford University Press, 2003).

[83]   Ibid., 14.

[84]   Alain Badiou, *Theory of the Subject* (London, UK: Bloomsbury Academic, 2013).

[85]   Ibid., 277.

to Badiou only to the extent that he interprets him along these lines. Does this though take our understanding of religious practice any further when it comes to trying to explain or describe how and why people are motivated to take committed ethical or political action? The best way to answer this is to take our exploration of Badiou forward to see how he now describes his understanding of the human subject and the engagement with current political action.

Badiou and Entangled Fidelities

In 2011 a translation of a text written two years before and summarising Badiou's current position was made available.[86] This will provide a helpful conclusion to this section as it touches again upon the key ideas already mentioned. Picking up once again the connections with Plato, Badiou uses the term 'Idea' to express his own thoughts. So an Idea is that upon which an individual's representation of the world is based, once s/he is bound to the faithful subject type through incorporation within the process of a truth. The Idea is then the mediation between the individual and the Subject of a truth, and by Subject Badiou means that which orientates a post-evental body in the world.[87] This is his own interpretation of Plato's use of this term, but replacing 'the Good' with 'the True'. The problem though is still that of how our experience of a particular world can open up access to eternal or universal truths. Remember that this is the classic philosophical question of the universal and the particular which haunts the relationship between philosophy and theology, and indeed the concept of the incarnation. It is also the reason why Badiou finds St Paul of interest, as he is seen to point towards a universal from within a particular commitment. Perhaps it is as well the main point of challenge for contemporary religious practice which can be focused upon the individual journey or search for truth and the tense relationship with all sources of tradition and the authority that has gone with this in the past. Are those currently engaged in spiritual exploration and a much more eclectic or freely chosen individual path still making claims to have accessed some universal truth – that which is of value for others as well as for themselves?

For Badiou, only that which is set out in the element of truth can be a means of creating a Subject, and is therefore not simply an individual decision. Unlike Plato, however, this must be a materialist understanding of the Idea. The worlds that are exposed by human animals capable of eternity do not present anything true by

---

[86]   Alain Badiou, *Second Manifesto for Philosophy* (Cambridge, UK: Polity Press, 2011).
[87]   Ibid., 105.

themselves, but are a matter of their transcendental logic: 'and we are examples amongst others of the play of differences and identities between multiples ruled by these logics.'[88] It also requires that we pass from the individual to the Subject, but in place of philosophy we now have art, science, politics or love, philosophy being only a means of capturing these in the light of a concept of Truth.

This begins to sound more like Deleuze, particularly with the reference to difference, and it could even be closer to his idea of assemblages where it is the particular configuration of components that constructs the possibility of action and change rather than the activity of lone individuals. It needs to be emphasised that Badiou is not talking about transcendence in a religious manner, but it is rather what he calls an immanence to the True through the Idea: 'the individual is not the author of this thought but merely that through which it passes, and ... would nevertheless, not have existed without all the incorporations which make up its materiality.'[89]

Then comes a critical comment where Badiou acknowledges directly that he is in agreement with Deleuze:

> Deleuze forcefully maintained – that thinking is never a matter of voluntary decision or natural inclination. We are always, he declared, forced to think. Thought pushes us, as it were, from behind. It is neither lovable nor desired. Thought is a violence done to us. I utterly agree with this view.[90]

So there is the brutal contingency of the event which exposes us to a choice that we have not desired – could this be what a person of faith might describe as 'a calling'? – and there is a response then of either incorporation, indifference or hostility. One is either a faithful subject, a reactive subject or an obscure subject. Badiou will explain these in a moment. Then there is the cost to the individual of following this calling, to use the faith term for it, and Badiou uses the example of one of his heroes from the field of mathematics (Cantor) to show that even though the thought of something new and radical had occurred to him, yet he still could not and did not want to believe it, and subsequently went mad. This is surely very close now to an experience that one might call 'conversion', with both the sense that this is something one has not chosen, and that then leads to consequences that one would certainly not have chosen for oneself. This sheds a new light upon the current tendency to see religious practice as a matter of choice rather than one

---

88   Ibid., 108.
89   Ibid., 109.
90   Ibid., 110.

of a commitment which one cannot ignore but feels compelled to pursue. It also highlights the collective dimension of this response and the need for a Subject to be incorporated into something greater than themselves, which, again, is a challenge to contemporary practice to the extent that it becomes a matter for the individual rather than the assemblage or community.

What are the differences between these three types of subject, now that Badiou has extended this beyond the 'faithful subject'? We know what the latter describes, but the reactive subject is 'everything that orientates the conservation of previous economic and political forms (capitalism and parliamentary democracy), under the conditions of existence of the new body'.[91] In other words, it tries to go on as before as if nothing had really changed – this perhaps sounds familiar as a response to the Global Financial Crisis? The obscure subject wants the death of the new body, so is implacably opposed to the changes. This would be an interpretation of Fascism in the twentieth century. One can analyse political approaches according to this terminology and also question where specific religious practices which engage in political activity stand on this spectrum. Many I suspect would look like reactive rather than faithful subjects, as they tend to collude with the existing economic and political structures even while claiming to challenge and critique them.

We turn then to Badiou's closing comments on politics itself to see where he now stands. He begins by saying that his former philosophical opponents, such as Derrida, would no longer be such as they had made peace with one another before Derrida died. The challenge to philosophy now is against a poor dogmatism by way of analytical philosophy; against cognitive science and the ideology of democracy and human rights. So his earlier manifesto from 20 years before which was arguing for philosophy's continued existence now talks instead about its revolutionary pertinence against any form of servile dogmatism. The previous argument mentioned four truth procedures: emancipatory politics; formal and experimental sciences; the arts; and love. Badiou says that these still stand but are now much more difficult to illustrate. The sciences, for instance, are increasingly reduced to their impact upon technologies' marketability. Art has been diluted by reference to the media and 'communications'. Democracy is now not much more than a cross between economy and management: 'let's say that technology, culture, management and sex have taken up the generic place of science, art, politics and love.'[92] All one can do in response is to protect the active autonomy of each of these areas. In other words, Badiou presents a bleak and

---

[91]   Ibid., 93.
[92]   Ibid., 121.

depressing interpretation of each of these spheres of public and private life and their current lack of emancipatory potential. He is especially pessimistic about the prospects of any form of parliamentary democracy being able to deliver the better world that he would strive towards. It is as if the universal or eternal dimension of these ideals had been lost, and were now appropriated by the mechanisms of global capitalism – what Hardt and Negri have referred to as the 'full spectrum dominance' of neoliberalism. In his own political practice, Badiou now gives his attention to the small-scale, local and micropolitical interventions that, once again, seem closer to the approach of Deleuze.

What then might a study of religious practice learn from the work of Badiou, Latour and Deleuze? Returning to the opening section of this chapter and the idea of rhizomatic religious practice, one can perhaps begin to see that the networked approach is very much in evidence. The use of technology to both disseminate ideas and organise resistance now characteristic of current political movements such as Occupy is to be found in the faith-based equivalents. Whilst this might be an effective way of organising though, it leaves the challenge of someone like Badiou who seeks a more radical or revolutionary response based in a faithful subjectivity, or sense of calling, hanging in thin air. Are these responses going to be no more than 'reactive' in Badiou's terms? Is this in fact all that faith responses will ever be, if those of faith can and do live 'in two worlds at the same time'? Is it possible to translate faith commitments into more direct political action which has an immanent rather than transcendent goal in view? What happens when the references have to stop circulating and decisions have to be made? Can one become so 'entangled' that it is impossible to 'see the wood for the trees'? A relational Christian realism must address these issues through practical examples, and these will form a later part of this book.

Chapter 3
Engaging the Theological I: God

In our gathering of speculative resources for a relational Christian realism in recent materialist philosophies, we have already begun to engage and interpret religion as a complex social reality that is characterised by fluidity and by the capacity to operate rhizomatically, forming connections and shaping fidelities across multiple realms and spheres of life. The next two chapters will build on this working interpretation, drawing on resources already brought to bear and invoking others, in order normatively and somewhat more systematically to engage religion as a kind of fidelity that can be appropriately entangled with other commitments, especially for post-secular communities characterised by multiple entanglements within a way of life that is pluralistic and this-worldly. We will do this first by rendering a general and very brief interpretation of the practice of worship as a means of being oriented to other material practices, and secondly by a re-engagement of classical theological themes from a philosophical perspective shaped by the new materialism. It is this latter task which will occupy most of our attention over the next two chapters.

Construing Religion

What, then, is religious devotion, or worship, and how can it be conceived as different from a mere distraction, sublation or obfuscation of material interests? We should be wary of essentialist interpretations of religion that supposedly hold across all traditions. But is there a way of conceiving religious practice normatively that would answer to these charges? One could hold, with Kant, that the material practice of religion has no value outside of a pictorial representation of the rational postulations that are maintained for the sake of ethical practice.[1] Worship in this idealist framework would function simply as

---

[1] Immanuel Kant, *Religion Within the Limits of Reason Alone*, trans. Theodore M. Greene and Hoyt H. Hudson (New York, NY: Harper and Row, 1960), 100–105. See Kant, *A Critique of Practical Reason*, trans. T.K. Abbott (Amherst, NY: Promotheus Books, 1996), 138ff.

a means of reinforcing and motivating commitment to rationally derived moral principles and the postulates that support them. While having to adjust to a subordinate role vis-à-vis philosophical reflection, worship in this view is at least spared the opprobrium of obfuscation or distraction. The problem is that this kind of idealist interpretation of worship removes it from materiality. Worship here becomes mere ritual, performed simply to build up a fund of motivation to engage in material practices: essentially unrelated to practice except as a method of releasing energy toward it. There is therefore nothing critical or constructive involved in religion: it says nothing about life. Oddly, there is a kind of autonomy ascribed to religion in this view that in fact shadows the absolute autonomy of idealistic ethics vis-à-vis empirical, material realities. Just as ideal norms are not checked or reinterpreted in terms of the material world, so here religious practice is not engaged in any way with the material practices by which we negotiate the world.

More critical attitudes toward religious practice are possible, of course, and we see them in materialist thinkers as diverse as Marx and Meillassoux. Marx's account of religion as the 'opiate of the people' is well-known. Meillassoux's account, seen in his still mostly unpublished *The Divine Inexistence*,[2] is somewhat different but bears some striking resemblances to Marx, as well as (oddly enough for a materialist) to Kant. For Meillassoux, religion is essentially awe in the face of overwhelming cosmic power. This awe does not support human agency, nor does it motivate commitment to moral principles. In fact, it dampens or even withers our moral sensibilities altogether, as we learn simply to accept what we might otherwise find unacceptable. According to Meillassoux, we ought to be haunted by the spectres of past injustices, of lives cut short (and, as for Kant, for Meillassoux all lives are cut short). Religion, he argues, is a matter of worshipping the source of that which is. But, since 'what is' is shot-through with injustice, to worship such a source is to bow the knee to unjust, amoral power.[3] In order to understand this point, it is crucial to recognise that Meillassoux already presumes the death of the theistic God. A divine being conceived in a theistic manner is supremely personal, and divine power is never abstracted from the divine vision of goodness. In other words, God is a moral being – indeed, for Augustine, the goodness of God is more theologically important and more fundamental to the divine reality than

---

2   The work has been partly translated by Graham Harman, and included in his *Quentin Meillassoux: Philosophy in the Making* (Edinburgh, UK: University of Edinburgh Press, 2011), 175–238.

3   Ibid., 236.

God's power.[4] Following modernity's excision of purpose from cosmology and of the twentieth century's experience of profound and unrecompensed evil, Meillassoux does not entertain classical theism's attempted union of power and goodness in a concept of God. So, the God of religion, in antithesis to Augustine, is for Meillassoux a God of sheer, amoral power, and thus worship is a matter of acquiescing or perhaps celebrating power, being drunken with it so that the bitterness of injustice is quietly endured or perhaps ignored. Since we engaged the Radical Orthodoxy of John Milbank in Chapter 1, we should mention here that Meillassoux plays right into Milbank's hands on this point. The idea of God conceived as power, for Milbank, is not Christian, but pagan. Again, we may call Augustine as witness. But of course, Augustine's position is off the table for Meillassoux: power and goodness are not reconcilable under present conditions, and thus we can either hope for the actualisation of goodness (such hope would be the achievement of philosophy, which has its own version of God, which we will deal with shortly), or we can worship the power which repeatedly crushes goodness (religion).

The problem here, as we can already see, is historical. Does Meillassoux's account of religion fairly describe the content of faith in dominant strands of Western religion? Hardly. Almost no practitioner of any religion would recognise Meillassoux's interpretation of it. On the face of it, Meillassoux's account is historically skewed. Simply put, religions and their advocates have over and over again linked what they call 'faith' to commitment to moral actions, habits and values that are very far from endorsing or even acquiescing in current configurations of power.[5] Of course, Meillassoux's point is not directly historical, but structural: whatever practitioners of a religion may report, they are in fact acquiescing to raw power if they hold that there is a transcendent being who supports the current order of things. But this begs the central question: is it possible to have a religion that does not cling to such a transcendent being, and therefore does not simply bless the current order? The fact that religions often link faith to revolutionary social and political programmes suggests that things may be more complicated. So, are we back to Milbank, then, at least for a more historically plausible account of religion? But the problem with Milbank's

---

4   Augustine, *The Trinity*, trans. Edmund Hillk, O.P., ed., John E. Rotelle, O.S.A (New York, NY: New City Press, 1991), Book XIII, ch. 4, 353–8.

5   Among a myriad of examples of religious thinkers who have challenged the political and even ontic *status quo*, one could cite Gustavo Gutierrez, *A Theology of Liberation: History, Politics, and Salvation*, revised ed., trans. and eds Sister Caridad Inda and John Eagleson (Maryknoll, NY: Orbis Books, 1988) and John Howard Yoder, *The Politics of Jesus: Vicit Agnus Noster*, 2nd ed. (Grand Rapids, MI: Wm B. Eerdmans Publishing Co., 1994).

account, as we have already seen, is that it is both monolithic and idealistic. Its idealism differs from Kant's, since it is not a matter of holding postulates that support deduced moral certainties. But it is still idealist in the important sense that it abstracts a core of normativity from the welter of practice and exempts it from rational scrutiny. It does this, as we argued previously, on the strength of the correlationist logic inaugurated by Kant.

So what other, more realistic and empirically defensible philosophical interpretations of religion are possible? Of course, if we are to respond to Meillassoux's thinking (and, indeed, to incorporate it) we need more than a conception of religion that avoids both the static character of Radical Orthodoxy's account and the distorting abstractions from historical religious practice that we find in both Kant and Meillassoux. We need to answer his 'spectral dilemma': how is it that injustice can be accounted without despairing or despising power?[6] In other words, how to reconcile power with goodness? But preliminary to that is a conception of religion as a fidelity that can engage other material loyalties and commitments with the social, economic and political spheres.

First, we need some account of religious practice itself. We have already begun to characterise a certain capacity of religion to operate fluidly and rhizomatically in this book. It is important to recognise that this is a normative and not simply descriptive account of religion: we are seeking to uncover powers inherent within religious practice that can be developed and further actualised. So, let us try to make this account somewhat more explicit. Religious practice, we suggest, is a particular kind of practice whose function and intention is to orient us towards other kinds of practice in distinctive ways. Religious devotion, let us note, is in this view just as material as are practices that are not tied to religion (that is, 'secular' practices): they interact with, negotiate, rework, are limited by objects within the plane of immanence which constitute the real. There is no transcendent, extramundane reality to which religious discourse and material ritual point. As Latour says, the discourse of religion does not refer to a beyond: in fact, it does not *refer* at all. Rather, religion calls our attention to the near.[7] It highlights the immediate presence of things, directing our gaze to the objects in front of us rather than engaging us in lengthy chains of inference toward a beyond. In his inimitable fashion, Latour points out that it is science that deals in

---

6   Quentin Meillassoux, 'Spectral Dilemma', *Collapse* IV (May 2008): 261–75.

7   This is the central book of his book on his recently translated book on religion. See Bruno Latour, *Rejoicing: Or the Torments of Religious Speech*, trans. Julie Rose (Cambridge, UK: Polity Press, 2013).

transcendence and not religion: religion's concern is with the wholly immanent.[8] As we saw in the previous chapter, the analogue to which Latour frequently appeals is love. The discourse of love, he tells us, is constantly being constructed in order to fend off the threat of distance. Love relationships are fragile, and there are times in which everything seems to hang on small gestures or minute inflections or differences in phrasing. All could be lost in a moment, and a chasm of distance sets in which hollows out all of our memories and hopes.[9] 'I never really knew this woman.' The other is now the end of a chain of references, or at least is along the chain somewhere and thus removed from the immediate circle of intimacy we have tried so hard to maintain. Like love, the relationship we have with our objects of worship, our gods, is fragile and beset by the possibility of final loss into transcendence. God can cease to be a present reality for us and vanish into a chain of references, ever circulating and never secure. We might say that, like love, religion changes everything. It colours our perceptions; indeed, it makes everything look different. In other words, religion orients us. To orient, literally, is to face toward the east, to turn oneself so that one's vision is framed by looking in a particular direction (from which, it is assumed, truth will become evident). For relational Christian realism, it is too much to say that there is one particular direction which discloses truth. It is also too much to say that a basic orientation such as religious participation has a privileged and unilateral relationship with other discourses, sources of insight or knowledges. As we have seen, religious practice may draw on multiple perspectives and traditions whose basic orientations are irreducible yet capable of deep interaction with each other. As a result, the orienting function of religion is fluid and dynamic, not given once for all once a person or community adopts a tradition. Moreover, distinguishing religious discourse from other kinds does not make it incommensurable with them, since discourses and practices are intimately entangled with each other and these entanglements are productive in all directions. In other words, though it is a function of religion to orient its practitioners to other material practices, whatever (scientific, political, social and so on) commitments that take shape (loves, in Augustinian terms) as these other material practices are engaged also to have effects on the practice of religion itself. Nevertheless, it is important to recognise that orientations, including those embodied in religious participation, make a difference in how we see.

---

8   Of course a qualification is in order here: 'transcendence' in Latour refers to a particular kind of 'beyond.' It is not an additional realm to the plane of transcendence, but simply an elsewhere to which chains of inference lead us. See Latour, *Pandora's Hope: Essays on the Reality of Science Studies* (Cambridge, MA: Harvard University Press, 1999), 98–108.

9   Latour, *Rejoicing*, 52.

We have not fallen once again into correlationism here, because this inevitable colouration need not be confined to the relationship between human knower and known object – that is, to epistemology.[10] We may generalise, and ontologise, this Augustinian and originally psychological point: all objects, human and non-human, confront each other in terms of their own internal structures. They do not in all cases have psychologies, but they do have ways of being which are decisive for the ways they encounter other objects. We will have much more to say about this later in the chapter, but for now we may call to witness some strange, and yet unexceptional, examples: a baseball encounters a swinging stick of hardwood much differently than a half-rotten pumpkin does, or a human skull. A hammer's blows are received differently by a ten-penny nail and by a cold human thumb. A deer encounters a three-inch layer of autumn snow differently than a beetle, or a wooden deck. There is nothing particularly exceptional about the case of religion, or even of human perception. Generally, what we are shapes how we encounter things. It is only beings with eyes that see things, to state an obvious but philosophically important point. And among humans, who we are – what lies in our personal and cultural histories, what we expect or hope for in the future – shapes what we see.

If we join this inevitability of orientation to Latour's interpretation of love, we have to modify the picture on the question of love's fragility. Though the content of love, or our specific relationship to a particular love-object, is fragile, *that* we love is not. This is both an ontological and a psychological point. Ontologically, all beings have a structure that influences how other things are encountered. Psychologically, this structure in humans includes what Mary Midgley calls an 'emotional constitution' that is, among other things, mammalian, and thus strongly shaped by interest in and need for attachment.[11] Even if our actual attachments are fragile, our drive toward attachment is relentless, and thus our emotional constitution is always seeking connection. Thus every object we encounter is interpreted in relation to that to which we are attached or seeking to be attached – 'that' referring here in most cases to a plurality of what Augustine called 'loves'. In Latourian terms, for each of us there is a near whose presence we seek to establish and maintain. And this near is more

---

[10]   Harman says he has no problem with correlationism; he simply wants to universalise it. See Graham Harman, *The Quadruple Object* (Alresford, UK: Zero Books, 2010), 126–8. But we cannot universalise it without escaping its orbit altogether, since in order to render an account of all interactions between objects as correlations we have to break the spell of the primacy of the human subject-object correlation as constitutive of all knowledge.

[11]   Mary Midgley, *Beast and Man: The Roots of Human Nature* (London, UK: Routledge, 1979), 321–6.

than an immediate experience: it is also a lens through which we interpret and appropriate all that we encounter through the long and circuitous mediations we call knowledge. We have made a strong claim here – that religion or something like it is both a product of what we may call, by means of a generalisation and abstraction, 'human nature'. Let us remember that we are offering a normative interpretation here, one that inevitably spills over into claims about what it means to be human. In this way, an interpretation of religion does not ground what a religion or theology will say about substantive matters such as the nature of human beings. Rather, these claims are reciprocally related. As striking is this claim about the inevitability of religion, it is of course not a new one. It has been characteristic of a strand of theological thinking known as 'theological liberalism', so called because it has sought to understand theological ideas as arising from and ultimately normed by human experience rather than by what one liberal theologian calls the 'house of authority'.[12] But of course, it must be admitted that appeals to human experience already reflect some particular account of the human. Liberal theology, and a relational Christian realism that follows it, seek intelligibility and accountability to other ways of construing the world and human experience. They do not seek nor do they establish certainty nor rational autonomy.

Among the many objections that have been raised by this procedure has been what we might construe as a theological precursor of the philosophical critique of correlationism that has arisen recently. The theological critique is that liberal theology seeks to domesticate the real (God) in terms of the categories of human understanding, thus undermining the wholly otherness of the divine[13] (compare Meillassoux's 'great outdoors' that we considered in Chapter 1). However, as we have already argued, the problem with correlationism is its imprisonment of the real within the human-world correlation. To say that religion is an all-but-inevitable product of the human emotional constitution in no way limits the real to what human loves can capture. What religion opens us toward, the presence of the near, is encountered by all beings, human and non-human, without doubt with radical differences, as we have suggested. Our perception

---

12   Edward Farley, *Ecclesial Reflection: An Anatomy of Theological Method* (Philadelphia, PA: Fortress Press, 1982), 166–8.

13   Karl Barth's famous invectives against the domestication strategies of liberal theology are of course the most well-known. See Karl Barth, *The Word of God and the Word of Man*, trans. Douglas Horton (New York, NY: Harper and Row, 1957), 9–27. For a more recent version of this argument, seen William C. Placher, *The Domestication of Transcendence: How Modern Thinking about God Went Wrong* (Louisville, KY: Westminster/John Knox Press, 1996), 1–17.

of the great outdoors is limited by our nature – but that is true of all beings who encounter other beings. Such relativism is not the opposite of realism – but, as Latour argues, the only way to have it.[14] Realism is not a matter of having absolute knowledge (we are parting sharply from Meillassoux here, as we shall see), but of acknowledging that our knowledge does not confine what is.

Theology as it is understood here is a set of concepts and procedures which serve this orienting function of religion, drawing together the various features of our experience together with our motivations, our fears and our aspirations so that we can be oriented coherently toward and within our present worldly tasks. In order for these concepts to work, they must be open concepts, never 'freeze-framed'[15] but constantly open to renegotiation in light of the various kinds of practical and intellectual entanglements in which we find ourselves. It is the freeze-framing of concepts in regnant forms of theological non-realism that we are seeking to contest and, ultimately, to undo. Though it was devised in the context of a theology which is perhaps too much tinged with idealism to suit our purposes without revision, there is no reason not to learn from Paul Tillich's 'correlational' theology on at least the following point. Tillich's distinction between 'preliminary concerns' and 'ultimate concern' accounts very well for the capacity of religious commitments and practices to become fruitfully entangled with other material practices as well as for the distinctive role played by religious practice.[16] What we call our 'ultimate concern' is the centre of value, to employ a Niebuhrian term from Chapter 1, that frames the way we perceive and engage other concerns. Or, in Julian Hartt's phrasing, religious belief is 'construing' belief in so far as its content is not so much a discrete, knowable object as it is a construal or interpretation of all components of human experience in light of its object.[17] Ineluctably, when we try and place God within the circulating references of human knowledge, God remains an unknown 'X': we do not know the ultimate referent of our religious speech. But, in the account of religious discourse we are adopting, reference is not its significance. Religious discourse, including theology, shapes the way we view other things – for us, material practices within our economic, social and political lives.

---

[14]   Latour, *Pandora's Hope*, 1–10.

[15]   Bruno Latour, *On the Modern Cult of the Factish Gods* (Durham, NC: Duke University Press, 2010), 122–3.

[16]   Paul Tillich, *Systematic Theology, Vol I: Reason and Revelation, Being and God* (Chicago, IL: University of Chicago Press, 1951), 10–15.

[17]   Julian N. Hartt, 'Encounter and Inference in Our Awareness of God', in *The God Experience: Essays in Hope*, eds Joseph, P. and Whalen, S.J. (New York, NY: Newman Press), 51–4.

First Theologeme: God

But of course the crucial critical question we must face is whether resort to talk about God is worth the risks it entails. Does it not entail transcendence, and thus obfuscation and alienation? Postmodern philosophy of religion has been devoted largely to a critique of the ontotheology of highest beings, and so trying to address the idea of God in a philosophical mode immediately raises the spectre of an uncritical return to theological metaphysics. In addition, as we have seen in our reading of Meillassoux thus far, there is an opposite danger that attends philosophical discourse about God in a postmodern mode – an equally uncritical return to religion in the form of a fideism which leverages 'correlationism' to license any number of theologemes, so long as they are not interpreted ontotheologically. Instead of a highest being, for example, there is a God 'beyond being', the affirmation of which is not touched by material or empirical pressures.

This project eschews both what Meillassoux calls the 'dogmatic' metaphysics of pre-modernity and early, pre-Kantian modernity (ontotheology) and the fideism of postmodern, postmetaphysical turns to religion. But we nevertheless need to address the question of God, both for practical reasons and for constructive/theoretical purposes. First, for a material religious practice that seeks orientation in the world, a way of framing or interpreting the broad range of material entanglements in which we find ourselves, we need a concept to draw together our motivations and our perspectives on the immanent real. Our point here recalls theologian Gordon Kaufman's account of the idea of God as that by which we human beings can imaginatively draw together the many facets of our knowledge and experience so that we can focus our attention coherently and thus fruitfully on the tasks at hand. We human beings need to construct some kind of unified, though revisable, framework by which to engage the ungrounded multiplicity which is the world. The idea of God, with its unity and its 'relativising' proviso that disrupts any particular content we might ascribe to it, is able to anchor such a framework.[18]

But beside this practical necessity for such a concept, there is also the constructive and theoretical matter of whether or not it makes sense to talk of God within a philosophy of immanence. Is there a way to reinterpret and redeploy the concept of God that is consonant with the philosophical position

---

[18]   Gordon D. Kaufman, *In Face of Mystery: A Constructive Theology* (Cambridge, MA: Harvard University Press, 1993), 78.

being outlined here? Without such a concept, it is hard to see how relational realism can sustain its identity as 'Christian'.[19]

So, how may we think about God from a relational Christian realist perspective that is informed by the return to the real in contemporary philosophy? Two quite distinct and rarely related sources will guide our thinking around a single theme: radical immanence. The revisionary strand of modern theology associated with classical theological liberalism running from Friedrich Schleiermacher through Ernst Troeltsch to Paul Tillich and more recent theologians like Gordon Kaufman has sought to reconfigure thinking about God in ways more consistent with the findings as well as the assumptions and implications of modern science.[20] Finding sufficient resources for causal explanation within the range of empirical knowledge, the idea of a transcendent agent who imposes purposes upon the world from the outside gives way in this intellectual trajectory to a power that is immanent within the cosmos though not reducible to it.

There is perhaps no better example to cite here than Friedrich Schleiermacher himself, whose thought lies behind the thinking of our theological interlocutor of the first chapter, H. Richard Niebuhr. Schleiermacher was impressed with the causally self-contained cosmology he inherited from the eighteenth century and sought to reinterpret Christian doctrine in light of it. Theology, he held, has to be carved out from within the religious experience of being dependent on powers greater than us.[21] It was, as Brian Gerrish puts it, a theology 'within the limits of piety alone'.[22] This procedure produced a theology that is highly disciplined, attaining a high degree of rigor but carefully delineating the subject matter and distinguishing the proper domain of theology from other forms of

---

[19]   See Langdon Gilkey's critique of 'Christian atheism' in *Naming the Whirlwind: The Renewal of God-Language* (Indianapolis, IN: Bobbs-Merrill, 1969), 147–78.

[20]   For monumental expressions of this project, see Friedrich Schleiermacher, *The Christian Faith*, trans. H.R. Mackintosh and J.S. Stewart (Edinburgh, UK: T & T Clark, 1999 (orig. 1830)), Ernst Troeltsch, *The Christian Faith*, ed. Gertrud von le Fort, trans. Garrett E. Paul (Minneapolis, MN: Fortress Press, 1991 (orig. 1912–13), Paul Tillich, *Systematic Theology*, three volumes (Chicago, IL: University of Chicago Press, 1951, 1957, 1963) and Gordon D. Kaufman, *In Face of Mystery: A Constructive Theology* (1993).

[21]   Schleiermacher, *The Christian Faith*, 76–93.

[22]   B.A. Gerrish, 'Theology Within the Limits of Piety Alone: Schleiermacher and Calvin's Doctrine of God', in *The Old Protestantism and the New: Essays on the Reformation Heritage* (Chicago, IL: University of Chicago Press, 1982), 201. See also Gerrish, *Continuing the Reformation: Essays on Modern Religious Thought* (Chicago, IL: University of Chicago Press, 1993), 147–51.

discourse. Drawing on this historic Christian piety, Schleiermacher's theology rendered an idea of God as the 'whence' of the feeling of absolute dependence: a God whose action is to ground and sustain the 'nature-system', the nexus of finite causes, rather than to intervene within it in discrete acts.[23] Relational Christian realism has no interest in attempting to sustain the level of scientific rigor exemplified in Schleiermacher's program, because it is purchased at too high a cost: limiting the range of sources for theological construction to the experience of piety cuts off its entanglement with other fidelities. Nevertheless, what is instructive about Schleiermacher's method in its actual exercise is that it takes causal immanence for granted, and is thus able to render an account of God that is shorn of the anthropomorphisms of conventional theism.

A recent term that captures the basic logic of the Schleiermacherian trajectory is 'panentheism'. God is not a being who is separable from and beyond the world. Indeed, there is no 'beyond' with respect to the world: all causes are part of the 'nature-system'. In this sense, transcendence has given way to a wholly immanent God. Nevertheless, God is not to be identified with the universe as a whole or with any proximate feature within it. As Kaufman suggests, the very meaning of the word 'God' resists identification with any mundane reality, thus providing a sort of imaginative purchase on the universe which allows to characterise it as a whole and thus to take up a posture toward it.[24] An example here would be the idea of 'grace'. In his *Principles of Christian Theology*, John Maquarrie suggests that to believe in God is to experience being itself as gracious.[25] There is no supposition here of a being outside of being, or, with Marion, of a God who is somehow beyond being.[26] Rather, there is simply an affirmation that being is susceptible to a distinctive, non-obvious interpretation. And, so interpreted, we may take up a posture toward being – we may experience it in a particular way. Such is the semantic upshot of talk about God. Articulated in ontological rather than merely linguistic and/or phenomenological terms, we might say that grace inhabits being while not being identical with it. We might even say that grace 'transcends' being while not being beyond or somehow behind it – if we limit the term 'transcendence' to non-equality within immanence.

---

[23]   Schleiermacher, *The Christian Faith*, 170–78.

[24]   Kaufman, *In Face of Mystery*, 328.

[25]   John Macquarrie, *Principles of Christian Theology*, 2nd ed. (New York, NY: Charles Scribner's Sons, 1977), 113.

[26]   Jean-Luc Marion, *God Without Being, Hors Texte*, 2nd ed., trans. Thomas A. Carlson (Chicago, IL: University of Chicago Press, 2012).

Part of what drives relational Christian realism is the conviction that this strand of liberal theology with its theme of immanence is capable of being brought into fruitful conversation with the theme of radical immanence in materialist philosophies, especially those that resist the postmodern linguistic turn and engage ontological questions once again. Without taking sides on too many intramural disputes, we can identify a 'philosophy of pure immanence' in recent continental philosophy extending from Gilles Deleuze's vitalist metaphysics through Alain Badiou's subtractive ontology, Quentin Meillassoux's speculative materialism and the object-oriented ontologies of Bruno Latour, Graham Harman, Levi Bryant, Timothy Morton and Ian Bogost. The rest of this chapter and the next attempt to engage these thinkers to re-engage the project of theological liberalism, especially as it was steered away from the Kantian idealism that continued to shape Schleiermacher's theology by the twentieth-century movement of Christian realism.

So how, going back to Macquarrie's conceptuality, can grace (or God) be construed as inhabiting being but not identical with it, or with any particular aspect or component of it? The first step we will make is to distinguish actual states of affairs from what we call, following Gilles Deleuze, the 'virtual'.[27] We will have to trouble this term, offering various refractions of it, shortly, but for now we will simply suggest that Deleuze's concept of virtuality allows us to talk about a feature of the real that is not limited by the actual but that does not constitute a transcendent domain. A number of things need to be clarified here. First, this conceptualisation depends upon a non-coincidence of the real and the actual. Actual states of affairs do not exhaust what is real. What is actual, rather, *expresses* the real. Another way to say this is to say that actual states of affairs, as well as aggregates of them, are contingent. Astir amid any state of affairs are powers or potentials which states of affairs express. What we call 'laws' or even 'tendencies' within nature provide a useful example. The state of affairs described by such terms as 'entropy', 'inertia' or 'evolution' are contingent expressions of what the world is capable of. To say that such things are contingent is to say that there is no metaphysical necessity for what Graham Harman calls the 'molten core' of objects, their 'volcanic' essence, to express themselves in those ways.[28] Ontologically prior to evolution, there are things that evolve. The relations, the interactions, the causal influences exchanged between things are secondary to

---

[27]   Deleuze's most celebrated account of the virtual is found in Gilles Deleuze, *Difference and Repetition*, trans. Paul Patton (New York, NY: Columbia University Press, 1994), 100–103. See also his essay, 'Immanence: A Life', in *Pure Immanence: Essays on A Life*, trans. Anne Boyman (New York, NY: Zone Books, 2001), 25–33.

[28]   Harman, *The Quadruple Object*, 17.

the things themselves. The powers hidden in things are not reducible to the particular ways these powers are actualised. The point is that actual events are real, but do not exhaust the real: hidden within them are powers that forever withdraw from complete actualisation.[29] This hidden power is the virtual.

Note here that there is a non-equivalence of reality with actual states of affairs without having to appeal to an additional realm of actuality which is regarded as somehow beyond or as more fundamental than the actual in which we traffic in our ordinary material interactions. The distinction between the virtual and the actual does not require two layers or levels to reality that could be assigned labels of immanence and transcendence, a 'here' and a 'beyond', or nature and supernature. Virtuality is not a realm: it is a power that stirs within the only world there is.

Our next move is to identify God with this virtuality. There are some options here for how to think of this identification, depending on which account of the virtual we accept, as we will see in a moment. First, we need to recognise the possibility of thinking about God without leaving, if you will, what Deleuze calls the 'plane of immanence'. Again, if we think of God as virtual, we do not have to posit an additional realm of actually existing entities that transcends the material world in order to engage this first and primary theologeme. For a theology of radical immanence, there is no such realm – which is to say that the ontological content of the idea of God will have to be filled out without attributing actuality to God in addition to material states of affairs. As Tillich once insisted, God, while real, does not exist: God is not an entity, a being who helps to populate an inventory of existing beings.[30]

Divine virtuality tracks the contingency of actual states of affairs. To believe in God the virtual is thus both to hope and to fear. That is to say, God as the virtual real both offers hope that the world as we now know and experience it is not necessitated, and it undermines ultimate confidence in the stability or reliability of things. This is where our point of view is radically different from Schleiermacher and also at least a conventional reading of Tillich: the attraction of belief is not the security of an eternal ground of being but rather the hope that arises from the ungrounding of being. Of course, the flip side of hope is fear: that the world is fundamentally ungrounded means that it is menaced as well as promised. The world's contingency means not only that it could be better, but also that the fragile securities of life as we have them, the social formations on

---

[29] Levi Bryant, *The Democracy of Objects* (Ann Arbor, MI: Open Humanities Press, 2011), 87ff.

[30] Tillich, *Systematic Theology, Volume I*, 235.

which we rely, even the biological and physical trends which carry us (somewhat) benevolently through environmental challenges, or at the very least make life plausible for a time, may be swept away without any reason at all. Such is the nature of contingency, as we will see more clearly below as we engage Meillassoux again: thought in the most rigorous fashion, it troubles even such metaphysical comforts as the principle of reason itself.[31]

Of course we still have not said what we mean by saying that God is 'virtual'. On this point, as we have already suggested, there are several options. One of them, theologising Deleuze (who is in turn appropriating Spinoza, Bergson and Nietzsche) would be to embrace a vitalist notion of virtuality. In *Anti-Oedipus*, Deleuze and Félix Guattari write about 'pre-personal forces' that circulate and vie with each other amid the struggles of individuals and societies. This 'molecular' (contrasting with 'molar') account of both class conflict (Marx) and intrapsychic conflict (Freud) suggests that there is a level of the real that is more fundamental either than economic substructure or the elements of individual personality, and that this level is composed of irreducible multiplicities.[32] What is equally important for Deleuze and Guattari as compelling description is adequate clinical, political and philosophical engagement. If a molecular analysis (also called 'schizoanalysis'[33]) is correct, then various ways of leveraging some kind of unity or solidarity to effect personal and social change are not only bound to fail because they run against the grain of the multiple real which is expressed in personal and social conflict, but also are a kind of oppression itself, suppressing the 'schizoid' character of life, driven as it is by pre-personal vitalities or forces that are seeking unfettered expression in the face of efforts to impose various forms of control. The clinically, politically and philosophically appropriate articulation of the deep, unmitigated multiplicity of vital forces is not a definite revolution or breakthrough to deep insight, but the permanent state of revolutionary self-expression of the play of surface effects they call 'nomadic'.[34]

What we are suggesting is that one option for thinking of God as virtuality would be to identify God with this unmitigated pluralism of circulating pre-personal forces that are continually astir amid actual states of affairs but that

---

[31]   Quentin Meillassoux, *After Finitude: An Essay on the Necessity of Contingency*, trans. Ray Brassier (London, UK: Continuum, 2008), 64.

[32]   Gilles Deleuze and Félix Guattari, *Anti-Oedipus: Capitalism and Schizophrenia*, trans. Robert Hurley, Mark Seem and Helen R. Lane (New York, NY: Penguin Books, 1977), 1–8.

[33]   Ibid., 322–9.

[34]   Deleuze and Guattari, *A Thousand Plateaus: Capitalism and Schizophrenia*, trans. Brian Massumi (Minneapolis, MN: University of Minnesota Press, 1987), 351ff.

never settle into any one of them. God is the movement of 'deterritorialisation'. Again, states of affairs are expressions of these forces, but the relationship between expression and expressed is contingent. Thus God as vital multiplicity is within the actual though the two are not identical or collapsible into each other. God is the immanent milieu of the actual, but is not one of the items to be counted among the actual, nor a kind of summation of the actual itself. An advantage of this way of conceptualising God is that it undermines hierarchies in a radical way. The centre of value, to recall Niebuhr's phrase, is not a singular transcendent being, but the swarming multiplicity that dissolves attempts to reify selves which would set themselves over against or above other selves, communities or environments. God is not one: or perhaps, God always fails to be one.[35] The concept of God does not describe a unified being, but rather does unifying work. In Alain Badiou's terminology, it 'counts [God] as one', imaginatively unifies multiplicity for the purpose of orienting human beings in the world.

The constructed character of this unity is important to recognise in light of Badiou's criticism of Deleuzian metaphysics as a subtle kind of monism. Badiou's claim is that beneath the clamour of the multiple in Deleuze lies the repose of being. For Badiou, this incipient monism undermines human agency in face of larger political and economic forces, and is thus inherently conservative, even fascist.[36] Peter Hallward leverages a similar critique, charging Deleuze's philosophy with otherworldliness. In ironic contrast to his explicit motif of immanence, Deleuze allegedly calls our attention to a realm that is abstracted from the material struggles of actual human existence.[37] The problem with Hallward's critique, however, is that it begs the question against Deleuze, whose claim is precisely that there are powers astir within rather than beyond the actual. That is what the contrast between virtuality and actuality means. Nevertheless, the force of both Badiou's and Hallward's critiques calls for an acknowledgment that any theological appropriation of Deleuze, or Deleuzian appropriation of theology, must avoid any association of God with a realm that is any sense beyond the swarming multiplicity of immanence. The unity of God is not a given ontological reality: it is a construction.

---

[35]   Laurel C. Schneider advances this claim in *Beyond Monotheism: A Theology of Multiplicity* (London, UK: Routledge, 2008), 153ff.

[36]   Alain Badiou, *Deleuze: The Clamor of Being*, trans. Louise Burchill (Minneapolis, MN: University of Minnesota Press, 2000), 102.

[37]   Peter Hallward, *Out of This World: Deleuze and the Philosophy of Creation* (London, UK: Verso Books, 2006), 55.

A different critique is levied by Ray Brassier, who charges Deleuzian metaphysics with vitalism.[38] We have already characterised the Deleuzian option as a kind of theological vitalism, and we have thus accepted Brassier's point at least at the descriptive level. The virtual in Deleuze is dynamic: it resists territorialisation (that is, it 'deterritorialises'), it flows, it swarms. While not all of these are biological metaphors, they suggest countermovements to the entropic processes that lead to death and the end of meaning. For Brassier, the test of mettle for any philosophy is its ability to resist any defensiveness in the face of the encroach of the nothing upon and within human experience. Brassier seeks to 'theologise' cosmology – that is, to ingest its austerity in order to face squarely the destruction of meaning by physicalist naturalism and the entropic scenarios it forces upon us.[39] It is in light of this test that Deleuzian's vitalism is problematic. We need not accept Brassier's nihilism to grasp the force of his point. For a relational Christian realism that welcomes entanglement with other discourses and seeks to do justice to non-theological sources of insight, any appropriation of Deleuze must reckon with the deflating realties of entropic dissolution.

A second possibility for thinking of God as virtuality is less open to the charges of monism and biocentrism, though in a way it is perhaps more open to the charge of dualism and otherworldliness. This second way can be described as a 'subtractive' option, and it is suggested by Badiou's subtractive ontology and also by his student Meillassoux's philosophy of radical contingency. As Hollis Phelps argues, Badiou's ontology is anti-theological,[40] and it is therefore difficult to derive a theological position from it, unless one counts atheism as a theological position. But there are moves which are suggestive nevertheless, especially when refracted through the philosophy of Meillassoux. For Badiou, being is irreducibly multiple. By 'irreducible' here we mean not subject to an order, or, as a Badiou calls it, a consistency. Being is inconsistent multiplicity, and it is only made consistent when it is ordered or 'counted-as-one'.[41] But the count is a constructive act. In the terminology we have suggested, it is a matter of construal: we 'take' or 'see' the multiple 'as' this or that ordered whole in order to be oriented toward it in a coherent way. Badiou's point, however, is that inconsistency always escapes the consistent multiplicities we construct

---

[38]   Ray Brassier, *Nihil Unbound: Enlightenment and Extinction* (London, UK: Palgrave Macmillan, 2007), 162, 222.

[39]   Ibid., 231.

[40]   Hollis Phelps, *Alain Badiou: Between Theology and Anti-Theology* (Durham, UK: Acumen Publishing, 2013), 13.

[41]   Alain Badiou, *Being and Event*, trans. Oliver Feltham (London, UK: Continuum Books, 2005), 23–5.

by counting-as. There is no ontological unity that transcends or governs the multiple.[42] Being is ungrounded, we might say. 'Void is the proper name of being.'[43]

What is suggestive of a possible account of God here is the notion that the real escapes our count – or, perhaps, menaces or threatens it. In a manner that is not all that different from a theologised Deleuzianism, in fact, we may say that the divine just is the ungrounding, the deterritorialising, of various configurations or orderings of being. The inconsistent multiple assigns the status of contingency to any count-as-one. More clearly than Deleuze, Badiou's ontology resists not only the ontotheological subsumption of the multiple under a highest being but also the congealment of multiplicity in a flowing vitality: there is no being, no set of sets, but only beings in their inconsistent multiplicity. So, if God be equated with the latter, then this central theologeme would lose its consistency, its unicity. God would refer neither to a highest being, nor to a unified ground of being underneath beings, a 'God beyond God' in Tillichian style, but to the fact that being is not, that only beings exist, and thus that counts are contingent and orders are ontologically fragile. God, here, would not be ground, but ungroundedness.

The speculative materialism articulated in Meillassoux's *After Finitude* does not mention God or the possibility of thinking about God in a rigorously philosophical manner, but what he writes about contingency and virtuality, like Badiou's void, is quite suggestive. As we noted above, virtuality tracks the actual world's contingency. For Meillassoux, virtuality does not so much refer to a kind of hidden, shadowy reality that is expressed in the actual without ever being collapsible into it, as in Deleuze. Rather, the virtual indicates possibility space. For Deleuze, possibility does not constitute the virtual, because possibility is always a function of actual states of affairs. For Meillassoux, however, virtuality is nothing more than possibility space, the non-totalizable (transfinite in the Cantorian sense) plurality of possible universes.[44] Actuality is only one possible instantiation of the virtual. Key here is that the word that links virtuality and actuality is not expression, as if there is something anterior to express, but instantiation, since what is instantiated is one particular possibility amid a transfinite plurality of universes. The virtual is the uncountable multiplicity of universes. This, essentially, is Badiou's 'inconsistent multiplicity'. Meillassoux most often refers to it as 'hyper-chaos'.[45] It is 'chaos' because it is not governed

---

[42]   Ibid., 24.
[43]   Ibid., 52.
[44]   Meillassoux, *After Finitude*, 62.
[45]   Ibid., 64.

by any law or any order. Laws and orders are contingent actualisations of certain possibilities, and as ultimately contingent (Meillassoux argues), there is no reason for them to be what they are. Thus, they might change at any time, for no reason whatsoever. This chaos is 'hyper-' because it applies not to a particular universe (our universe is clearly not chaotic in this sense), but to the uncountable multiplicity of possible universes. Thus, there is no reason why this universe is rather than some other one – and, further, there is no reason why this universe cannot be replaced in a moment and without reason by another with different laws and possibilities inscribed in its architecture.

In a trivial but metaphysically troubling example of radical contingency, Meillassoux notes that there is no reason that billiard balls do not sprout wings and fly off the table.[46] We might easily imagine less homely, entertaining examples: water may become poisonous without reason; air pressure may crush rather than support the human frame, without reason. Or, human hunger may end, without reason; a supernatural being may arrive to destroy death, without reason. The liturgical repetition of 'without reason' in the above examples captures a central feature of Meillassoux's speculative philosophy: the principle of unreason. Directly contradicting a central 'dogma' of classical metaphysics or ontotheology, the principle of sufficient reason, the principle of unreason sets the sign of contingency over the ordering of the universe, thus ensuring that any such ordering is menaced by the threat of dissolution or profound transformation.[47] By ungrounding the world, hyper-chaos grounds both fear and hope.

In *The Divine Inexistence*, it is the supernatural being who abolishes death that is brought forth as the properly philosophical hope for God, a hope grounded in the principle of unreason. Hyperchaos, or virtuality, is repudiated as a potential object of worship. Indeed, the problem with 'religion', as we saw above, is that it tends toward worship of chaos, the raw power to make things happen without (moral) reason. We will address this critique below, but for now we simply want to suggest that construing Meillassoux's virtual as divine is indeed a possibility, even it is not one that he himself approves of. As with the vitalist option, this subtractive position does not construe the divine as a singular transcendent being. Neither, however, does it regard the divine as a shadow reality that is somehow astir within the actual, as the expressed in its expression. Rather, hyper-chaos simply indicates the lack of reason for the instantiation of this particular world from among the transfinite possibilities that could be instantiated.

---

46   Ibid., 95–8.
47   Ibid., 71.

There are problems with Meillassoux's philosophy for a relational Christian realism, however. First, while it overcomes the biocentrism and monism that threaten Deleuzian positions, the subtractive option in general and Meillassoux's version of it in particular tends toward dualism. For Badiou, there is a break between ontology and event: indeed, the meaning of event is precisely to break from an ontic situation. Meillassoux's philosophy radicalises this break with the notion of 'advent'. The later is not just an exception, subtraction from or non-participation in a predominant situation or ordering, but is the arrival of a whole new ordering. The dualism here is between the two situations riven by the advent. As in all dualisms, the question would be how one gets from one to the other – and of course in Meillassoux the answer is no reason at all. This is a dualism that offers no chance of dissolution or even mitigation: the break is sudden, non-rational and unanticipated.

This characteristic of Meillassoux's philosophy leads to a second and more troublesome difficulty: it seems to undermine agency. In Badiou, an event arrives and we construct our agency in faithfulness to the event in order to bring about revolutionary change. In Meillassoux, on the other hand, revolutionary change happens in sublime indifference to agency of any kind: it is pure contingency, pure accident. There is an advent – a complete transformation of one contingent situation so that it becomes another one – and particular agents have nothing to do with its arrival and no role to play in maintaining the world that it inaugurates. As in Deleuze, oddly enough, it is the virtual which seems to perform the action. In this case, virtuality is possibility space rather than a pre-individual substance. But the effect is the same: out of the infinite well of possibility space emerges a world, without reason and without cause, and what it includes are merely the expressions of just this possibility. We don't construct new worlds: we are the constructs of them. This raises a question about order in Meillassoux. In general, some kind of order would seem to be the only possible context of productive agency. Even if agency is understood as response to the Badiouan event, that is, as a subtraction from some regnant order, it would seem that such subtraction is just one more of several possible relations to order, each of which presupposes the existence of an order of some sort to relate to – positively or negatively.

However, is it really true that there is no order in Meillassoux's speculative system? It is true that, as in an intra-cosmic matter, order is undermined by the constant menace of order's absolute contingency – an order can fall apart or be replaced at any time for no reason. But in *The Divine Inexistence*, Meillassoux describes a succession of what he calls 'worlds', by which he means something like 'universes', complete with a set of laws that govern them. Each world is utterly contingent, but there is a logical succession from one world to the next.

For example, the first world consists simply in being, and it is comprised of inorganic objects that exist (importantly, for Meillassoux) without any subject to know or to describe them. The emergence of life, for Meillassoux, constitutes an event, or 'advent', that is not fully accounted from by the previous world. A new world comes with the event, with new laws (biological ones) that can actually work against the physical laws of the prior world. From this second, biological world arises, again for no reason and without cause, a third world, a human one in which there are new, intellectual principles that hold sway. In the third world, there are beings who can come to contemplate meaning, and thus can come to know the meaninglessness of the world – that is, its utter facticity, its lack of reason. Importantly for Meillassoux, it is impossible to imagine any innovation in this third world that would not remain with the basic parameters of a third world. Billiard balls could sprout wings, but that would mean we have just a stranger third world on our hands. Nothing essentially new would have arisen – there would have been no advent. The only advent that is now possible, given the actuality of the third world, would be the arrival (without reason, of course) of a supernatural being who would do justice to humanity's absolute knowledge of facticity by overcoming death and imparting the immortality to human beings that they 'so richly deserve' as rational beings who have come to know the absolute. This would be something new, because it would convert meaninglessness to meaning, or to justice, as there would now be a world of beings who can know absolutely (as we have now) but who have an eternity to enjoy their knowing. There would be no more (what inevitably seems to us) arbitrary cutting off of knowers from the possibility of knowing.[48]

What we want to call attention to here is the fact that, even in Meillassoux's radically contingent world, there is not a complete absence of order. The advent of worlds is not and cannot be random, but follows a definite logic. It may not be a completely satisfactory account of order, to be sure. Indeed, it is an order of cataclysmic changes and not one of constant negotiation, as we find in other ontologies. It thus cannot account for fine-grained interactions and exchanges with the kind of precision as we find, for example, in object-oriented approaches, which we consider next.

Beside vitalist and subtractive modes of construing the divine as virtuality, there is finally a pluralist option. One may leverage the thinking of a group of philosophers who are thinking through the metaphysical implications of Bruno Latour's philosophy of objects. 'Object-Oriented Ontology' (OOO), including the work of Graham Harman, Levi Bryant, Ian Bogost, Timothy Morton and

---

[48]   Meillassoux, 'Divine Inexistence', 217.

others, is built on the seemingly innocuous premise that the world is made up only of objects of various sizes and kinds.[49] The radical implication of this supposition, however, is that there are not metaphysically distinct entities called 'subjects'. This is not a denial of subjectivity as a human experience *per se*, but an insistence that even human consciousness, and its intensionalities, fall into the category of objects, along with a list of more homely realities, including rakes, derivatives, belt buckles, the colour blue, gum and femurs. OOO tends to generate what Ian Bogost calls 'Latourian litanies' that simply list objects in their insistent non-connection because it holds that the world is not the correlate of a subject which somehow escapes it, as idealist philosophies have long suggested, but a swarm of entities in relationships of constant negotiation and resistance.[50] At a fundamental level, all objects, including the objects we call 'subjects', are on the same ontological plane: hence a broader, more inclusive name for what OOO advocates is 'flat ontology' (all proponents of OOO are flat ontologists, but not all flat ontologies embrace OOO).

Like vitalist and, less clearly, subtractive options, OOO views all reality as inhabiting a single 'plane of immanence'. Suspending for a moment the question of whether any meaning can be given to the term 'transcendence', there is for OOO no great beyond, no realm of reality that is in some definitive way higher, more real, or more permanent than the pedestrian one we inhabit day today. Like other flat ontologists, OOO radicalises this claim of inclusive secularity by denying any sense of metaphysical uniqueness, including the singling out of human beings and/or their subjectivity. However, OOO is also characterised by a clearer, and more homely, sense of transcendence than either the vitalist or subtractive options. Since reality is comprised of discrete objects whose relations to each other are contingent and not exhaustive of the identity of each of object (more of this in a moment), one can say that transcendence is relocated rather than simply renounced. If traditional ontotheology locates transcendence in a distinct sphere that is in hierarchical relation with our own 'immanent' one, and if idealist philosophy locates it in the transcendence of the ego – or, alternatively, in the transcendental or 'constituting' character of the subject – OOO locates it in the particular ways in which specific objects resist being defined fully by their relations to other objects or to collectives. Transcendence is not the prerogative

---

[49]   For representative examples of this position, see Graham Harman, *The Quadruple Object*, Levi Bryant, *The Democracy of Objects*, Ian Bogost, *Alien Phenomenology: Or What It's Like to Be a Thing* (Minneapolis, MN: University of Minnesota Press, 2012), and Timothy Morton, *Realist Magic: Objects, Ontology, Causality* (Ann Arbor, MI: Open Humanities Press, 2013).
[50]   Ian Bogost, *Alien Phenomenology*, 38.

of the great beyond or of the subject in its alleged distinction from objects, but it is rather a feature of each and every object comprising the real, precisely in its singularity. As Graham Harman writes, there is a 'volcanic' inner core of objects that is never captured in the ways other objects encounter them.[51] For OOO, one cannot speak of 'Transcendence' with a capital 'T', but of small-t transcendences which are individual, particular and local.

Bryant's version of OOO is particularly interesting for our purposes, because he draws on and modifies Deleuze's (vitalist) account of virtuality. Bryant does not interpret the virtual as a shadow reality behind the actual, as if one can talk coherently about a virtual 'world' that is somehow more real than the actual one. Rather, the virtual categorises particular features of individual objects. According to Bryant, every object has an 'internal structure' which is never fully grasped or operationalised in its relations of negotiation and resistance with other objects. Here, virtuality refers to the essential non-relatedness of objects, a stubborn reserve or unseen potential or power that remains unrevealed or unexpressed within the actual. The virtual is thus the capacity of an object or an alliance of them to engender change, its capacity for revolution both in its constructive and destructive dimensions. Crucially, this capacity is not a shadow reality behind or beneath the actual, nor subtracted somehow from it; rather, it is a power that is attached to actual, material conditions in the world.

It is actually more difficult to use OOO for theology than it is the other speculative philosophies we are examining here, precisely because of its insistent littleness: the virtual is always distributed, attached to objects rather than serving as some great reserve that is beyond or beneath them. Drawing on OOO in order to reconstruct our first theologeme, we might say that the idea of 'God' indirectly refers to the plural powers of the actual world. It thus gathers into a singular concept that which is irreducibly plural. Again, for the pluralist option, virtuality is not a shadow reality behind the actual, nor a way of describing possibility space that is indifferent to the actual, but is a property of actual – and thus God would be understood here to be a property – or, more precisely, the set of properties – of actual, material conditions in which objects interact in various and contingent ways.

A distinctive advantage of this approach is that it is not susceptible to the charge of monism in the way that Deleuze's Spinozist/Bergsonian vitalism is. Here, there is clearly no ontologically singular referent of the 'expressed'. Virtuality is a general term that designates certain features of objects – it is not readily reified into a distinctive realm or object in its own right. In fact, a

---

[51]   Harman, *The Quadruple Object*, 17.

divinity construed in object-oriented terms would have more in common with Badiou's inconsistent multiplicity than with Delueze's virtual. Thus, to speak of the virtual, or God, is to construct rather than to describe: it is to employ a way of construing the inconsistent real so that one may oriented toward it in a consistent way. This way of taking the idea of God has a strict parallel in the constructivist theology of Gordon Kaufman, according to whom the word 'God' refers not to a distinct object but to a set of general observations about the universe. In Kaufman's case: the facts that creativity occurs and that this creativity often gets channelled into some kind of trajectory, as creative momentum gets built up along a particular pathway.[52] Further parallels will be drawn below, as we discuss the second theologeme (creation), but here the point is simply that recourse to theologemes in general is warranted for its constructive promise rather than its descriptive power.

A second advantage of an object-oriented approach is that it does not threaten to fall into dualism of conditions and event (or advent). Again, it is the littleness of OOO that is helpful here: there is no great reserve of virtuality or possibility which stands over and against the world of objects. Virtuality is integrated within them, so that the divide between the virtual and the actual cuts across objects themselves. In Harman's terms, objects have a real dimension and a sensual dimension: the real is the object's volcanic inner core whose potential is never exhausted or fully articulated; the sensual is the object's presentation as it is related, perceptually and otherwise, with other objects.[53] The actual is the object in its relations, its place in what Timothy Morton calls the 'mesh' of interacting objects; the virtual is Morton's 'strange stranger', the object's irreducible singularity and irreducibility to the relations in which it appears.[54]

The obvious problem for theology that an object-oriented ontology as we have described it poses is whether its use of the term 'God' to describe the multiple real, the virtual, is warranted. If the term 'God' speaks in the singular of an irreducible plurality of partial objects, why use this term at all? Is not its singular form profoundly misleading? There is an object-oriented way out of this difficulty, and we may have done well to take it. Adam Miller, in *Speculative Grace: Bruno Latour and Object-Oriented Theology*, suggests that God is one object among others, perhaps a very great one, but one that is, like all objects,

---

[52] Kaufman, *In Face of Mystery*, 281–97.

[53] Harman, *The Quadruple Object*, 20–34.

[54] Timothy Morton, *The Ecological Thought* (Cambridge, MA: Harvard University Press, 2010), 38.

limited in 'his' knowledge of other objects and even of 'him'self.[55] Latour himself makes similar suggestions in his writings on religion and the 'factish'.[56] For Latour, all religious objects, all gods, are real precisely because they have been constructed: thus the term 'factish'. But they are also of necessity limited, not because of their having been constructed by humans, but for the deeper and more pervasive reason that all objects are limited: there is no unilateral power in the world, since objects leverage power by means of negotiation with other objects. This idea of God as an object that exemplifies rather than serving as the unique exception of a general ontology is a well-trod path in recent theology, blazed in part by the process theologies inspired in the twentieth century by Alfred North Whitehead and Charles Hartshorne.[57]

However, in this book we have determined to take a different path, thinking of God not as an actual being, but as in some way virtual: as a power or powers that are somehow hidden within the actual, along the same plane of immanence with them but not among them as one actuality among others. We have taken this path to preserve something about the idea of God that makes it recognisable as the God of classical Western theism: a kind of non-identity if not transcendence, a capacity to play a causal role in the world that is unique if not unilateral. Simply put, a God who is submerged within the play of objects is not what the tradition has meant by 'God'. Much better to think of God as the play itself: this is what the notion of God as virtual effects.

Taking this less conventional path raises complications, to be sure. A loss, from the perspective of a more classically Whiteheadian process theology, is actuality, as we have already admitted. Another loss, closely related, is unity. God's unity, for us, is not that of a discrete actuality. In saying that God is virtuality, especially if we interpret this claim in object-oriented terms, means that God is not one, that unity is a counting operation we use in order orient ourselves to this multiple power and possibility, and that it is always only a provisional human construction for which we must take responsibility.

But that does not mean that there is no such thing as the one God. Here, we can appeal to Latour and Badiou in the same breath: God-in-the singular is the factish we construct in our attempts to navigate inconsistent multiplicity. A God-in-the-singular, we might say, helps to cope with reality of divine multiplicity.

---

[55]   Adam S. Miller, *Speculative Grace: Bruno Latour and Object-Oriented Theology* (New York, NY: Fordham University Press, 2013), 9ff.

[56]   Latour, *Cult of the Modern Factish Gods*, 22.

[57]   See, for example, Alfred North Whitehead, *Process and Reality: An Essay in Cosmology* (New York, NY: The Free Press, 1929), and Charles Hartshorne, *The Divine Relativity: A Social Conception of God* (New Haven, CT: Yale University Press, 1948).

As factish, a concept which has its own objectivity and reality precisely because we have constructed it and deployed it in the world, God-in-the-singular is a real being whose causal efficacy, like Whitehead's God and Harman's objects, is limited by its place in a mesh of relations with real others. Factishes may be born, arise to become regional or even global powers, be rebuffed and rebuked and of course die. And, we may engage in new works of construction, seeking to build better factishes, whose reality will be more durable in the face of the challenges we anticipate. But these factishes are made in human factories, invoking and mobilising other objects, powered by real multiplicity, a pervasive virtuality that is volcanic and not susceptible to exhaustion. It is this power that drives construction, and enables us to hope for a God who may come that will faithfully and fruitfully express the multiplicity from which it arises, and direct us toward a better life within it.

But we need to take a step back. There is a glaring weakness in any of these attempts to inscribe the divine on a plane of immanence, whether in a vitalist, subtractive or object-oriented mode. The problem is that, as a matter of actual (material) practice, one cannot serve such a God. Empirical realist theologian Bernard Meland wrote approvingly of 'appreciative consciousness'[58] that recognises the profligate creation of value throughout the universe, but we cannot commit ourselves to such profligacy. In actual practice, we require a specific direction or trajectory within the mélange of powers and goods that proliferate amid the infinity of interactions within the world in order to orient and commit ourselves consistently and coherently. Kaufman, from the perspective of constructive theology, understood this, and that is why 'creativity' alone never sufficed for him as a metaphor for God. In various ways and with limited success Kaufman took up the more difficult issue of what he called 'directionality' as well.[59] If we are to speak of God in a way that is both religiously appropriate and adequate to the tasks of life, we have somehow to risk a greater degree of specificity than we have so far found in our reflections to this point. We have to go beyond talking about virtuality, and look for an actualisation, or the beginnings of one. We have to go to work and construct a factish.

To recognise this is to appreciate the force of Meillassoux's critique of a religion of 'awe' which simply worships power. There is nothing particularly attractive about such passive reverence, and in the end it stultifies human initiative. Moreover, one cannot be trusting of and loyal to such a divine in a

---

58   Bernard E. Meland, *Fallible Forms and Symbols: Discourses of Method in a Theology of Culture* (Philadelphia, PA: Fortress Press, 1976), 57.

59   Kaufman, 'On Thinking of God as Serendipitous Creativity', *Journal of the American Academy of Religion* 69 (2001): 409–25.

direct way, because it is expressed in great evils as well as goods.[60] Rather, we can be faithful only to certain concrete events which express it. So, while awe is without doubt a component of a genuine interaction with the real implied in the idea of God, it has to be complemented by something like faithfulness to a particular trajectory within the world, a particular configuration of values and historical/cosmic possibilities.

Again, awe is a real component of religious experience, but by undirecting, or by bracketing any particular direction to which we might be committed with the sign of contingency, it actually threatens faithfulness. So, the question is how to recognise the validity of awe before an unmitigated multiplicity of values and powers, and yet press on toward a more coherent orientation that can guide or at least positively shape engagement with the material world? Here, Badiou's analysis of fidelity is instructive. Whatever we make of his subtractive ontology (and we prefer the pluralist ontology of Latour and his object-oriented interpreters, if we have not made that clear), Badiou's account of agency as an historic construction produced by enduring faithfulness to a revolutionary event is suggestive of how we might account for something like directionality within the confines of an ontology of pure immanence. One need not think of this event as subtractive in an ontological sense – or, in Meillassoux's terms, the 'advent' of a new world. Rather, we may simply think of it as a happening among others that is quantitatively more powerful than most because it creates a higher than usual number of productive links between objects or elements within the plane of immanence. Pasteur's mobilisation of professional societies, public opinion, medical practices, laboratory instruments and microbes in the form of a theory of infectious disease is an event in this sense.[61] So is Jesus of Nazareth's mobilisation of Jewish tradition, revolutionary hopes and ancient frustrations in the formation of a new social group with a distinct sense of a universal mission. Even this more pedestrian account of an event, we suggest, is capable of explaining the motivations we might have for remaining faithful to it long after is has receded into history. For Christians, of course, the most illuminating fidelity-producing event is that of Jesus and his new community. This event, for most theologians, is not simply the birth of the man Jesus or even the 33 years of his life taken as a whole, but the complex of historical confrontations and engagements which includes a Roman imperial government in the 1st century CE, its methods of controlling its outposts, the socio-economic conditions of

---

[60]   Ibid., 410ff.

[61]   This example is frequently cited throughout Latour's writings. For his fullest account, see Bruno Latour, *The Pasteurization of France*, trans Alan Sheridan and John Law (Cambridge, MA: Harvard University Press, 1993).

Galilee, the various political and religious factions gathered around Jerusalem, human nature, the social functions and the temptations of wealth, Mary, agriculture, manual labour, water pots, weeping sisters and so on. In fact, the 'Christ-event' is made up of a veritable Latourian litany of swarming objects of various size and scope and in various kinds of negotiated relationships with each other. But the assemblage takes a particular shape or gestalt. Out of this swarm, connecting these objects in provocative if not revolutionary ways, emerges a picture of one taken to be the very 'form of God' (Phil. 2).

By way of interpretation in terms of a philosophy of immanence, we may say that Jesus is the divine form (the 'form of God') insofar as he unsettles the actual and mobilises the volcanic powers of the virtual into the already-formatted (actual) world with a particular direction or aim. Both elements are crucial here: divinity, setting the sign of contingency upon arrangements of the actual, or upon material conditions; historical form, shaking up the world not simply to watch it fall to pieces but to beckon, lure or perhaps force a region of human experience in a particular direction. It is this direction which invites faithful participation and loyalty, and it is the acceptance of such an invitation over time that shapes human agency and makes Christian faith a matter of ethics as well as metaphysics.

At this point once again we have multiple options for how to think about this event. We may characterise them in terms of two ancient traditions within Christian theology regarding how to understand the relationship between Jesus and the divine. We will characterise the first as the 'Alexandrian' option, recognising that neither the first nor the second options simply repristinate orthodox representations, but rather redeploy their logics in terms of a very different way of conceptualising God. In Alexandrian logic, the relationship between what we are calling divine virtuality and the human figure of Jesus is characterised as a *union* between the virtual and the actual. The actual bodily reality of Jesus, together with the relationships in which he is entangled, expressed the divine. In theologian Laurel Schneider's version of this logic, this entanglement is crucially important: God becoming flesh means that God embraces the deep relationality of embodiment, and so the divine is expressed and actualised not in a discrete individual with sustained and well-defined boundaries (a 'chaste' incarnation), but in the unmitigated multiplicity that is the actual world of relationships. For Schneider, to say that God is in union with material reality means that God is 'promiscuously' in union with all of reality.[62]

---

62   Laurel C. Schneider, 'Promiscuous Incarnation', in *The Embrace of Eros: Bodies,*

And so the practical question of how one is to be oriented – what direction such orientation should take – is answered quite ambitiously. God is expressed in all of the dirty details of life – therefore we are to value and give voice to all of them.

It is conceptually difficult to distinguish Alexandrian logic, at least in Schneider's version of it, from the religious awe critiqued by Meillassoux. No doubt there are tonal differences: Schneider is not interested in acquiescing in whatever happens to be the case, surrendering her agency in an act of passive devotion. Rather, the 'promiscuous' kind of orientation she seeks to articulate actively searches out relations with others, to extend or at least to become aware of the extendedness of the incarnation in both personal experience and, likely, public policy. However, what is stubbornly similar between Meillassoux's awe and Schneider's promiscuity is a certain oceanic (the Freudian reference is intentional) vagueness about what the centre of value to which one is committed really is. 'Embodiment', we may say. Yes, but to what purposes are bodies set in motion? For what particular transformations do we hope? As we noted earlier, the multiple as such cannot coherently organise human motivation, cannot gather it into an efficacious agency. We need, rather, something more concrete, and if Christology cannot give it that, it is hard to see what it really adds to devotion to the virtual.

And so, we turn instead to the second option, which redeploys ancient Antiochene logic. Here, the divine virtual is not expressed in the material body of Jesus so much as in his total person, including most importantly his distinctive subjectivity. Object-oriented ontology, we will remember, does not rule out the value or the force of subjects – it only insists that subjects be included among other objects. Thus, we may say that the subjectivity of Jesus is a powerful object that is able to exert significant force on other objects, mobilising them in order to effect changes in the configuration of things. For 'Antiochene' spirituality in materialist mode, what is important is not the impartation of divine power to physical flesh, but the formation of this particular object we may call revolutionary consciousness, a subjectivity that is rooted in ancient Hebrew piety but extended toward a universal transformation of social, political and economic structures, and indeed to life on earth as far as it is impacted by human intervention.

Like Alexandrian logic, what is key is that the divine virtual achieve a foothold, a uniquely luminous expression, within actuality. The difference is not, as it may first seem, one of materiality versus ideality. Both logics, in fact, focus attention on the material – at least in our materialist appropriation of them. The difference

---

Desire, and Sexuality in Christianity, ed. Margaret D. Kamitsuka (Minneapolis, MN: Fortress Press, 2010), 242–4.

is between a focus on relationality, a potentially infinite web of connections which is hard if not impossible to lift just because it is so profoundly entangled, and a focus on a particular historic trajectory, one object within a Latourian litany gaining influence by leveraging the virtual powers inscribed in Israel's real, material history to create linkages and associations, and possibilities. This incarnation is an emergence of a concrete, historical object (Jesus) that gains the very natural and traceable power to reinscribe itself within the internal structures of other objects, so that they re-instantiate the Christic trajectory and its universalising intent.

Theologians have used different conceptualities to articulate this logic. Friedrich Schleiermacher's romanticism yielded a discourse of sympathy in which Jesus' unique power of God-consciousness had the lateral effect of drawing others in so that they by degrees would replicate it.[63] Paul Tillich's Schellingian-inspired existentialism yielded the language of 'spiritual presence', a still ambiguous but nevertheless genuine historical expression of the 'new being' revealed in Christ.[64] Dietrich Bonhoeffer, somewhat more crudely but perhaps more provocatively for a secular age, wrote of forms of Christ (*Gestalten Christi*) that may have nothing to do with institutions or with persons associated with the Church. Thus, for the secularising Bonhoeffer, the Christic reality is able to re-inscribe itself within ostensibly hostile forms of community and action.[65]

Bonhoeffer's important innovation points toward a larger theme of non-enclosure that must accompany any invocation of Christology to support entangled fidelities. First, the divine virtual, even if it is expressed in the event of Jesus, the formation of a revolutionary subjectivity and its transmission to various historical trajectories, cannot be enclosed by it. Especially if we embrace the pluralist option for thinking about divine virtuality, we must be able to account for the presence of an unsettling power that is attached to every actuality. Thus, the virtual might be and likely is expressed elsewhere. We cannot affirm all of these expressions as capable of providing orientation (that is, being the locus and referent of faithfulness), because some of them will undoubtedly be troublesome if not evil, while most will likely be indifferent. But those expressions that do

---

[63]   Schleiermacher, *The Christian Faith*, 431ff.

[64]   Tillich, *Systematic Theology, Vol. III: Life and the Spirit, History and the Kingdom of God* (Chicago, IL: University of Chicago Press, 1963), 138–41.

[65]   Perhaps the clearest connection Bonhoeffer makes between his Christology and ethics appears in *Ethics*, trans. Neville Horton Smith (New York, NY: Simon and Schuster, 1955), 186–204. For an account of the way the reference of the term *Gestalt Christi* broadens over Bonhoeffer's career, see Larry L. Rasmussen, *Dietrich Bonhoeffer: Reality and Resistance* (Louisville, KY: Westminster/John Knox Press, 2005), 32–73.

invoke a like faithfulness, that point toward a universal transformation toward justice, can and must be recognised as sites of 'the spiritual presence' or as *Gestalten Christi*. In fact, the presence of *Gestalten Christi* in the various arenas of late modern society and culture is a major (though not the only) warrant for the entangled character of fidelity that we are advocating in this book.

Second, the virtual is not only able to be embodied in analogous ways in other places or along other historical trajectories, it is also expressed, as we mentioned above, in ways that do not directly provide adequate human orientation in the world but may even undermine it: earthquakes, tsunamis, bloody coups by rising tyrants, child sex trafficking, infectious disease, to begin a tortuously long Latourian litany of objects we likely want to marginalise. They do not invoke or shape subjectivity toward faithfulness of the kind we are talking about. However, the broad category of such expressions of the divine is crucial to acknowledge. Their non-enclosure within a Christic logic suggests the latter's profound limitation and even fragility. Faithfulness, even the entangled kind, does not operate without restrictions or limitations, and is not necessarily supported by the predominance of forces that express the divine. We cannot responsibly and realistically say that God is on the side of the oppressed, for example, nor, unfortunately, that the arc of the universe is long but that it bends toward justice. There is simply no warrant for that, even if there are more circumscribed hopes, in a realistic perspective.

Finally, and most ambiguously from a human point of view, we have to acknowledge that absolute contingency is not enclosed by the Christic trajectory, but rather the other way around. The latter could stall out, or be co-opted without remainder. Simply put, the Christ event could come to an end, no longer re-inscribing itself within the internal structures of present and future objects. Such is the possible fate of any object, since causality in OOO is indirect and non-constraining.[66] More generally, any or all of the best values we associate with human flourishing could meet a similar end. None is necessary, or guaranteed. God would still be God in the sense of there being a real that powers the actual from within – virtuality would still be attached to every feature of actuality – but the things we are faithful to or for would be gone. The God we have known would be dead.

To recognise the limitation and the contingency of values, and of the efficacy of events which invoke and form faithfulness, is itself an important feature of faithfulness, we are suggesting, because it acknowledges that those features of our experience which serve as the focus of our confidence and our loyalty do

---

[66]   Timothy Morton, *Realist Magic*, 72. See also Harman, *The Quadruple Object*, 69–81.

not enclose the powers that give life and take it. To recognise the mortality of our God is part of what it means both to acknowledge a divine power beyond ourselves and to hope for God who may yet come. We are ultimately dependent ('absolutely dependent', according to Schleiermacher) on a vast, inhuman real, and to acknowledge that fact means that what we love and serve are only its contingent and partial expressions. To be devoted to the real means that our faithfulness is always marked with a sign of reservation, even of unbelief. In the end, Meillassoux's awe continues to haunt faithfulness. What Reinhold Niebuhr often called a sense of the 'beauty and terror of life' is the price, and the reward, of realism.[67]

So, by way of summary, there are three motifs that characterise the idea of God as we have framed it. First, there is the restless ungrounding that evokes religious awe. The referent of our speech about 'God' is in the first instance not an actual object, but an infinite milieu or network or mesh of relations in which and through which objects interact for good or ill. God 'is' in the mode of virtuality, and thus is not susceptible to reification, or to anticipation. One might call this first motif 'hope', since the ungrounding of actual states of affairs, its being menaced by contingency, is what affords hope for radical, systemic change. In Meillassoux's words, it is the 'inexistence' of an ontotheological ground of the present order of things which allows us to hope for a new world.[68] The second motif highlights a characteristic expression of God (a form of God) that evokes faith, understood as loyalty and trust. Following Badiou, we could say that fidelity is a particular kind of subjectivity that is evoked by a decisive event. The form of God is a particularising, a concretising, of that vast, ungrounded virtual real that churns within the actual. The latter is not capable of evoking subjective commitment because it provides no object on which to focus. But the form of God is an expression of the virtual amid the actual world of objects and their relations, and so it is the making possible of a stance of subjective commitment to the God beyond objects. Needless to say, this second motif may be called 'faith', since the form of God is what makes concrete commitment to God possible. Finally, there is within the idea of God an affirmation of what Paul Tillich called the 'spiritual presence'. This is the transformative power that is actualised in the world by a new relation that is established between the objective form of God and our subjective commitment to it. As a gathered

---

[67] Characterising life in terms of its 'beauty and terror' was a favourite rhetorical strategy of Niebuhr which reflected his sense of its fragility and contingency. See, for example, Reinhold Niebuhr, 'The Sickness of American Culture', *The Nation* 166/9 (6 March 1948): 269.

[68] Meillassoux, 'The Divine Inexistence': 232.

people whose imagination is framed by commitment tinged with awe, religious communities can discern in a wide variety of concatenations of forces and objects a power to bring new possibilities, new structures and new orientations. This 'presence' within the actual world is 'spiritual' because it contains not only the dynamism of the virtual which ungrounds and therefore menaces actual structures and objects (such dynamism is universal in any case), but also and more importantly because it repackages and redeploys the specific power toward transformation that characterises the form of God. In other words, there are *Gestalten Christi* everywhere for those who see the world through faith. This final motif may simply be called the motif of love, since such perceptions enable a basic generosity toward the actual as everywhere a potential conveyor and site of radical transformation.

The relation of the first and third motifs to the second is decisive for the sort of relational Christian realism we are constructing. It is easily seen that the three motifs together constitute a kind of functional or economic trinity, and this is to be welcomed so long as this construction does not attempt to re-inscribe relational Christian realism within a new (or old) orthodoxy. For orthodoxy, as for its contemporary apologists, trinitarian logic simply explicates adherence to a high doctrine of the Son or Word. And, as is often the case with narrow orthodoxies of the word, it is the non-subsumable powers of creativity and spiritual presence that threaten to undo our brittle certainties and narrow fidelities. The reality of the multiple is never captured in its written traces. But since the form of God is the form of *God*, the christomorphic focus and origin of distinctively Christian faith cannot be allowed to harden into a christocentrism which rejects other fidelities as unfaithful and/or unwarranted. Rather, a relational Christian realist account of God supports the acknowledgement of an entanglement of multiple fidelities on the basis of the insight that God is expressed in multiple communal and social trajectories and thus produces multiple subjectivities which are present within the commonwealth in which we participate, and thus that circulate as well in us as persons.

Chapter 4
Engaging the Theological II:
Creation, the Human and Redemption

The idea of God is of course the most difficult among those that need to be retrieved and reconstructed for a relational Christian realism. But within the conceptual universe of Christian thought, the idea of God never stands alone but is aligned with other theologemes that lend it specificity and contour. We already saw the religious inadequacy of a bare concept of God in the previous chapter: we needed to provide texture and directionality to it by invoking the Christ event and the spiritual presence. Here, we must go further and relate the idea of God to the flat, wholly immanent infinity of non-divine objects that are synoptically invoked in the (problematic) concept of world.[1] If we assert the reality of God, what can be affirmed about other things in light of God? The classical categories that must be engaged here are those which depict 'the world' in terms of a cosmic and historical drama in which a transcendent God was held to be involved: creation, fall and redemption. Since we have parted company with the idea of a transcendent divine being, we must ask whether and how these categories, as well as those that attend them, can be reshaped in light of the divine immanence we are describing here.

Second Theologeme: Creation

Besides God, first of all, we need to engage the idea of 'creation'. The importance of this second theologeme for a relational Christian realism is two-fold: first, it renders a degree of specificity to the first intention of the idea of God as we have described it: inconsistent multiplicity, hyper-chaos or virtuality. One might say that it is, in fact, the correlate to the first intention. If God is first

---

[1]   Strictly speaking, there is no 'world' in OOO, because a reality made up of objects in various kinds of contingent relationship with each other does not admit a final sense of inclusion or containment. See Levi Bryant, *The Democracy of Objects* (Ann Arbor, MI: Open Humanities Press, 2011), 270.

of all a transcendental virtuality (rather than transcendent being) that renders all things radically contingent, the idea of creation is that of an order that is under ontological threat. That is to say, creation means that all things – all objects, but perhaps more importantly all relations between them – are in a strong sense contingent. The world, to speak synoptically and improperly, is not self-sustaining but dependent upon sources of creativity that both encircle and menace it. And secondly, the idea of creation is important because it indicates a texture to finite existence that makes it a site of directional movements and capable of producing the spiritual presence. That is to say, creation also connects with the second and third intentions of the idea of God.

The theologeme of creation as it is reformulated by relational Christian realism interprets the world not as a static order guaranteed by a fixed, supra-mundane transcendence, but as an enclosed and inclusive ontic domain (a 'plane of immanence') that is characterised by a flexible but genuine ordering toward the possible emergence of meanings and values. To invoke again the first motif of the idea of God, it assumes that current states of affairs (the actual) are menaced by a restless divine virtuality, for worse but also for better.

Relational Christian realism can thus connect with and radicalise a point made by Radical Orthodoxy here, even if qualifications have also to be introduced. For the latter, creation is to be construed as gift. Its existence and character are utterly gratuitous, and reflect the character of God who is perfect charity.[2] 'Gift' then becomes a prominent motif in Radical Orthodoxy's interpretations of politics and economics: it points to real possibilities for challenging capitalism and constituting an alternative, non-agonistic economic and political order.[3] Relational Christian realism radicalises the gratuitous character of the creaturely order(ing) because it removes its fixed, transcendent point of reference. God is not actual, and thus the gift is not grounded in a singular transcendent being and fully realised in this 'over there'. The upshot for us is that we do not, as in Radical Orthodoxy, participate in an actual and final realisation of gift with varying degrees of adequacy and fullness. Gift, for relational Christian realism, names a decisive character of the everlasting, ungrounded circulation of goods that is the created ordering. Every good could just as well not be: it is contingent. Therefore, in the circulation and distribution of goods there is acknowledged a fundamental ungroundedness about that which is exchanged. It is gift all the way

---

[2]   John Milbank, *Theology and Social Theory: Beyond Secular Reason*, 2nd ed. (Oxford, UK: Blackwell, 2006), 392. See also Milbank, *Being Reconciled: Ontology and Pardon* (London, UK: Routledge, 2003), 154–61.

[3]   Such is the ambitious agenda of the last chapter of *Theology and Social Theory*. See Milbank, *Theology*, 383–442.

down. Nothing guarantees it, and thus the gift is a characteristic that pervades the circulation of goods itself. Gratuity is taken to extremes.

The notion of gift in relational Christian realism, it should be said, is as hostile to capitalist exploitation and to its ideology of possession and ownership as the parallel concept in Radical Orthodoxy, but it does not point to a singular alternative polity and economics: it can support socialisms of various kinds, but it does not lead by a kind of ontological deduction to a repristinated Christian Socialism. Rather, relational Christian realism is nomadic and to some degree pragmatic (provided that by pragmatism we don't mean a blunting of critique and acquiescing in the picture of the world that neoliberalism seeks to portray as necessary and obvious). Whatever political and economic structures emerge as a result of robust critical engagement with them, relational Christian realism assumes, will be complex, situational and characterised by multiple entangled fidelities. More about these matters will follow in subsequent chapters.

As we have already hinted at, the creation theologeme reconstructed in this way can do more than emphasise and specify contingency. Drawing here on the work of Bruno Latour, Levi Bryant and other exponents of OOO, we may say that creation is also textured by the many circuits or connections between the irreducibly multiple objects that it is. This is perhaps the key theological point for a specifically *relational* Christian realism. The object oriented ontology that we are drawing on insists upon the non-reducibility of objects to their networks of relations, but its insistence upon the integrity of objects without relations does not diminish but rather enhances the genuinely relational character of the created order(ing). It can affirm that persons, T-shirts, dead plant leaves, hyena hairs and hubcaps are not merely ephemeral expressions of intersecting lines of force, defined and produced entirely out in terms of the network of relations in which they are enmeshed, but rather genuine participants in a series of negotiations with other such objects, each of which relates to the other in terms of its own internal structure. In the words of Graham Harman, OOO refuses to 'undermine' objects by reducing them to their place amid the forces created by relationships.[4] But it is just this refusal that makes networks contingent upon an undissolved multiplicity of real objects; and, more importantly, it is that which makes the specific negotiations between them undetermined and their outcome all-important.

An important feature of a relational Christian realist account of creation is the notion of change at the level of the actual: the force contingency leverages is not just a power of virtuality that stirs beneath the actual and is expressed in

---

4   Graham Harman, *The Quadruple Object* (Alresford, UK: Zero Books, 2010), 8–10.

it, but a power that is embodied *within* the actual – in actual exchanges and negotiations. This is what keeps relational Christian realism from a form of otherworldliness or Spinozist occasionalism where nothing really happens at the level of actuality that is not simply the expression of some reality behind, beneath or above it. Since the virtual is not a unified substance but a dimension of every object, the ways its forces get unleashed has to do with real relations between objects – alignments, disjunctions, oppositions and so on. In terms of the second intention of the idea of God, contingent forms of God can emerge, enter negotiations with other objects and have a decisive impact on subsequent events.

Classical Christian theology insisted, against ancient Gnosticism, that creation is good. Relational Christian realism echoes this claim in a new key by insisting that the power of transformation not be confined to virtual shadow world, but that actual, material states of affairs be sites of embodied virtuality. There are real moments of revolutionary historical change, forms of God that enter the pervasive series of negotiations that constitute the created order and that overturn, reconfigure and reconstruct power structures as their potentials are unleashed.

How does this work? For classical Christian theology, creation was regarded as the site of divine interventions on the part of a singular transcendent being. For relational Christian realism, on the other hand, creation names the contingent and dynamic order(ing) that is constituted by an infinite series of ongoing, finely textured and open-ended negotiations between objects. For OOO, on the one hand, every object has an essence that is independent of relations and always withdraws from them. In Levi Bryant's rendition, the essence of an object is virtual rather than actual precisely because of its independent reality which is neither overmined nor undermined by its relations; but, again, this account of virtuality does not locate it in a spectral realm but in the hidden fullness of the object.[5] Thinking of God as the virtual in this particular construction, we would say that the virtual (God) is present to each object as its unexpressed plenitude – as the infinity of its possible expressions and relations. Because of this, the explosive power of every object's unexpressed plasticity, patterns within creation could always be different than they are.

Care is needed here. We cannot identify God with the hidden core of every object itself without undermining objects in precisely the same way that worries Harman and without adding the additional difficulty of a theological occasionalism that destroys the integrity of the created ordering. Rather, we must be more circumspect and say that God simply names a fact about the

---

[5]   Bryant, *The Democracy of Objects*, 105ff.

inner cores of objects: their inexhaustibility. Especially in an object-oriented mode, with the idea of divine virtuality we gather together the multiple under a singular concept. We do not evacuate objects of their mundane essences, but we characterise the infinity that attaches to them. One can think of God here as the dis-ordering potential embodied in every object which makes static orders among them impossible.

Every object is embroiled in networks of relation that stretch to infinity but that can take specific local shapes. The various 'trials of strength' in which things are perpetually involved yield larger patterns of inclusion and exclusion. And thus there emerges an evolving 'commonwealth' or 'parliament' (Latour) in which things struggle to find their places.[6] This commonwealth assigns things a status, both ontological and normative. Latour writes about this activity in terms of two moments or elements within an ongoing process: (1) taking into account, and (2) putting in order. The first of these is a matter of recognising the existence of new beings that appear before the commonwealth and, as it were, petition for admission. The proper exercise of this function amounts to a perpetual openness to an outside that is far more supple, and inevitably more densely populated, than the commonwealth can discern at any one moment.

The second function, 'putting in order', is a matter of integrating new objects into the commonwealth's existing structure – a structure that inevitably changes as new objects are added, but that has continuity across time. Putting in order expresses, we will note, a feature of objects in general, including not only large ones like commonwealths but also comparatively small ones like the objects they welcome – inner structure or essence. Bryant's account of this inner structure correctly underscores its indeterminate plasticity – since we only have one angle of vision on a thing at any one time, no one can tell 'what a body can do'.[7] Nevertheless, the commonwealth, like all objects, remains what it is even as it changes. That fact that it must impose its structure on the newly welcomed object is what Latour means by 'putting in order'.

Thus orderings develop as objects enter into relations with each other, and descriptive evaluations and evaluative descriptions become possible. Understood this way, the creation can be affirmed as good, corruptible and renewable (that is, as created, fallible and redeemable). It is good in so far as it is both open and ordered. It is thus characterised by a flexible ordering that undermines

---

6   Bruno Latour, *We Have Never Been Modern* (Cambridge, MA: Harvard University Press, 1993), 142–5.

7   Bryant, *The Democracy of Objects*, 157. The expression quoted is Spinoza's. See Baruch Spinoza, *Ethics*, part III, prop. 2, scholium, trans. Samuel Shirley (Indianapolis, IN: Hackett Publishing, 1992), 105.

hegemonies on the one hand and mitigates isolation on the other. The good of the creation, as a commonwealth of beings, is that of a democratic ordering where the individuality of each object is respected while also integrated into a common life. Such an ordering is corruptible in two ways, to which we have already alluded: by isolation, in which ordering is incomplete and fragmentary so that some objects are effectively left out of the commonwealth or barred access to it; and by unmitigated hegemonies. With respect to isolation, we can think of undocumented immigrants at the level of human politics, or of subatomic particles which are invisible because of some failure or glitch in a research programme that could have conceptualised them. With respect to unmitigated hegemonies, we can think not only of political and economic hegemonies, whose effects are all too clear, but also hegemonic thoughts, research programmes or even physical objects, all of which can come to have so central a place in a commonwealth or in some region of it that all other objects in the vicinity are effaced or overrun.

An important point here is that Latour's conceptuality allows us – requires us, in fact – to sidestep two modernist distinctions: fact and value, and also human and non-human. The tasks of taking into account and putting in order cut across either of those distinctions. Taking into account, ostensibly a matter of discerning 'facts', actually is both evaluative and descriptive, since acknowledging existence also embodies a decision to attend to the integrity and uniqueness of an object as object. As H. Richard Niebuhr pointed out, even allegedly value-less scientific description depends upon confidences and loyalties that maintain that objects under investigation are sufficiently interesting to sustain the rigours of investigation and conceptualisation.[8] On the other hand, 'putting in order', ostensibly a matter of assigning values, is both descriptive and evaluative, since assigning things a place in relation to other things within the framework of a commonwealth is not only a matter of ranking but also of discerning the contours of an object so that its potential relations to others can be clearly articulated.

The distinction between human and non-human, while clearly viable as a sorting device, loses the importance ascribed to it in modern thought when confronted with Latour's conceptuality for two related reasons. First, Latour's notion of commonwealth simply ignores the distinction, including all objects whatsoever as ontologically equal members (even if admittedly of unequal strength). Smokers and cigarettes, shooters and guns, microbes and biochemistry researchers, each both act and are acted upon in local trials of strength that, in

---

8   H. Richard Niebuhr, *Radical Monotheism and Western Culture, With Supplementary Essays* (Louisville, KY: Westminster/John Knox Press, 1960), 86–9.

the aggregate, determine their places in the body politic of humans and non-humans. Secondly, and by implication, the two scientific-political (describing-evaluating) activities of the commonwealth are the aggregate functions of trials of strength in which both humans and non-humans participate. In other words, it is not simply humans who perform knowing and evaluating acts. As Latour points out, reflecting on a comic strip, cigarettes are not passive or inert objects acted upon by their consumers; nor are smokers simply passive victims of the charms of cigarettes.[9] Rather, each object acts on the other, and receives the actions of the other, always in light of its own internal structure. The same is true for guns and their owners, for microbes and the researchers that try to understand them, and for hosts of other relations between objects. One important implication of this is that there is no final, absolutely hegemonic power. Another is that non-humans exert constructive influence in the expansion and formation of the commonwealth in just the same way as humans do.

A final point needs to be made about the creation theologeme and its role in orienting material practice. Here we need to delve a bit more deeply into explicitly theological modes of explication and argument. We have previously engaged Radical Orthodoxy with respect to its account of 'the gift' as a way of constructing an alternative, non-capitalist, polity and economics by way of claims about participation in transcendent actuality of gift or 'charity'. We have suggested that relational Christian realism radicalises the theme of gift by removing its transcendent grounding and locating its gratuity in the contingent character of material exchanges, but that such a reframing does not lead to a ready-made alternative polity. We need at this point to bring in another theologeme that often follows 'creation' in order to understand why this is the case.

The classical theologeme of a primordial 'fall' is a philosophical surd. As historical (that is, actual) event it is nonsense. And yet it is an important symbol for understanding the conflicted, agonistic and often tragic character of the actual world, especially if we have already asserted its essential goodness. However, it is hard to separate the symbol of 'fall' from the thought of an event: it does not seem simply to indicate a pervasive ontological condition. If its meaning does not entirely eviscerate Christian claims about the goodness of creation, it must invoke some sense of contingency. It is in so far as we grasp it in terms of a contingent outcome that it plays an important role in rendering a full account of the possibilities and limitations that are woven into the process of gathering and refining a commonwealth.

---

[9]   Bruno Latour, *On The Modern Cult of the Factish Gods* (Durham, NC: Duke University Press, 2010), 55–6.

Here, the theologeme of a primordial fall is taken to indicate the open-endedness of negotiations between objects. With negotiation there arises the possibility of dominance. Radical Orthodoxy accuses almost every viewpoint other than itself of an ontological agonism that holds that the struggle of individual wills is necessary. The only way to combat this pervasive agonism, we're told, is to hold that ultimate reality is peaceable, fundamentally non-agonistic: the full actualisation of gift. Measured against Radical Orthodoxy, we must say that a cost of our reconstruction, where gift (or 'grace') is assigned a non-actual, virtual, status, is that there is no guarantee of an actualised non-agonism. The spiritual presence may exemplify it in part, but as with Tillich we would have to say that all such exemplifications are fragmentary and ambiguous. But, what we say is that agonism, like any other relation between objects in the commonwealth, is also contingent. Negotiation there must be – but agonism is only one of its possible outcomes.

But in our claim to realism we must go further, and recognise that actual material reality, at least at the level of sentient life, is in fact infected with deep hostility and possessiveness. The 'in fact' points to the contingency of this state of affairs, while recognising that it is an expression rather than a contradiction of the open-endedness of negotiation. As we have said, Latourian negotiation is not yet agonism: only a facile romanticism would see the assertion of individual interests as necessarily conflictual and destructive of wholesome relationships. Nevertheless, it is a fact that the primordial situation of constant negotiation everywhere, within human and mammalian life, at least, yields the facticity of agonism.

'Creation' and 'fall' function in Christian theology together to account for the fundamental contingency of objects and their relations, and for the fragile capacity for commonwealth that characterises the endless negotiations in which objects take part. Fall is reflected in the human condition of Hobbesian conflict which seems to require political repression and to entail the necessary truth of ideologies of privatisation. The affirmation of goodness of creation, the non-agonism of perpetual negotiation, however, affirms that capitalist polity and economics are contingent rather than necessary and thus susceptible to radical critique and reconstruction. Acknowledging the fall of human life into agonism, as Reinhold Niebuhr understood, rules out any simple possibility of love being embodied in the structures of human social life. Any redemptive movement in history will have to be more subtle, more wily and we might say more nomadic than that. But the fact the redemption arises as a topic at all is a function of the way in which creation and fall work together: the reconstruction of the commonwealth is possible because agonism is not ontologised as a necessary feature of creaturely negotiation; and it is needed, because the trials of strength have in fact yielded isolation and hegemony. To questions of human nature and the quest for redemption we now turn.

Third Theologeme: The Human

The third and fourth theologemes we will reconstruct are each crucial to our substantive account of entangled religion. The first, theological anthropology, or simply 'the human', is really a rubric under which several theologemes are traditionally grouped. Under this heading fall notions of the *imago dei*, for example, and the idea of sin. Together, these form the basis of what is really an extension of theological ideas of creation and humanity, the notion of redemption – our fourth and final theologeme.

The first thing that must be said about the human in a late modern/ postmodern context from our perspective is negative. Against modernist (specifically Kantian) conceits, relational Christian realism denies that humanity is characterised by a transcendent freedom that makes us uniquely agential in face of a world of relatively inert objects. Obviously, there are actually two denials here: first, a denial of transcendent freedom, and second, a denial of a certain picture of human-nonhuman relations.

Why deny transcendent freedom? The first answer must be that relational Christian realism as we have constructed it has no room for any form of transcendence that is not expressed in actual, empirical states of affairs. There is no transcendent fulcrum against which we may gain leverage to move things within our humanly lived realm of immanent relations between objects. If agency is to be effective, it must negotiate the mesh of connections in which agency arises. This means that Kant's account of the subject is rejected in favour of developmental, social, relational accounts that take into consideration the many ways in which agency takes shape in contexts already characterised by significant relations and thus that it is constructed to respond to those relations. Much more about that will follow.

But the second denial is equally important for our purposes: relational Christian realism denies anthropocentric accounts of the relation between human beings construed as rational, purposeful agents and an environment of allegedly inert objects which has been regarded as obvious to much of modern thought. We have already witnessed this rejection in our use of Latour's 'actor-network' account of human agency. There are, as we saw, any number of 'actants' that co-determine outcomes, and in our actual negotiations in the world only a small fraction of these are human agents. The point is not to embrace a kind of panpsychism that attributes an integrated subjectivity to inanimate objects (or for that matter, to a higher mammal – including ourselves), but simply to insist that objects are not inert. They leverage influence, and this means that our relations to the non-human world are far more complex than typically modern accounts suggest. The real relationship, as we will describe it further in a moment, is entangled rather than unidirectional.

Drawing on ontologies of immanence, especially object-oriented ontologies, and expanding on classical Christian tradition, a relational Christian realist account of the human holds that we are objects and actors among hosts of others, constantly negotiating relations with non-humans of all kinds. A more radical notion of kinship with all of creation is affirmed, and thus of humans as creatures who participate in rather than control the world. Because of the denials in which our affirmations are themselves entangled, there is a definite sense in which our reinterpretation or reconstruction of the human is, while not anti-humanist, then at least consonant with recent articulations of what has been called 'posthumanism'.[10]

However, if these denials, along with affirmations such as kinship with creation that go with them, were the only things that could be said under the heading of the human, then we really would have no theologeme but simply a taking of sides on a philosophical controversy. So, to get to the specifically theological content of the human, we have to ask about the meaning of such theological language about humanity as 'image of God' and as 'sinful'. We need an interpretation of these ideas that is consonant with relational Christian realism and that substantively contributes to it. Hence, the agenda for this section will be to reconstruct the notions of the image of God and sin in a way that deepens the affirmation and description of human entanglement that we have suggested in prior chapters.

So then, what about the 'image of God' (*imago dei*)? From the perspective of relational realism this is a deeply problematic theologeme because it suggests a subtraction from the world, an identification of some capacity or some relational quality of human beings that separates them from the rest of the world or at least puts them in a special class. Platonic conceptualisations of this separation employ the idea an immortal rational soul that is a metaphysically separate apparatus from the body and the possession solely of human beings. Other conceptualisations

---

10   For an account of a version of posthumanism that is compatible with a materialist insistence on full embodiment, see Katherine Hayles, *How We Became Posthuman: Virtual Bodies in Cybernetics, Literature, and Informatics* (Chicago, IL: University of Chicago Press, 1999), 283–91.

are possible, including the idea that the divine image is a special relation or role of human beings vis-à-vis the divine. Whether humanity's alleged uniqueness lies in the possession of a transcendent apparatus or component or in its unique position vis-à-vis the divine, these arguments for uniqueness are problematic because they each undermine the entanglement of human beings with other objects. In the Platonic/Cartesian version, there is an extra something that strictly and absolutely eludes entanglement; in the relational one, while there is no absolute exemption, there is a special relationship enjoyed by human beings that is abstracted out of the morass of relations in which such a relationship would have to be placed. To be more specific, a view which holds that human beings are unique because of their role as God's appointed stewards over the earth loses its coherence when the distinction between humans and other creatures is replaced by a view that sees only constant negotiations between various kinds of actants. What becomes problematic is the unequivocal sense given to the word 'over' in the traditional view of stewardship. For a relational Christian realism employing a flat ontology, there is no single sense of positional terms like 'over' that would signal transcendence, superiority or even power or size. In a sense, as we saw in a previous chapter, the universe itself is an object that is in my mind as I contemplate it. In the same way, there is a real sense in which the animals that we tend (three dogs, in the case of one of us) are also tending us, since their internal structures as canines are oriented toward anticipating and capitalising on human behaviour. Submission to particular commands, for them, is simply a way of getting exactly what they want from us. The point is that, from the perspective of a flat ontology, we are each in a mesh of entanglement in which there are specific senses of influence or even dominance but no single meaning to such terms. Therefore, there can be no status or role that makes any object unique in a general sense.

Nevertheless, from our perspective the *imago* theologeme is warranted insofar as it serves to highlight the fact that humans embody, along with other creatures, the reality of the virtual. The modal distinction between virtuality and actuality, as we have said, is the way that relational Christian realism conceptualises the relation between God and the world, and so the term 'image of God' may be translated as 'image' or 'embodiment' of the virtual. How might a theological anthropology be developed along these lines? Following the pluralist account of virtuality that was described in the last chapter, we may say that the virtual is both within human beings as the infinity that characterises their withdrawn, never fully expressed essence (that is, their power or potential) and in the world as the infinitude of configurations and relations that are possible in a contingent ordering among humans and other objects or actants. The embodiment of this non-localised virtuality occurs with special vividness in the exercise of human agency, since we form explicit purposes that draw from our inner resources and yet interact in complex ways with environmental possibilities and limitations.

But, again, this is not a capacity that separates humans from other creatures. Rather, again drawing on Latour, relational Christian realism affirms that agency does not depend on conscious intentionality, or even on being alive, but characterises all objects insofar as they have effects. Hence, *imago* language needs to be extended to all creatures. This linkage of creaturehood and the image of God allows us to redeploy a famous Christian realist duality[11] within the non-dualist, material theology being developed here. Things are 'creatures' insofar as they are participants in and dependent upon a wider ordering of being and value, and they are 'images of God' insofar as their participation is inflected by their own unique essences or internal structuring.

One is tempted to say that the creaturehood of things corresponds with their mode as actual, and their status as *imago* reflects their being in the mode of virtuality. However, the difficulty with such a neat way of sorting these terms is that it tends to obscure the ways that the virtual is embodied (actualised) not just in what we tend to think of as individual objects, but in the shifting networks in which relations between objects are being negotiated. From the pluralist perspective of OOO, of course, both the objects included in a network and the network itself are objects with their own internal structuring. Therefore, the wider ordering of being and value is also a site of its own, irreducible virtuality. Thus, the distinction between modes cuts across the distinction between objects and wider orders in which they are embedded: both are actual and virtual. In theological terms, both are sites of the interaction between God and the world. This is an important point theologically because it allows us to distinguish God from the wider order of being and value without separating them. God is neither collapsed into the overall structuring of the world nor into the individual objects that are its elements.

Readers will have seen that a relatively deflationary account of human beings vis-à-vis the non-human world threatens the viability of a distinct topic for understanding human beings. And it must be admitted that, for a deeply relational Christian realism, the doctrines of 'creation' and 'humanity (as created)' simply affirm the same things. A separate treatment is required only

---

[11]   For a classic modern account of this duality, see Reinhold Niebuhr, *The Nature and Destiny of Man, Vol. I: Human Nature* (New York, NY: Charles Scribner's Sons, 1964), 150–77.

explicitly to address and counter-act centuries of anthropocentrism in theology and culture. The picture will be altered somewhat when we get to the next theologeme under the topic of human beings, sin, because here the traditional language is rooted in the distinctive internal structuring of the class of objects that we call human beings. Nevertheless, relational Christian realism is a form of posthumanism, embracing the reality of co-constitution of our humanity by the non-human objects with which we interact as we arrive at and perpetuate our humanity.

How might this picture be filled out? Here we will not an attempt an exhaustive picture of a posthumanist theological account of the human, but will simply draw attention to three related strands of philosophical thought that may be brought to bear in constructing a posthumanist account of humanity as creation. The first we may call the theory of 'distributed cognition', arising from cognitive science (especially the work of Francisco Verela) and integrated into posthumanist philosophy by Katherine Hayles.[12] Distributed cognition holds that what we call subjectivity is really a function of relations between the brain and many other things. In terms of recent technology, my (James's) consciousness is shared with or distributed across several processors and conveyers of information – at the moment, my brain, the texts that it is recalling, the laptop on which I am working, the Amazon.com search function that allowed me quickly to recall the spelling of Verela's name and so on. Thinking, in this view, is not confined to a Cartesian *res cogitans* nor to a Husserlian ego, but is a matter of links being established and developed between one particular object (the human brain – though it certainly could involve non-human brains or perhaps even non-carbon-based processing units) and others. But the theory is not simply about technology – according to Verela and his colleagues, cognition is essentially about making such connections: that is what 'embodiment' means.[13] Humans have always thought, felt and acted in concert with shifting assemblages of others. Subjectivity is necessarily not only inter-subjective (Merleau-Ponty) but in fact 'inter-objective'.[14]

From a theological point of view, what this means is that relations between God and humans, or between humans and other humans, is not a matter of isolated, self-contained centres of consciousness (and of course we have denied that God should be thought of in this way), but are confrontations and

---

[12]   Francisco J. Verela, Evan Thompson and Eleanor Rosch, *The Embodied Mind: Cognitive Science and Human Experience* (Cambridge, MA: MIT Press, 1991), 40–42. Also, Hayles, *How We Became Posthuman*, 288.

[13]   Verela, et al., *The Embodied Mind*, 147–57.

[14]   Bryant, *Democracy of Objects*, 217.

negotiations between complex, highly distributed networks of objects: one's perception of as spouse necessarily involves shared relatives, animals, cookware, microbes, the paper out of which cheques in a shared banking account are made and so on. In other words, Latourian litanies pervade the ways our relationships are realistically articulated, and this means that the meaning and vocation of created humanity are conveyed with the help of lists that include a horde of non-human members.

The second philosophical resource we will bring to bear here is Catherine Malabou's notion of 'plasticity'.[15] Malabou derives plasticity from a reading of Hegel, the contours of which need not concern us here. The important point is that plasticity as an account of the human affords a way of talking about human 'nature' or 'essence', its distinctiveness as a species but also the distinctiveness of individual cultures and persons, without claiming that human nature or personal identity are fundamentally static. Though Malabou does not likely intend it, her account fits well with and can be explicated to some degree by OOO's notion of withdrawn essence. In Harman, there is a distinction between the inner structure of an object and its outward manifestation: he even contrasts 'real' and 'sensual' objects. Plasticity describes the inner dynamism of the 'real object'. Think of a ball of silly putty. It can stretch and contract, twist and turn, contort and return to shape, and yet still it bears the same structure, a structure that contains within itself indeterminate possibilities for being manifested in various shapes and also limitations that are functions of the way the structure is organised.

For Malabou, as for OOO, plasticity has broader application than just human beings, but her analysis of the plasticity of the brain is especially instructive for an account of the human. In much neuroscientific literature, neuroplasticity suggests surprising degrees of flexibility in the brain, as it continually rewires itself, forging new connections between individual neurons and between regions of the brain in response to environmental opportunities and threats. Malabou counters, however, that flexibility is perhaps too passive to characterise the explosive possibilities that thinking has in relation to the political and economic environments that provoke us. Indeed, an important aspect of the meaning of the word 'plastic' is borne by its association with explosives. Thus, plasticity is not flexibility but it is an inner dynamism that is creative and destructive: plasticity is the brain's remaking itself – not just in order to adjust to an environment, but

---

[15]   For the clearest account of her notion of plasticity, see Catherine Malabou, *Plasticity at the Dusk of Writing: Dialectic, Destruction, Deconstruction*, trans. Carolyn Shread (New York, NY: Columbia University Press, 2010).

to reconfigure it.[16] This remaking is not necessarily positive. Indeed, in the case of traumatic events and catastrophic illnesses, the 'synaptic self'[17] may become completely other in relation to its prior state.[18] In any case, the political payoff here is obvious: we human beings are not simply quiescent creatures at the mercy of larger forces – our very materiality (our brains) are objects that forge new possibilities that challenge, undermine and possibly overthrow and reconstruct those forces. Importantly, there are limitations – plasticity does not mean lack of structure. But what is limiting – the distinctive character of the brain with its insistent identity, including its visions, hopes and desires – is also precisely its specificity, enabling, possibilising and also threatening.

Malabou's notion of plasticity is felicitous for relational Christian realism because it allows us to revisit once again and perhaps to revise Reinhold Niebuhr's characterisation of human nature as finite and free. The similarity is perhaps obvious: plasticity involves both being limited by an internal structure – a wiring handed on by evolution, in the case of the brain – and an indeterminacy about how that structure can express itself. Appropriating and revising a famous line from Spinoza, Malabou affirms that 'we don't know what a brain can do'.[19] Plasticity means finite freedom and free finitude, stretching and torquing in an utterly contingent display of Niebuhrian 'beauty and terror'.[20] The revisionary element in reading Niebuhr in light of Malabou has to do with the confinement of Niebuhr's two polar features to an immanent, material domain. Paul Tillich had argued that Niebuhr needed an ontology of finite freedom for his system to work, and Niebuhr resisted Tillich's point because he believed the paradoxical quality of an unresolved polarity was important to account for the anguished quality of human agency and would be undermined by an ontology. The paradox, for Niebuhr, was a matter of being confronted at once with transcendent and immanent features of the human condition – our standing before a transcendent, supramundane God and our embeddedness within a natural order.[21] Interpreting Niebuhr by means of Malabou puts us on the side of Tillich on this point. We

---

[16]   Catherine Malabou, *What Should We Do with Our Brain?*, trans. Sebastian Rand (New York, NY: Fordham University Press, 2008), 54.

[17]   Joseph Ladue, *The Synaptic Self: How Our Brains Become Who We Are* (New York, NY: Penguin Books, 2002), 304ff.

[18]   Catherine Malabou, *Ontology of the Accident: An Essay on Destructive Plasticity*, trans. Carolyn Shread (Cambridge, UK: Polity Press, 2012), 2–4.

[19]   Malabou, *What Should We Do with Our Brain?*, 78.

[20]   Reinhold Niebuhr, 'The Sickness of American Culture', *The Nation* 166/9 (6 March 1948): 269.

[21]   A famous written exchange of criticism between Niebuhr and Tillich can be found in *Reinhold Niebuhr: His Religious, Social, and Political Thought*, eds Charles W. Kegley

thus lose the internal anguish Niebuhr thought crucial to a realistic account of the human. But again, from our point of view, the anguish of human as well as non-human agency is not a matter of being situated amid both transcendence and immanence, but is a product of external relations within a wholly immanent commonwealth, as trials of strength are negotiated with multitudes of others. What Malabou adds to this account is the radical possibility of otherness that haunts human selves.[22]

The third philosophical resource we will employ toward developing a posthumanist anthropology is a series of images used by Gilles Deleuze and picked up by Rosi Braidotti and others to account for the ways in which human life continually transgresses boundaries and wanders beyond various schemes of organisation and control. Deleuze writes about the 'schizoid' character of life that defies or transgresses regimes of normalcy, and about the 'nomadic' and 'rhizomatic' character of a philosophy that follows the schizoid through her various permutations and becomings. The schizoid, in an important metonymy for human life in general, continually becomes-other in its eccentric acts and movements of association, affinity and solidarity. In *Anti-Oedipus*, writing with Félix Guattari, Deleuze tracks larger movements of 'deterritorialisation' within cultures and histories. Cultures carry substantive norms and traditions: their formation and codification is a movement of 'territorialisation' or perhaps 'reterritorialisation'. But a recurring feature of life is that these territories, or secure and normalised cultural spaces, are being continually transgressed, abstracted from or bypassed. An example that is central to Deleuze and Guattari's analysis is the way in which capitalism replaces local traditions and substantive commitments and values with the abstract value of money and globalised homogeneity. Capitalism, in other words, deterritorialises, and a necessary countermovement of continual reterritorialisation only serves to continue producing cultural fodder for the market, as the local becomes commodified over and over.[23]

But of course becoming in Deleuzian vocabulary is not just a trap effected by the wiles of capital. It is also a generative and liberative power, as Rosi Braidotti shows in a number of works, including *The Posthuman*.[24] Humans, according to

and Robert W. Bretall. Tillich's essay in the volume is 'Reinhold Niebuhr's Doctrine of Knowledge', 35–44. Niebuhr's reply is in 'Reply to Interpretation and Criticism', 432–3.

[22]   Malabou, *Ontology of the Accident*, 7ff.

[23]   Gilles Deleuze and Félix Guattari, *Anti-Oedipus: Capitalism and Schizophrenia*, trans. Robert Hurley, Mark Seem and Helen R. Lane (New York, NY: Penguin Books, 1977), 222ff.

[24]   Rosi Braidotti, *The Posthuman* (Cambridge, UK: Polity Press, 2013).

Braidotti, participate in larger movements of becoming that reach down into what we used to call 'nature' and also into technological and cybernetic realms. The becoming-other of humans and others is a power that can liberate us from the discipline of culturally enacted genders and classes. We can certainly think of this becoming-other in terms of queer and transgender experience, but we can also think of it in terms of solidarity and affiliation. Becoming-woman is a proper vector for heterosexual men who ally themselves with women, and becoming-animal is within the possibility space of humans ('animal' here meaning non-human animal) as they discover their ontological solidarity with non-human others and seek to deploy it in political practice.[25]

The theological importance of these Deleuzian terms for a relational Christian realist account of the human is that their open-endedness is an expression of the *coram deo* character of life, its before-Godness. Religious traditions in the West are filled with themes of wilderness wandering, of pilgrimage. These narratives and images suggest that there is a powerful sense in which human beings have no home but God. We would add, of course: a God who is not above in a transcendent super-nature but who is identified in part by movements of departure from actual states of affairs. The term 'deterritorialisation' is distinctively apt here, because it suggests departure without transcendence: wandering away, escaping along the plane of immanence. Of course, as we have insisted a number of times already, human beings can be no exceptional or unique instance of this feature but simply an exemplification that is most visible to us. Deterritorialisation occurs at all levels and among all groups of objects. If God is restless virtuality, then home for us who are expressions of the virtual is the road itself.

This is not to say, as theologian Kathryn Tanner has said, that human nature is to have no nature – that we are essentially those beings that are conformed to that with which we associate ourselves.[26] In an OOO-inspired theology, no object could ever achieve that kind of transparency, or one might even say non-objectivity. Besides that, who would ever want to? Being nomadic, as Deleuze and Braidotti have each shown, can mean a 'becoming-animal' or 'becoming-woman', as identity shifts in response to new associations, affiliations and solidarities. But it is always a matter of becoming, and never of being. That is to say, becoming-animal is a trajectory and not a fixed terminus, and the trajectory is traversed by an identity – a nature, a self. Again, from the perspective of

---

25   Ibid., 51.

26   Kathryn Tanner, 'Grace without Nature', in *Without Nature? A New Condition for Theology*, eds David Albertson and Cabell King (New York, NY: Fordham University Press, 2010), 363–75.

OOO, objects are never exhausted by their relations, though they may express themselves in highly distinct and variable ways as they enter them.

At this point it may be helpful to summarise. We have mined three spatial descriptors and evaluators of the human as a good creature within a wider ordering: humans, like many others, are distributed, plastic and nomadic. We are pilgrims across the plane of immanence, the desert of the real, perpetually finding and losing our way as we seek to embody the virtual, to become spiritual presence, to participate in the assembly of the many objects which we find along the way, and which find us in our finding, into a dynamic community of beings-before-God.

But, as with the theologeme of creation, there is a contingent actuality that must be explored in order to achieve a full-orbed account of the human. To creation we had to append 'fall'; to humanity, made in the divine image alongside hosts of other creatures, we must append the notion of 'sin'. Sin in a relational Christian realist framework refers to the multiple forms of reality distortion of which we are capable and toward which we are in fact oriented in our distribution, plasticity and nomadic wandering. In the older Christian realism of Reinhold Niebuhr, sin is a matter of responding improperly to the basic human anxiety of finitude to secure oneself by either 'pride' or 'sensuality'.[27] Niebuhr's 'pride' redeploys Kierkegaard's 'in despair wanting to be a self'; 'sensuality' recalls 'in despair not wanting to be a self', losing oneself either in disconnected experiences or in overweening devotion to some kind of other.[28] Kierkegaard's rich phenomology of sin, in turn, is rooted in Augustine's account of sin as 'pride' and 'sloth'.[29] In this tradition, liberated from Augustine's contortions over the temporal beginning of sin, the 'fallenness' of human beings is our tendency to fall into either of these abortive, destructive strategies, either pridefully seeking to hide our finitude through dominance and exploitation or slothfully seeking to hide ourselves by attaching ourselves dependently and uncritically to some other or else by failure to participate in the responsibilities and opportunities of life. Of course, the obvious objections to this Augustinian-Kiergaardian-Niebuhrian account of sin from the standpoint of a relational Christian realism are that it is too preoccupied with the self (thus eliding the

---

[27]   Niebuhr, *Nature and Destiny of Man*, 186, 228.

[28]   Søren Kierkegaard, *The Sickness Unto Death: A Christian Psychological Exposition for Edification and Awakening by Anti-Climacus*, trans. Alistair Hannay (London, UK: Penguin Books, 1989), 50.

[29]   Augustine, *The City of God against the Pagans*, Book XIV, chs 12–17, ed. and trans. R.W. Dyson (Cambridge, UK: Cambridge University Press, 1998), 607–17.

collective) and that it is too focused on human relations, thus abstracting history from the wider order of things.

However, using the Latourian language of collection offers another, less anthropocentric, way to conceptualise sin while maintaining the rich phenomenology of Kierkegaard's account of sin as either positive or negative: 'wanting' or 'not wanting', desire or quiescence. The 'prideful' route into sin, we might say, is a premature completion of the work of collection. The perpetual open-endedness of the commonwealth of being's task of accommodation, negotiation and integration into diverse collectives of objects causes a pervasive anxiety, and this invites a response of simply shuttering the process and deeming those objects seeking incorporation irredeemably outside the pale. 'Illegal aliens' are shunned, persecuted and abused. Non-human forms of life are treated as instruments of human pursuits of utility without their own value or interest. The ecology of which we are a part is ignored or it is ransacked for the sake of values that are attached to human, or perhaps European or North American, interests alone. A variant here would be that the process of negotiation within the collective for position and influences is curtailed. Women or members of ethnic or religious minorities, or persons from certain geographic regions or socio-economic classes, are kept in place by a rigid system of control and discipline. In all of these cases, this form of sin is a form of prideful self-assertion on the part of an individual or collective agent. In despair, we attempt to be the commonwealth we imagine as the fulfilment of our own particular, self-referential interests.

The 'slothful' or 'sensual' route, on the other hand, is a failure to participate in the collective process. It is a failure of desire, a 'hiding' of one's interests within a place either outside or within the commonwealth with which one has become comfortable. In order for the process of collection to go on, objects must petition the collective for a place and a role, and the collective must be nimble and accommodating enough to respond. Failures of the collective or of powerful actants within the collective to do so constitute the sin of 'pride'; failures on the would-be petitioners' parts represent the sin of sloth (or 'hiding').[30] It is a different manifestation of the temptations inherent in the anxiety of collection. Petition is demanding, and there are collective pressures that resist. It takes courage (the 'courage to be', to borrow a phrase from Paul Tillich)[31] to assert minority interests amid a collective already structured by negotiations that

---

[30]   Susan Neslon Dunfee, *Beyond Servanthood: Christianity and the Liberation of Women* (New York, NY: University Press of America, 1989).

[31]   Paul Tillich, *The Courage to Be* (New Haven, CT: Yale University Press, 1952).

preceded, trials of strength whose outcomes are encoded in the collective's sense of its own interests, capacities and limitations. Here a qualification must be made, however. Participation, in the sense of asserting minority rights, can take the paradoxical form of resistance through refusal to participate. In some cases the most elegant way to leverage influence is simply to withdraw from the scene, making one's absence itself a kind of insistence, a registration of minoritarian power in the face of collective intransigence. The point of participation is to refuse despair of the process, and in this sense a compliant belonging is less participatory than a defiant resistance. The larger point we are making is that if the process of collection itself is the collective's good, and thus the good of the wider order of being in which we are always already entangled, then to curtail the process or to acquiesce in its curtailment is what we must mean by sinful resistance to the good.

What have we done here? Have we simply appropriated the traditional Augustianian account of sin (as interpreted through Kierkegaard and Niebuhr), and dressed it up with Latourian language without substantial change? Yes, in a way. Augustinianism represents an important aspect of the meaning of realism. Relational Christian realism, we will recall, means in part that we seek to ground theological and philosophical thinking in the real. It means resistance to various forms of fideism and the correlationalisms that support them. But part of the effort to ground thought in the real is an attempt to grasp the realities of our situation in an existential and moral sense. What are the possibilities and limitations of our agency? How are we biased and even skewed by pervasive pressures to act or to be in ways that do not advance but rather hinder the collective interests of the wider commonwealth of beings in which we are enmeshed? The power of the Augustinian tradition on this question is that it advances a phenomenology of interest that grounds destructive possibilities in our basic situation of not knowing and not controlling outcomes. In a situation of anxiety, we are either driven or pulled, almost with inevitability, toward destructive choices. Realism in collective self-understanding is a crucial piece of the relational Christian realism we are advancing in this book, because it helps us toward a sober assessment of our possibilities and limits; and, more importantly, it undermines the overconfidence in our own power and wisdom that tends to lead us to underestimate our entanglements.

But there is more to say on this question. The Latourian language we are adopting to modify the Augustinian-Kierkegaardian-Niebuhrian picture is more than window-dressing. While retaining the structure of sin in the tradition, it relocates the driving force of sin. Sin no longer emerges from the contradiction between immanence and transcendence, finitude and freedom. Indeed, the flat ontology we are adopting here removes that contradiction: freedom is a capacity of finitude, and transcendence is always within and never beyond immanence. The anxiety that raises the spectre of failure in our account of sin is not the product of an internal clash but of an external process of negotiation. We are anxious because we are in a network of contingent relations that is open-ended. We are anxious because we do not know what shapes the commonwealth will take, or our own place within it. In other words, the Latourian appropriation of the theme of anxiety we are offering is computational and ecological rather than existential in the classic sense. Sin arises in a world of objects with their own internal structures who are in constant negotiation with each other for place and role. It is not a feature of their internal structures, but of the process of negotiation. It is a disease in the process, a glitch in the machinery that threatens to bring it to a grinding halt.

But to whom or to what does this account of sin apply? The prejudice of a posthumanist theology that is constructed with the aid of a flat ontology is toward an ontic democratisation of sin, seeing it as a capacity of every object. Can we not observe non-human objects, especially in the animal world, engaged both in excessive self-exertions and in failures to participate, embroiled in dominance patterns and slinking off in defeated isolation? Moreover, if sin is seen as a disease or failure within the network of objects rather than an internal problem within the objects themselves, why not see sin as more general, and not as a human problem alone?

But caution is in order here. We need to take into account the original conceptual content of the term and see how it might be fitted for a new one. When we do that, it is not clear that the term can be applied so broadly as 'creaturehood' and 'the image of God'. In classical theology, as we have said, sin is understood as a matter of internal structure: the term 'sin' is used both for self-conscious acts that are immoral and/or religiously improper (that is, acts of worship in which self or other creatures are the focus rather than the creator), and for an overall affective, intellectual and bodily orientation or bias that is expressed in such acts. The more circumscribed meaning of 'sins' as self-conscious acts (either of pride or of sloth) cannot of course apply more generally to objects, since not all of them are self-conscious. Nor can the more robust but still quite circumscribed notion of an affective, intellectual and bodily orientation apply more generally to all things, since not all objects are structured by affective and intellectual capacities. So, the category of sin in the tradition appears to be relevant to only a select class of objects – those that are internally structured by certain capacities enabling them to be characterised by a pervasive orientation which gives rise to a wide range of acts that are seen as sinful: idolatries, violence, hiding or failure to participate, to name a few general sub-categories.

But of course the main feature of our reconstruction of the notion of sin is that it is not simply a matter of internal structure, and this shift means that that 'sin' in our context is open to a different and much broader application. Again, however, the question is how the more classical Augustinian notion of sin and ours are linked. What are the continuities between the two concepts? As we have said, a Latourian reconstruction relocates the force of sin in faltering processes of negotiation between objects rather than in the internal structures of particular kinds of objects (that is, humans). But on this account it still may be maintained that self-conscious acts of sabotage (in the forms of pride and sloth) and affective orientations that frame and motivate such acts are particular expressions of sin as failed negotiation. Thus it is not that we are rejecting the Augustinian account of human sin, but rather we are reframing it in terms of a wider ecological and cybernetic framework.

Moreover, there is a way of characterising the effects of sin upon the wider ordering of human and non-human objects that has nothing to do with its sources. Here the ecological and cybernetic aspects of sin are especially visible. Whatever sin's source, the whole commonwealth of being is affected by it. In the Bible, we have the language of being 'subjected to futility' (Romans 8:20) for example. It is not clear how to interpret this way of speaking, and thus it is not immediately obvious whether and how it might or might not fit into an object-oriented relational Christian realism. But it does point toward an affirmation that non-human objects, and the networks of relations between them and between the non-human world and human beings, are negatively affected by evil acts and skewed orientations. Articulating this negativity by means of OOO, we might say that the objects are inhibited from expressing the virtual that is attached to each of them in the actual world. The volcanic powers that reside in them as distinctive objects, whether they be individual things or collectives that are defined by their internal organisation, are choked off, devitalised or simply killed. Trees cannot grow properly in the wash of acidified rain, rivers cannot flow in desertified lands, computer networks are choked with viruses. The 'futility' hinted at in the Bible is just this frustration and inhibition of the powers that animate the non-human members of or petitioners to the commonwealth. It is not limited to the organic, but infects all things with frustration, incapacitation and disorientation.

This frustration, of course, is not simply episodic, but structural. In cybernetic terms, we may say that negative feedback loops begin to take shape within the networks in which objects are enmeshed. Such loops of negativity effect a diminishment of objects' capacities to express themselves: they limit what bodies can do. Desertification amplifies itself when it gains a foothold; melting of Antarctic glaciers is a self-perpetuating process that can reach a point of no return; the frenzy of a mob or the forward inertia of a whisper campaign can compound political and economic resentments, leading to further destructive behaviour. When these things happen, collection falters because objects are either overwhelmed or left isolated. Their integrity as objects is compromised or else it is ignored or cast out. Things, from glaciers to fragile ecosystems and the organisms that depend upon them to resident aliens and ethnic minorities, suffer diminishment in the process.

This notion of the ecological, cybernetic effects of sin is important because it accounts for the inherently frustrating and inevitably frustrated character of the process of collection. Collectives are not necessarily characterised by violence – such inflictions are contingent. Nevertheless, despite such contingency it seems everywhere the democracy of objects breaks down in terms of the actual configuration of beings. Hierarchies form and harden. Oppression takes shape, and violence ensues as a means to enforce or to resist it.

It is not possible to judge such hierarchies as 'bad' in some generic sense. After all, a hierarchy is a way of collecting objects that can benefit all of those who are in it – it is one way of marshalling strength for the ongoing processes of negotiation between objects. And there is no kingdom of peace put forward here as the archetype that has now been defiled. In a Latourian framework, contra Radical Orthodoxy, struggle is primordial and ontological: objects are everywhere engaged in trials of strength, even if resort to violence is contingent. It does no good, for example, to think that human well-being can co-exist with the unrestrained success of certain viruses, or for that matter with the unconstrained proliferation of firearms in our cities and schools. We have to join issue and take up power struggles with objects of all kinds, inorganic as well as organic. But it is when such struggles eventuate in frozen hierarchies, power arrangements that have become impervious to challenge, that bad things happen. As earlier Christian realism was wary of concentrations of power because it regarded the inevitably sinful human heart as the engine of injustice, so relational Christian realism is wary of them because it knows that the anxiety of collection gives us every reason to stop short, to shutter the process and thus to take advantage of our relative positions of power and privilege in order to oppress other members of the commonwealth.

Fourth Theologeme: Redemption

In this conceptual context, what is redemption? Here again, as with our account of humanity as created, our first point must be negative. Relational Christian realism, because it recognises an ongoing process of collection in a commonwealth of objects as ultimately real, holds out no hope for any final sense – or perhaps more accurately, any final reference – to the notion of redemption. In other words, there is no expectation, or even desire, in relational Christian realism for a final beatific end for human beings, for the earth, or for the universe. Or, if there is an end, it is the process itself, precisely in its unending.

What we are rejecting is any notion of redemption as completed, whether in the present as realised eschatology or in the future as in theologies of 'hope'.[32] While realised and futurist eschatologies tend to ground a completed view of redemption in a high Christology, according to which the victory over sin has already been in principle if not in fact secured, relational Christian realism embodies a much more restricted, less ambitious Christology. As we saw in the previous chapter, Christ cannot in a relational Christian realism enclose or even get a full purchase on divine virtuality. Christ as event within the actual is one expression of virtuality among multitudes of others, and so the only way for Christ to leverage power within the world is through alliance with other such actualities. To cite the theme of this book, fidelity to Christ is entangled with other fidelities, or else it is abstract, otherworldly and ineffectual.

Given this non-enclosure of the real within a Christology, there is no warrant for claiming that the real is tied definitively to a state or even a process of redemption. Redemption in other words remains stubbornly contingent – it is never guaranteed. To this negative point a positive one may be attached: we are giving an account of redemption that is not static but utterly dynamic and open-ended.

What more might we say about redemption, other than it is always incomplete and undecided? There are general characteristics and there are those that are a part of a special subset, applying to the human class of objects. The general sense is simply unblocking the process of collection. Among non-human objects, this happens, for example, when established evolutionary pathways lose their necessary character and give way to new evolutionary possibilities and strategies. Some aleatory event occurs: a chance that takes

---

[32] The seminal text in recent theology privileging eschatology is Jürgen Moltmann's *Theology of Hope: On the Ground and Implications of a Christian Eschatology*, trans. James W. Leitch (New York, NY: Harper and Row, 1967).

hold and gets connected to objects in their mutual entanglements, thus creating a new opportunity for collection and connection: a meteor strike, a random fluctuation in temperature, a chance encounter between objects that have never met in such propitious circumstances before – some event that allows a reconfiguration of relations between objects, a shuffling of the deck. Or, to borrow from Meillassoux, it happens when there is a breakthrough to a different 'world': a different regime of cosmic law or governance through the contingent appearance of a new reality.[33] The appearance of life, for example, took up and reoriented the conditions that prevailed in a pre-biotic world, incorporating what went before within a new configuration that represented radically new possibilities. Sites for creativity emerged, but the emergence was out of what had been a series of cycles of bare repetitions of previous configurations. What is redemptive about the emergence of new creative sites is that through them bare repetition is exchanged for a more genuine repetition: the virtual is active again in a new way, taking that which is old and using it to bring forth that which is new.[34] Thus the process of collection is started on a new level: new objects emerge, and with them new possibilities for negotiation and exchange.

At its deepest level, this is what redemption means. The old is no longer simply recycled. Existing patterns are not simply reproduced or kept secure. Repetition is not simply bare repetition. Rather, previously existing and circulating actualities are lifted into a new context in which new realities emerge from the creativity which is found to adhere to the old collections. The virtual leaps forth as originating power, but the origination is not total: it is from the throbbing, immanent power within the world of objects that is already there. Thus redemption rather than simple creation is in play.

Two points need to be made here. First, there is a close connection between creation and redemption in relational Christian realism, following a well-known trajectory within Christian theology that is not without its critics but is still viable and widely authorised. H. Richard Niebuhr associated such an affiliation with a 'Christ of culture' type of theology – for example, classical liberal theologies and also liberation theologies which align Christ's redemptive trajectory with a certain pathway or a certain constituency within human history, whether it be the cultural elite or the poor and marginalised.

---

[33]   Quentin Meillassoux, 'The Divine Inexistence', in *Quentin Meillassoux: Philosophy in the Making*, Harman, G. (Edinburgh, UK: Edinburgh University Press, 2011), 187ff.

[34]   For a classic discussion of the difference between 'bare' and this more genuine, or 'clothed', repetition, see Gilles Deleuze, *Difference and Repetition*, trans. Paul Patton (New York, NY: Columbia University Press, 1994), 20.

Niebuhr was critical of this type because of its tendency to exchange the tension between God and world with a conflict between elements within the world – culture vs. nature, for example.[35] In the elite version in classical theological liberalism, the humanistic, enlightened cultural vanguard is pitted against the 'cultural lag' of benighted, primitive instincts which remain close to 'nature'. In the liberationist version, the raised economic and political consciousness of the revolutionary vanguard is pitted against the reactionary forces in culture which think of themselves as protecting and articulating natural economic and political patterns of free exchange and meritocratic hierarchialization. In either case, God's creative activity is regarded as drawing order out of chaotic nature, and redemption is simply a matter of breaking up the obstacles to the ongoing work of creation.

Obviously, a Latour-inspired relational Christian realism does not fall prey to the pitfalls of crudely humanistic versions of this type because it resists any ontologisation of the differences between human beings and other objects – or, to put it another way, it undercuts the division of reality into 'nature' and 'culture'. But the immanent God of our perspective may seem to minimise if not eliminate Niebuhr's all-important tension if not outright conflict between God and the world, and this does tend to undermine the strong distinctions in much of classical Christian theology between creation and redemption, distinctions that Niebuhr wished to maintain because of his commitment to the sovereignty of God and to a radical account of human sinfulness that together called for a radical account of redemption as an altogether new act.

For relational Christian realism, as we have seen, God is not a personal agent who performs discrete acts that may be partitioned into categories like 'creation' and 'redemption', but is rather the immanent virtual that is always creatively at work, finding expression in the empowerment of novel configurations between objects, enabling new connections and collections into an increasingly vast commonwealth of being. The initial difference between God and world is modal: it is the distinction between virtuality and actuality (of course, in our revision of Trinitarian thinking, we went on to say in the last chapter that there are actualised expressions of God in the 'spiritual presences' of the world, as the form or possibility of God discerned in Jesus by Christians (and as something else by others, very likely) is taken hold of by objects or groups of objects in the world). The question is whether a modal distinction is adequate to maintain a tension between God and the world that unsettles, challenges, leverages

---

[35]   H. Richard Niebuhr, *Christ and Culture* (New York, NY: Harper and Row, 1951), 108ff.

influence upon the world as a whole – or at least, upon all of its components, rather than simply 'siding' with one component over and against others. It is a Levinasian point – without transcendence, can there be ethics in any meaningful sense?[36] But of course we have tried to argue that the concept of virtuality actually captures the needed tension or unsettling characteristic of discourses of transcendence. There is something astir within the actual that is not reducible to it. Following the pluralist version of virtuality characteristic of OOO, we say that that which is astir is not a lurking substance. Rather, it is a distributed mode that characterises all objects in their irreducible singularity. Still, the fact that there are such features of objects is what we mean by 'God', and that is enough to cause a general as well as particular unsettling: it infuses radical contingency within every situation.

Therefore, Niebuhr's worries about collapsing creation and redemption amount from our perspective to little more than defensiveness about orthodox accounts of the absolute sovereignty of God and the radical corruption of human beings. To protect the sovereignty of God, creation has to be creation *ex nihilo* – a radical and unique act. Because of the radical corruption of human beings, redemption has to be a unique intervention into the human situation, different in kind from the act of creation. Within Niebuhr's theological constructions, these points make good sense. But we have constructed the relation of God and world somewhat differently, and have accounted for the idea of sin more broadly (cosmically, in fact), and so we cannot and need not be detained by Niebuhr's orthodoxy.

A second point about the connection between creation and redemption in relational Christian realism is that it follows from a radical de-anthropocentrising of Christian realism such as we are trying to effect here. For classical Christian theology, redemption applies first of all to human beings, and only indirectly to the rest of creation. In the tradition we have creation, the fall of human beings and the consequent futility to which creation as a whole is subjected, and finally the reconciliation and redemption of human beings, by means of which the creation as a whole is healed. The fulcrum of the drama is what happens to and within human beings. But to place human beings squarely in the mesh of creation is to de-centre them and thus to un-centre the drama of creation-fall-redemption. For relational Christian realism, creativity is the process of negotiation between objects, and redemption is just the successful resistance to obstacles to the process. In other words,

---

[36]   Immanuel Levinas, *Totality and Infinity*, trans. Alphonso Lingis (Pittsburgh, PA: Duquesne University Press, 1969), 194–7.

redemption redeploys creativity. It is not so much a third thing, a surplus, as it is a recapitulation.

Now, to un-centre the drama of redemption does not mean that there is no way to specify what is unique about the human experience of it. As applied to humans, the process of redemption that recapitulates and resumes creativity has contours that are specific to the structure of human objects. In particular, redemption for human beings means a four-fold reorientation or restructuring of their structures: intellectual, affective, practical and material.

Intellectually, the reorientation and reconstruction of human beings that occurs when creativity resumes transformatively in the midst of human failure means a new vision of the commonwealth. Theologian James Gustafson has urged that faithful, God-centred piety 'relates all things according to their relations to God'.[37] This relating-to-God is more than intellectual, for Gustafson, but it does involve an intellectual reorientation: we are enabled under the power of redemption to see things differently, not simply as self-enclosed objects or as objects that have utility for us, but objects that are in relation to a vast network of objects that comprise a commonwealth of being.

Affectively, our emotional life is re-shaped to some degree by the appearance of a wider, more inclusive desire. As Jonathan Edwards argued, true virtue is 'benevolence to being in general'.[38] This is another and less obvious dimension, especially to the philosophically minded, of Gustafson's point about relating to all things according to their relations to God. Such relation means a reorientation of our affective or emotional lives. An important part of the inner structure of human beings is what Mary Midgley calls their 'emotional constitution', a set of interests and biases that are encoded in our brains as the sediments of a long, evolutionary history.[39] Through our emotional constitution our affections are ordered, prioritised: I (James) am inclined toward my children more so than to neighbours, and certainly more so than to persons on other continents (with due respect to my collaborators!). This is a way that the trials of strength characteristic of networks of objects has been internalised in my own inner structure, and adhering to its priorities has survival value and yields distinctive satisfactions to me and to those with whom I am connected.

---

[37]　James M. Gustafson, *Ethics from a Theocentric Perspective, Vol. I: Theology and Ethics* (Chicago, IL: University of Chicago Press, 1981), 158.

[38]　Jonathan Edwards, *The Nature of True Virtue*, in *The Works of Jonathan Edwards*, Vol. 1, rev. Edward Hickman (Edinburgh, UK: Banner of Truth, 1979), 122–40.

[39]　Mary Midgley, *Beast and Man: The Roots of Human Nature* (London, UK: Routledge, 1979), 321–6.

But the well-known trouble here, pointed about famously by an earlier Christian realist, Reinhold Niebuhr, is the pervasiveness of 'collective egotism'.[40] The emotional constitution gets *curvatus in se*, curved in on itself, resistant to challenge or expansion. Selfish accumulation of resources gets intensified when we are hoarding for a group. Violent conflicts gain powerful motivation when put into the service of love. As human beings we fail to register that the relations that we are conscious of are actually part of a larger set or mesh of relations that extend outward far further (indefinitely, in fact). Hence, we fail to admit new members into negotiations toward a fuller, more expansive commonwealth of objects. Creativity breaks down; collection is shuttered.

In this situation, the renewal and resumption of creativity inevitably means for us a reorientation of our emotional constitution, our affective lives. Our loyalties are extended beyond the narrow range they reached before, and this causes us to ask critical questions about our patterns of accumulation, consumption, defence and so on. We become biased in a different way – less toward our own narrow self-interests, community interests, national or even species interests, and more toward the interests of the whole, the developing and expanding commonwealth of being. Of course it hardly needs to be said that there are limits to the universalisation of our affective lives. Our emotional constitutions may stretch indefinitely ('indeterminately', according to Reinhold Niebuhr)[41], but they will also remain attached in particularly strong ways to the objects they have been biased to love by evolutionary and probably also social history. Nevertheless, it is the trajectory that is important here. Remember that we have said that we reject a completed picture of redemption. Love is process – it is not an actual state of affairs effected by a powerful theological fiat: rather, it is virtuality, a power that is at work in the human heart that reaches toward an indeterminate, always open and incomplete future.

Practically, redemption means for human beings a reorientation of 'will', or of the ends or choices that we pursue. Influenced by a reoriented and restructured vision and emotional constitution, we engage in practical activities that are pursued for the sake of a broader range of objects. Much more about this dimension of redemption as well as the material dimension will follow in later chapters as we consider alternative economic and political practices supported by relational Christian realism. Here all that needs to be emphasised is that the vision of redemption we are holding forth is not only a matter of head and heart,

---

40   Reinhold Niebuhr, *Nature and Destiny*, 209.
41   Reinhold Niebuhr, *An Interpretation of Christian Ethics* (New York, NY: Harper and Brothers, 1935), 97.

nor is it otherworldly in the least. Rather, it not only cashes out in, but actually consists in, practical actions that support and advance fairly specific political and economic agendas toward democratisation, ecological responsibility and just distribution of resources.

Materially, redemption means the restructuring of material structures. As in intellectual and emotion reconstruction it is the human mind and heart that is reoriented and reconstructed, so here it is the body of the commonwealth of beings, its institutions, its structural components including hierarchies and inequalities, its physical attributes (the flow of carbon, for example) that are restructured and reorganised. Relational Christian realism acknowledges the point of Deleuze's 'body without organs': there is a constant flow of singularities (for us, these are objects) that circulates nomadically through the body of the commonwealth, and therefore any structuring or ordering of them is de-ontologised, rendered inessential.[42] But it is just this flow that makes it possible to break up old structures and constitute new ones in the service of more just distribution of power and resources.

It is crucial to note that this restructuring may not necessarily be on a grand scale. It may occur in pockets, small-scale 'spiritual presences' in which material life (and non-life) is organised according to the relation of all things to the virtual real (to God) that inhabits them. It could occur in alternative forms of economic production and exchange, in protest movements, in collaborations that have a limited scope and range.

The limitation here points to something very important about redemption as it is understood in relational Christian realism. As we pointed out in the last chapter and have emphasised again here, our perspective resists the pull of a Christology that definitively encloses and determines the real. Christ represents a possibility, a form of a contingent actualisation (perhaps) to come, and not a realised actuality that unilaterally effects redemption. For redemption to become actual, in other words, the creative element that is resumed in it must link up, make connections with other actualities. It must leverage influence on the network of beings in which it finds itself. And that means that it inevitably faces limitations. Redemption arises whenever the opportunity for creativity resumes in the midst of stagnation and arrest, but its power to propagate itself is always constrained by the inertia that characterises other objects that accompany it, including its own local and extended networks. Intellectual reconstruction, the building of new, more inclusive, visions of the real, is always hindered by myopic habits and patterns of thought that have been built over the course of

---

42   Deleuze and Guattari, *Anti-Oedipus*, 9–15.

trials of strength. The reorientation of the human emotional constitution is limited by the very definite biases and predispositions that are structured into our emotional lives both by inherited biological factors and by our particular circumstances. The restructuring of human ends and of the material structures characteristic of the commonwealth of objects is limited by the accumulation of previous priorities and regnant structures.

But redemption seizes hold of the indeterminate possibilities that attend every object in its contingency. For human beings, it exploits the basic plasticity of the human condition that we described in our section on human beings as created in order to resume the creative process that rumbles in the heart of objects and reverberates through collections of them. Indeterminacy does not mean infinite flexibility, but rather the absence of actualised outer boundaries. Objects – human beings, in this case – have inner structures, but how those structures are articulated and realised through interaction with other objects is not predetermined. It is this lack of determination even for inwardly defined objects that makes the trajectory toward truth, love, goodness and fulfilment possible, even though unambiguous articulations of these are not forthcoming.

Because relational Christian realism holds to a cosmic, non-anthropocentric vision of redemption, we must emphasise again that this four-fold restructuring of the human object is not only redemptive for human beings: as objects that serve as nodes in a broader network of being, their own redemption adds to the resumption of creativity. In their own special way, humans experience and convey a redemptive trajectory that is redemptive for the commonwealth, though it is only part of the redemptive realities emerging in the latter.

Christian thought about redemption inevitably involves the question of whether or not there are there special agents of redemptive processes in the world. Having already concluded that the practice of worship itself requires that the inconsistent multiplicity that the first intention of the idea of God invokes be specified in terms of a specific direction which is depicted in the Christ event, we are bound to answer in the affirmative. There are indeed trajectories in the world that bear redemptive possibilities, and those trajectories take shape by means of particular institutional embodiments. One of these is the institution whose purpose is to point to larger movements both of creativity (and judgement) and redemption. It is the institution where worship as a material, orienting practice is housed: the church.

The church participates in the larger work of the commonwealth in that it collects members into an open, expansive order. Its work of collection includes both organisation, or the work of constructing a social order that reflects its vision of a larger commonwealth where both the integrity of objects as well as their participation in larger collectives is acknowledged, and witness. In a relational Christian realism, the church is not a sort of redemptive substance that is conveyed sacramentally or episcopally, by means of channels which are exclusively authorised and effectual. Governing traditions of the church and high sacramental theologies are not excluded or rejected, but ecclesiologies that seek to make the church an actualisation of redemption rather than its fragmentary and localised anticipation cannot be a part of relational Christian realism. What we are saying here is corollary to the notion that there is no completed and closed reality of redemption affirmed in our view. Because redemption is open, contingent upon various ways in which the divine virtuality is expressed amid the interplay of actual things, and always in process, there is no one route or pathway that redemption must be channelled. It is not an actualised reality at all – a substance – but an ongoing and open-ended process that can be and is attached to a plurality of expressions and forms.

Still, the actualised institution of the church, along with other communities whose variety of expression cannot be constrained *a priori*, plays a distinctive role in the commonwealth. As we have already said, its own internal organisation exemplifies the redemptive process of resuming creativity and collection in the midst of inert structures. As importantly, and at the same time and in the same way, its witness to the contingent, non-guaranteed appearance of further progress in redemption (the kingdom on its way, if you will) keeps hope for a better world, a more expansive and inclusive commonwealth, from collapsing into satisfaction with the present state of things. As theologian Max Stackhouse has said, the church is a human institution among others but one with the distinctive vocation of articulating and sustaining a 'metaphysical and moral' vision that holds other sectors or spheres of corporate life, including the economic, the political, the professions and the family, accountable, exposing their contingency and offering possibilities for reconstruction.[43]

But, in keeping with our insistence that the power of God (the virtual) is immanent within and not transcendent beyond or over the commonwealth of being, we must attribute primary redemptive agency not to a single institution but to the multitude of objects in their relations with each other. In other words, we must resist a sacralising or sacerdotalising of redemption. To do otherwise, privileging the church as the unique authoritative vehicle and mediator of redemptive possibilities, would be to invoke a kind of transcendence that relational Christian realism rejects. On the grandest scale, we may say that it is

---

[43]   Max Stackhouse, *Creeds, Society, and Human Rights: A Study in Three Cultures* (Grand Rapids, MI: Wm B. Eerdmans Publishing Co., 1984), 118–25.

the commonwealth of being itself which collects, and thus effects redemption, being kept open by the menace of the virtual to new candidates for inclusion, and being enabled to order and re-order and to establish new fidelities in terms of its distinctive character.

Only we must not reify or substantialise the commonwealth, either. The commonwealth is composed of actual objects and relations together with the virtualities that circulate in and among them. In this sense it is itself actual, but its actuality is an open-ended one. Neither its outer limits nor its internal structure, if you will, is determinate. So to say that the commonwealth collects is to say that it is the site of a collection which is performed as multiple agencies clash, interact and negotiate. In other words, relational Christian realism refuses to attribute a unique exceptionalism or transcendence to anything, including the collective process itself. Redemption is a trajectory that can be named and joined, but not contained or reified. It is movement, a dance, among objects, but in itself is no object, and has no substance. Thus it yields not a single coherent program, nor a single over-arching fidelity, but a nomadic existence in which fidelities are multiple, entangled and always being exchanged, expanded, revised and reconfigured. It is deterritorialising, in other words – not eschewing territories, but always taking off from them, designating lines of flight, over and again.

Chapter 5

Practices in Christian Materialism and Relational Christian Realism: Urban Community Empowerment

The following three chapters now move the arguments of this book into the area of practical engagement in the public square. We do this because we want to engage philosophical ideas of the Real with material religious practice. We do this because we cannot in all integrity construct the case for a new relational Christian realism based on an ethic of entangled fidelities without discussing in detail how this contributes to the relationality of public life.

Specifically, what this next section seeks to do is directly apply some of the richness of our new theologemes within existing Christian praxis. We do this with reference to four themes that carry over from the last section into this one.

The first of these is the principle of radical hospitality. The assemblage called the Church, we are arguing, exists to establish new fidelities that encourage the flourishing of minority or subjugated interests as part of the important task of keeping the commonwealth circulating, and thus preventing entropic or stratiating tendencies. The Church, as the assemblage of things called into unique constellations of being in specific places and spaces by fidelity to the Christ event, is there to introduce new members to the relational-ontology of the mesh and ensure that they are connected and embedded in webs of relationship.

The second is the principle of distribution; namely ensuring that the flows of interaction and engagement are not allowed to build up into static and frozen hierarchies within the commonwealth. When this happens the equal distribution and flow of power is disrupted and the well-being and flourishing of the fragile immanent plane that constitutes the divine commonwealth is always under threat from sclerotic consolidations of things that disproportionately skew the creative equilibrium of the system a whole.

The third principle is that of attraction. In what could be interpreted as an austere and minimalist vision of the created order presented in this book, the richness of orthopraxis (doing the right thing for the sake of the commonwealth as a whole) becomes all the more important. Fidelity is not simply following the call of the Event but is also about doing it in the most compelling, authentic and creative ways possible. This is so that the *ekklesia* (the assembly of those elements called forth to be the *Gestalten Christi* in a specific time and place), can act as attractors and bifurcators within the teeming multiplicity of the commonwealth. Within natural systems theories such as Maturana and Varela's concept of auto-poesis or self-renewal (which had an influence on Deleuze's work),[1] attractors and bifurcators help push systems of equilibrium to the point of chaos (and vice versa). At the point of chaos the system encounters bifurcation points (like forks in the road) leading to different futures. As we have written elsewhere, if an old attractor can dissipate the energy of the bifurcators, then potential changes get dissolved and the system reverts to a variation of its former state. If however a new set of influences gains the upper hand, it can attract other energies within the system towards new configurations. These attractors and bifurcation points always exist as latent (or virtual) potentials in any complex, non-linear system, and the smallest changes in the system, depending on loops of feedback (rather than lines of command), can often unfold into large effects.[2]

The fourth element relates to the notion of reassembling the public commonwealth so as to arrive at 'matters of concern' rather than 'matters of fact'. This reassembling is, as we have already surmised in our discussion of Latour, a deeply ethical and non-partisan position that nevertheless requires tenacity, patience, phronetic pragmatism and a commitment to empowering forms of political and collective action. This will entail a form of political analysis and leadership, particularly at local levels, that is visionary and progressive (in the sense of outward looking) but where necessary, also recognises the need for deconstruction and moving systems beyond a paralysing homeostasis. We propose four dimensions of reassembling as part of the living out of the principles of a philosophy of Christian materialism: a reassembling at the individual or internal level; a reassembling at the collective, social or political level; reassembling of the human with the non-human and, finally, a reassembling of the human with the divine.

These four elements represent a form of Christian praxis and witness that is deeply relational, deeply hospitable, deeply performative and deeply committed

---

    [1]   John Protevi, 'Deleuze and Life', in *The Cambridge Companion to Deleuze*, eds Smith, D.W. and Somers-Hall, H. (Cambridge, UK: Cambridge University Press, 2012), 255.

    [2]   Christopher Baker, 'Roots and shoots and the curious case of Schleiermacher's tree (aka 'Is rhizomatic truth seceding arborescent reality?'), *International Journal of Practical Theology* 17.2 (2013): 209–31.

to the just distribution of flows and connections. During this performance of relational Christian realism, the *ekklesia* forsakes an hubristic accommodation to the sense of its own importance and autonomy as a self-enclosed and entropic system. Instead it sees itself as an assemblage of things and a multiplicity of practices which seeks to both attract and bifurcate, to provoke chaos and restore equilibrium as the situation dictates.

The three areas of encounter have been selected to show these dynamics and represent areas of current public engagement by the authors. They are urban community empowerment and regeneration, education and the environment.

Urban Community Empowerment and Regeneration

In this chapter we will examine three case studies of faith-based urban engagement that epitomise some of the dynamics of a relational Christian realism outlined above: gathering; distribution; power of attraction; and reassembling. Whilst there is a claim that each of these case studies reflects a particular dimension of relational Christian realism, clearly they each reflect all four dimensions in various permutations. These case studies emerge from some of our own empirical work exploring the contribution of churches to urban regeneration in Manchester in the early 2000s, as well as the work of up and coming urban theologians and human geographers who reflect on urban materiality in very interesting ways.

Case Study 1: Gathering the Lived Experience – Visual Ethnographies and Local Circulations of Meaning

The first case study relates to the work of Scottish urban theologian and Baptist minister Derrick Watson. Watson's work aims to restore a deep connection between the lived materialities of urban space and the local church community (namely the body of Christ). His area of engagement is the former parish and now suburb of Cathcart in the South Side of Glasgow where he ministers. His way of restoring deep connection is not to present familiar narratives of the locality, but unfamiliar ones, that bring together different material objects that are impacting on the locality into arresting focus. He aims to create this arresting focus through the use of visual ethnographies, which in effect are pictures, and commentaries or narratives that pertain to each of these pictures, taken of different sites by different user groups in the locality. Watson refers to this methodology as a practice of 'photo-elicitation'.[3] The user groups he engages with include: tenants from a newly built housing association development which has been recently populated from other areas of South Glasgow and which contains a high percentage of residents from diverse nationalities and languages; a traditional men's barber's shop in the High Street; the dog walkers who traverse on a daily basis the open spaces of Cathcart Old Cemetery and Linn Park that sits across the White Cart river and act as breathing spaces for residents; and plot holders at Berridale allotments.

The main theoretical and methodological influence on Watson's approach is the interdisciplinary work of Sarah Pink, whose own output is generated by the central principle that 'everyday life' is a 'site of activist practice'.[4] In other words, flows and movements that belong to global circulations shape the localities and experience of daily life for ordinary citizens. Her work helps to critically engage with these everyday and mundane sites of practices, 'where we make our worlds and our worlds make us'[5] in the hope that different visualisations and perceptions of these everyday sites undertaken by citizens themselves will change their habitual (and perhaps disempowered) responses. Her work on visual ethnographies therefore engages in what Watson calls 'the messy contradictions of the everyday life'[6] in order to make a difference through research. He quotes Pink's work to further effect: '... the localities where activist projects are created become both the intersections of complex sets of power relations and frame the experienced realities where people live out their everyday lives ... offering alternative sensory embodied experiences.'[7] These changes in experienced realities played out as local circulations of meaning and experience, Pink suggests, will minimise the alienating influence of the global circulations.

Watson as an urban practical theologian develops Pink's language of 'intersections' and 'framing' into a warmer and more holistic concept; namely simply 'to gather'.[8] This word signifies an act of drawing disparate events together in order to bring about interactions that, in language reminiscent of Ingold, can become 'subversive, creative, disruptive, life affirming'.[9] Watson also

---

3   Derrick Watson, 'Critical acts of gathering: "Old Men of Cathcart", green guerrillas and new lines of desire', unpublished paper for *Urban Shifts 2 – Desire Lines? Joining dots in local communities* (Chester, UK: University of Chester), (2014), 6.

4   Sarah Pink, *Situating Everyday Life: Practices and Places* (London, UK: Sage, 2012), 5.

5   Ibid., 5.

6   Watson, 'Critical Acts of Gathering', 3.

7   Pink, *Situating Everyday Life*, 10.

8   Watson, *Critical Acts of Gathering*, 3.

9   Ibid., 4.

helpfully, from a relational Christian realism perspective, folds this language of gathering into the rhizomatic nature of Deleuzian thought – 'the placing side-by-side [of miscellaneous objects from visual ethnographies reflects] the subterranean supra-cognitive linking of disparity as a creative act'.[10] This intentional deterritorialising and reterritorialising of objects helps create new trajectories or lines of flight of perception and experience within individuals at a very deep level.

To help us make sense of (or 'hold together')[11] the existing and potential new orderings of objects and perceptions in a given locality, Watson makes use of another methodological tool – the dialectogram. The dialectogram is a visual representation of object spatiality and relationality devised by an associate of Watson, Mitch Miller from the Glasgow School of Art. Dialectograms are 'subjective passionate and open-ended sketches of relations and experiences' between objects assembled within that space. They attempt 'to carry disparate visual and textual material across local spaces'.[12] Thus, at the time of writing, Watson is working on three dialectograms to reflect some of the relationships that are 'gathered' by his user groups. The one reproduced below reflects the 'event of intimate space' that occurs as a housebound participant, on the newly built housing association development mentioned above, moves between a corner of the kitchen overlooking their rear garden and the rear garden itself, with links through that garden to other adjoining spaces and activities: community play, neighbours and a bowling club.

As can be seen from this dialectogram, Watson draws and inscribes material objects and their spatial interaction with each other, with fragments of subjective narrative and memory that create a temporary assembling of both within the everyday experience of the user of this space. Watson inscribes spaces where his interviewee can, as a housebound person, shout in conversation and connection across with a neighbour, where he can have a peaceful smoke, the space in the corner represented by the chair in which his wife used to sit, and where one senses she is still present. This mapping and reflection on a micro-commonwealth of objects and the responses/engagements between them is an exercise in empathy and incorporation into wider networks of recognition and valorisation.

However, Watson not only wants to faithfully record physical localities through these exercises of visual ethnography. He also seeks to interrupt the 'local hermeneutical security of the explicit body of Christ'[13] (namely the 'actual'

---

10   Ibid., 4.
11   Ibid., 10.
12   Ibid., 10.
13   Ibid., 8.

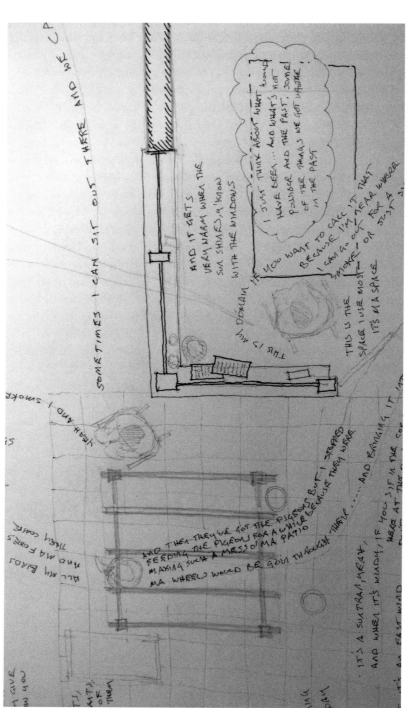

Figure 5.1   Dialectogram. Used by permission of Derrick Watson

expression of the Church) and extend that interruption back into the local site through visual and collage street expressions, exploring marginalising relations through temporary and fragile re-workings of everyday space. Watson's discourse and methodology, rooted in a collaborative search for meaning of the spatial text, is, we suggest, a prescient, parallel and suggestive rereading of what in the previous chapter we had identified as *Gestalten Christi*, that is, the temporary localised space that is assembled in activist fidelity to the Christ Event.

Watson's careful and painstaking logging and mapping of local peoples' visual and oral responses to their built environment is also a great example of Latourian-inflected urban theology that seeks to establish 'matters of concern' rather than 'matters of fact'. It highlights the emerging importance of the non-textual and more material readings of the city and reaffirms the *Missio Dei* theology emanating from the post- or open Evangelical ethnographic turn in theology; discerning the kingdom of God already at work in the materiality and connectivity of the urban. In the words of British Baptist theologian, Paul Fiddes, 'We live in the presence of the environment of the triune God, who is always opening and manifesting God's self to us'.[14] He continues,

> We need to get beyond the subject-object thinking to a kind of thinking characterised by engagement and participation. Such participation applies to all created reality, since everything created participates in the relations of the triune God, or exists in the space opened up by the interweaving relations of God. God makes room for God's self for us to dwell.[15]

Case Study 2: Community Pride – Distributing Knowledge and Critiquing Hierarchies

Our second case study of relational Christian realism involves a faith-based community empowerment network established in Manchester in 1999 called Community Pride. Their current work focuses on what they call 'Schools of Participation' which they run with groups who tend to be the most excluded from relationships with the wider community; refugees and asylum seekers; young single parents; postcodes of multiple deprivation; citizens living with sensory impairment. According to Community Pride, their Schools of Participation are 'alternative space[s] where people meet to reflect on their reality, share

---

[14]   Pete Ward (ed.), *Perspectives on Ecclesiology and Ethnography* (Grand Rapids, MI: Wm. B. Eerdmans Publishing Co., 2012), 26.

[15]   Ibid., 26–7.

experiences, gain skills, learn together and plan actions to have more control over what is happening in their lives and communities'.[16] This commitment to redistribution of knowledge, education and power is based on a liberation theology model, and owes direct acknowledgement to the participative pedagogies pioneered by Paulo Friere,[17] to whom we will refer later. Our research engaged with Community Pride at an earlier stage of their development when their focus was on more generic community empowerment in those parts of East Manchester undergoing massive urban regeneration under the then New Labour government's (1997–2010) plans for reviving city centres.[18] Vast swathes of East Manchester were originally constructed as the industrial powerhouse for the city which helped it secure its place as a pre-eminent global and colonial city for roughly a century between the 1830s and 1930s. East Manchester was home to the first industrial suburb ever built (Ancoats) whose collection of vast multi-storey mills surrounded by rows of cheap 'two-up, two-down' terraced housing became the blueprint for the industrial age city all over the world. This planning formula was repeated mile after mile east of Manchester's city centre during the mid- to late Victorian era. By the 1980s, owing to the drastic decline of manufacturing in the UK due to cheap global competition, much of East Manchester was a wasteland of derelict industrial sites and traumatised communities. Whole district populations were cleared from the Victorian slum terraces and decanted into large depersonalised housing schemes, which within a space of 20 years had themselves become modern-day slums. High levels of unemployment, mortality and illness rates and low educational attainment were exacerbated by drug-related crime and violence and a pervading sense of quiet despair and hopelessness. New Labour's plans for regenerating East Manchester relied on a three-pronged attack aimed at accelerated transformation within a 10-year time frame. First was the successful bid for the 2002 Commonwealth Games which allowed for the development of prestigious sports facilities. The former Commonwealth Games Stadium is now the Etihad Stadium, the home of Manchester City Football Club whose current pre-eminence in the English Premiership League (itself a world-wide brand) is predicated on the massive financial investment from oil revenues generated in the United Arab Emirates. Second, was attracting global retailers such as the US-based Walmart

---

[16]   Available at: http://www.communitypride.org.uk/?page_id=14 (retrieved 1st February 2014).

[17]   Available at: http://www.communitypride.org.uk/?page_id=14 (retrieved 1st February 2014).

[18]   Lord Rogers of Riverside, *Towards a Strong Urban Renaissance* (London, UK: HMSO, 2005).

conglomerate who constructed a very large flagship Walmart-Asda Superstore for the area. Third, was the construction of designer housing for the new urban 'creative' class (sometimes referred to as the New Bohos – or New Bohemians),[19] including one scheme called New Islington which proposed the joining up of two industrial canals to create more new water frontage against which to sell the new designer housing.

To help understand the nature of the impact of Community Pride's engagement in the public sphere, it is worth unpacking the material dimensions of this particular project a little more. The New Islington development, which was badly hit by the 2008 financial collapse, was unable to afford the ambitious canal joining scheme on which much of its iconic status was predicated, and it is struggling to be completed. The current view looks like this. The affordable housing (that is, shared equity or rental schemes), which was intended to house a small number of the previous high-rise and terrace housing tenants whose housing was demolished as part of the regeneration, has also been hugely delayed and indeed may never be completed. This housing, although of good quality, is stranded in the middle of overgrown and litter-strewn plots awaiting development, bookended by private entry and avant-garde designer housing. In the meantime, what the local press likes to label 'feral youths' from the neighbouring estates, which are in a permanent state of limbo awaiting their turn for regeneration, engage in nefarious acts of violence, drunkenness and drug dealing in the still derelict canal areas once designated to turn this (literal) wasteland into 'the Venice of the North'.[20] So what we have in this 'regenerated' space is an assemblage of objects; abandoned industrial buildings, new designer flats, detritus, graffiti and so on. There is also a multiplicity of place names that shape the perception and experience of this space. New Islington is a name intended as a rebranding of the 1970s Cardroom Estate, some of which has been demolished. This ill-fated high-rise estate was named after the card rooms used for stretching and cleaning cotton into strands ready for weaving in the textile factories that were demolished in order to make way for the high-rise flats. New Islington attempts to valorise local history by taking its name from a local street of terrace housing which was found on a map of the area dating back to the 1840s. However this name was also (presumably) chosen because of its specific echoes with an example of a successful urban regeneration project in North London (namely Islington). These changes in place name (and the conflicting

---

19   Richard Florida, *The Rise of the Creative Class* (New York, NY: Basic Books, 2002).
20   Available at: http://www.manchesterconfidential.co.uk/News/Ancoats-New-Islington-Marina-Failing-Manchester [accessed 21st February 2014].

signals they give out) engage with other assemblages of objects associated with such words as solidarity, poverty, globalised finance, local memory and so on. It is into this complex commonwealth of objects and object-object (OOO) relations that Community Pride inserts its participatory community empowerment. Research undertaken for the William Temple Foundation in the mid-2000s exploring the methodology and impact of Community Pride's key workers with the residents and tenants of East Manchester identified various dimensions to their work on knowledge and information distribution. The first was defined as local-global analysis.[21] As one key worker said, 'Our crunch points have been around the impact of globalisation on local people, and after five or six years we've been able to critique externally what we've seen happening and how things have or have not been changed for local people'.[22] This intervention shows the importance of political and economic analyses of power created by the dynamics of globalisation on local and embedded spaces. There is also an implicit acknowledgement that there have been some material benefits to the local community from the globally induced inward investment by the likes of US multinationals, Gulf petro-dollars and offshore pension funds.

A harder-edged critique was also voiced by the Community Pride key workers – namely that of colonialism. The renaissance of urban space for professional and higher-earning citizens at the expense of the physical demolition of 'redundant spaces' is reinforced by the demolition of local cultures which are deemed not to be compatible with the new materialist utopia. One Community Pride key worker described the regeneration industry as having a 'missionary approach'; arriving in a new area and telling existing residents how they should 'improve' themselves – for example, recommending prohibitions on smoking and eating meat pies within the localities earmarked for regeneration. The key worker continued their analysis:

> ... I don't mean this nastily, personally, but look at Mr X at the New Deal for Communities [the government private/public partnership programme designed to co-ordinate regeneration programmes]. The man has come to save East Manchester, and the way the residents relate to him is like a priest in some respects, they defer to his wisdom. And he comes and presides at meetings, there's loads of imagery like that.[23]

---

[21]   Christopher Baker, *The Hybrid Church in the City – Third Space Thinking* (London, UK: SCM Press, 2009).

[22]   Ibid., 113.

[23]   Ibid., 113.

This disciplining of the local population into the demands of the regeneration industry for sleeker, attractive, aspirational people to enhance the material value of their investments and minimise the risk of negative image or impact was interpreted by Community Pride as a form of collusion and surrender to a more omniscient power. This sharp critique of disparate flows in the commonwealth is however not a naïve endorsement of the superiority of one set of objects/actants over another set. In this case, the Community Pride workers were not blind to the inherent capacity for ossification and regressive tendencies within the local culture. They were also equally committed to open and transparent engagement with the power brokers from government, local authorities and businesses in an attempt to circulate references that reflected a fairer and more nuanced picture of the communities that some of these institutions had come to 'save'. But they were equally clear that their role was not to mediate a meaningless or uncritical consensus, which is the default position of much of the public policy rhetoric on localism. This rhetoric emphasises the new ideal of 'governance' rather than government, in which the State willingly secedes the chimera of its own expertise and competence to shape local affairs to the knowledge and wisdom of the 'market' and 'local civil society'.[24] As one key worker reflected, 'I think under the surface there isn't consensus ... and I think that somewhere conflict has got to come out. A consensus would only come from a really, really profound and deep engagement with people'.[25] So instead of a shallow and meaningless consensus, Community Pride saw its role as working towards what one of the key workers called 'a critical consensus'. In other words, to pursue deeper levels of engagement and acknowledge genuine diversity and plurality without perpetuating a system where the most powerfully presented view of a partnership holds sway. In these situations the silence of other partners might be suppressed expressions of frustration, exclusion or apathy rather than active agreement. A 'surface' consensus would possibly gain in expediency, but would lose in sustainability (that is, building networks and processes that will last into the future irrespective of the whims of public or private funding streams). This deeper level of engagement was analysed by an external review from the European Institute of Urban Affairs[26] into the work of Community Pride which suggested the intimate connection with what it defined as 'a firm value base' (that is, its Christian origins and ethos) and its commitment to 'going the extra mile' which,

---

[24]   Ibid., 57.
[25]   Ibid., 114.
[26]   European Institute of Urban Affairs, *Impact Report 2002–05* (Manchester, UK: EIUA, 2005).

in the opinion of the report, led to variety of impacts 'beyond its numbers'.[27] These impacts ranged from initiating processes of inclusion as well as delivering practical contributions to community empowerment based on sharing of knowledge, information, analysis and ideas. For example: role-modelling a sense of sharing that leads to moral support; a belief in partnership; a commitment to trailblazing and identifying needs that are not otherwise being met; creating self-sustaining structures, not dependency; creating a niche way of operating that mixes both analysis and group work skills; recognising the significance of power structures; keeping up to date with current policy initiatives and so translating knowledge and information for those who are affected by the decisions of others; feeding intelligence back to the policymakers.[28] This form of deep engagement is, from the perspective of relational Christian realism, about taking up power struggles with objects of all kinds in the form of material redemption, often at the small, pocket-sized scale, in order to free up frozen hierarchies and release virtual energies of change, located within the actual present configurations of objects.

Case Study 3: Drug Addiction Programmes – Postsecular Caritas and the Deterritorialisation of the Church

Our final case study is a spatial analysis of how different materialities comprised of non-human actants and human actants combine to produce new lines of flight within the commonwealth or assemblage of events represented by a Salvation Army (TAS) centre in the South-West of England. This centre provides emergency accommodation, maintenance, detoxification and rehabilitation facilities for people with drug dependency problems. The centre is a hybrid-funded space, representing a formal partnership between the Salvation Army and a local authority Drug Strategy Team. This faith-secular hybridity also stretches to the large interdisciplinary team that are employed at the centre, ranging from conservative evangelical Christians, more open evangelical and liberal Christians, Buddhists, pagans and a range of employees, often from faith backgrounds, but who would now characterise themselves as agnostic or atheist. The researcher Andy Williams is a human geographer based at the University of Exeter and he is keen to analyse spatially the persistent and re-emerging presence of religious discourse and practice in the twenty-first-century public sphere. This re-emergence, or perhaps more accurately, new visibility, of religion as a

---

[27]   Ibid. 4.

[28]   Chris Baker, 'Entry to Enterprise: Constructing Local Political Economies in Manchester', in *Through the Eye of a Needle – Theological Conversations over Political Economy*, eds Atherton, J. and Skinner, H. (Peterborough, UK: Epworth Press 2007), 198.

significant cultural and political force in public life has been labelled the postsecular. This increasingly ubiquitous term has been widely contested,[29] but Jurgen Habermas' definition from 2005 is considered to be the most empirically accurate and conceptually broad: namely the need to adopt 'a postsecular self-understanding of society as whole in which the vigorous continuation of religion in a continually secularizing environment must be reckoned with'.[30] Williams' research into this postsecular space challenges the popular and rather simplistic Marxist-led critique that the re-emergence of interest in religion in public life is simply as a result of governmental incorporation of FBOs into systems of neo-liberal governance. It also challenges however an equally narrow assumption, usually from faith groups themselves that any distinctive practices or discourses pertaining to faith groups who engage in partnership with secular agencies are hollowed out. Williams is interested in a 'subtle' reading of the different and multi-layered ways in which faith-based and humanitarian motivations 'accrete' around mutual ethical concerns and cross-over narratives.[31] This subtle reading has a number of features that are relevant to our discussion.[32] The first is the way that Williams identifies the macro discourses and circulating references which help shape these micro-spaces of what he calls 'emergent, transient and performative outworkings of caritas and hospitality'. These discourses include: the post-1970s shift in evangelical theology from 'quietist' to 'transformational' approaches whereby 'knowing what is right should lead to doing what is right in contemporary social contexts';[33] the renewed interest in Christian virtue ethics (that is, 'a character that is formed by practice, the choices that we make and the communities to which we belong');[34] and the mainstreaming of spirituality in British healthcare, with several medical staff at the TSA centre, 'specialising in

---

[29]   For example, James Beckford, 'Public Religions and the Postsecular: Critical Perspectives', *Journal for the Scientific Study of Religion* 51.1 (2012): 1–19.

[30]   Jürgen Habermas, 'Equal treatment of culture and the limits of postmodern liberalism', *Journal of Political Philosophy* 14.1 (2005), 26.

[31]   Andrew Williams, 'Postsecularism as Practice: theo-ethics and religion without religion in a Salvation Army Drug Programme', unpublished paper given at the *Compassion, Charity and Hope in the Postsecular City* conference (University of Groningen) (2012), 2. It has since been updated as a published article. Williams A (2014) 'Postsecular geographies: theo-ethics, rapprochement and neoliberal governance in a faith-based drug programme', *Transactions of the Institute of the British Geographers* ONLINE 27 AUG 2014 DOI: 10.1111/tran.12069.

[32]   Ibid., 2.

[33]   Ibid., 4.

[34]   Ibid., 4.

aromatherapy, massage and Buddhist philosophies of mindfulness'.[35] Williams concludes, '... the blurring boundaries between scientific and therapeutic practices create a hybrid space where the relationship between religious belief and practice and therapeutic care become increasingly complex'.[36] This blurring of practices and circulating of discourses create the conditions for new trajectories of Christian pragmatic (in the sense of empirical and experimental)[37] mission that help create new intensities of redemption in the form of hope and solidarity, receptivity and generous engagement. The second feature of Williams' analysis relevant to this debate is his identification of three moral and professional positionalities of the workers within the TSA centre. He characterises *Christian caritas* as the traditional conversionist stance within some of the Christian workers at the centre. This orientation focuses on Christian praxis as the opportunity to share the gospel, but is 'unable to recognise the radical alterity of those who live beyond, or reject the Christian narrative'.[38] *Secular humanism* identifies with residents' past experience of drug use and extols the duties of an 'avowed professionalism to service delivery based on reasoned beneficence and benevolence within conceptions of independence and self-sufficiency'.[39] However, this professionalism, like the Christian caritas, is also offered to the clients on the host's terms which has the effect of promoting 'particular conceptions of independence and self-sufficiency, without taking into account the specific position of the other'.[40] Finally, there is *postsecular caritas* which steers an alternative path between the other two positions by challenging the 'limitations of self-identifying giving' on both sides of the traditional secular/religious divide in favour of a 'pursuit to recognise the otherness of the other'.[41] This value is expressed in the notion of the 'stringless gift – an attempt to give without any expectation of reciprocity'.[42] This notion of postsecular caritas, it seems to us, is fundamental to the practical outworking of relational Christian realism, in its willingness to create new spaces for the virtual power of different objects to be expressed and contribute to the just flourishing of the commonwealth as a whole. Third, Williams identifies a number of episodes of postsecular caritas

---

[35]   Ibid., 4

[36]   Ibid., 5.

[37]   For discussion on the idea of pragmatics as experimentation, see the discussion in *The Down-deep Delight of Democracy*, Purcell, M. (Malden, MA: Wiley-Blackwell, 2013).

[38]   Williams, *Postsecularism*, 9.

[39]   Ibid., 11.

[40]   Ibid., 11.

[41]   Ibid., 11.

[42]   Ibid., 12.

which involve both human and non-human actants. These include the communicating of care and peacefulness to clients by the receptionist, a conservative Evangelical, who modelled what Williams defines as the 'emotional tonality'[43] of the whole centre whenever she was on duty; the atmosphere of prayer that pervades the whole centre after the non-obligatory daily prayer meeting in the chapel; the enabling testimony of the Salvation Army centre manager at the annual commissioning service which spoke powerfully across epistemological positions held by the staff. This last episode occurred because the manager's testimony was perceived to come from authentic experience and was couched in stories and narratives of hope and 'not as formal propositional belief'.[44] Williams characterises these examples as visceral and performative spaces of postsecular caritas, 'emanating from the interweaving of bodies, materials and affective environment which can connect the ethical proclivities of different actors in ways that constitute a space of *translation* wherein rigid identity divisions are reformulated'[45] (emphasis mine). Finally, in terms of the performative practice of postsecular caritas, Williams suggests that new expressions of Christian religion are emerging, involving the 'de-capitalisation of one's own truth claims and embracing theologies of common grace'.[46] Many of the Christian staff at the TAS drugs rehabilitation project, he observed, were willing to experiment in 'how to be church in the community – with homeless people – outside the four walls of a church building'. This experimentation coincided with a reformulation of the epistemological bases of belief, that is, 'a concession that absolute truth [which] cannot be known in any epistemological way leads to a more dialogical expression of faith-sharing premised on a culture of assurance of practice rather than conviction of right belief'.[47] Meanwhile, within the secular actants working in the TSA centre, Williams observed a movement from 'beyond merely tolerating religious belief, towards an open recognition of how religion and tradition articulate moral intuitions where they can share participation in theo-ethical virtues of agape and caritas'.[48] It is perhaps this dimension of faith-based mission that speaks most powerfully into the relationship between the actualised church and the virtual church. As we have already suggested, institutionalised, actualised and solid forms of church are not excluded or rejected as means by which to collect and organise a larger and more

---

[43] Ibid., 15.
[44] Ibid., 17.
[45] Ibid., 17.
[46] Ibid., 21.
[47] Ibid., 22.
[48] Ibid., 28.

inclusive commonwealth where both the integrity of the object and thus participation is acknowledged. However, these experiments in 'church' and Christian identity in postsecular space (as outlined by Williams) are vitally important expressions of the virtual church. The virtual church is (in terms that Messailloux would recognise) a 'menace' to the complacency and inertia of the actualised church. It constantly keeps the process of redemption open and recontextualised. In this form, the body of Christ connects with other creative and virtual forces within the commonwealth (which will be non-religious as well as religious objects) to create new assemblages of redemptive creativity. As we bring this enquiry into relational Christian realism in respect to urban and community empowerment to an end, we aware of the varying and dynamic operations of religious communities operating as they do across inter-religious and religious/secular boundaries. We are also aware, with respect of our final case study of faith/secular partnerships over drug addiction rehabilitation within a Christian setting, that this affirms the category of the postsecular as a productive and naturally occurring new space for relational Christian realism to flourish.

We are not reifying the postsecular as a monolithic form of public space that replaces the secular model. If one was to reify the postsecular, and label it as a proto category, one would simply fall into the trap of reiterating (but from a different epistemological base) the idea of a static one-size-fits-all secular model of the public square (or commonwealth) that emerges from Western enlightenment with its prescriptive formula of science (= public) and religion (= private). Indeed it was this static, sclerotic and rigid closing down of the commonwealth of ideas, objects and experiences within modernity that Latour most deeply criticises in his tirade against critical theories, that is, 'matters of fact' asserted by academic elites, as opposed to 'matters of concern'. So we prefer to see the postsecular as a fluid and non-essentialised space of virtual possibilities. Human geographers Paul Cloke and Justin Beaumont, in ways that freshen Habermas' functional and somewhat prosaic definition which we cited earlier, see the postsecular as an opportunity to 'trace new interconnection between diverse religious, humanist and secularist positionalities in the dynamic geographies of the city'.[49] These interconnections are likely to be reflected in the emergence of localised 'spaces of care, protest, tolerance, reconciliation and ethical agreement'.[50] It is here at the local level, rather than across the public commons as a whole, that geographies

---

[49]   Paul Cloke and Justin Beaumont, 'Geographies of postsecular rapprochement in the city', *Progress in Human Geography* 37.2 (2012): 32

[50]   Ibid.: 32.

of 'postsecular rapprochement' between religious and no-religion actants are increasingly occurring. Cloke and Beaumont describe spaces of postsecular rapprochement as 'opportunities for people of religious faith and none to "do something about something" over the plight of socially excluded people in the city' and in which the 'insider and outsider position are very fluid and porous'.[51] Taken together, these emerging geographies of postsecular rapprochement, they suggest, reflect 'new spaces of hope and new lines of flight that can be released into the politics and poetics of postsecular resistance in the contemporary city'.[52] These lines powerfully sum up the impact of what practices of relational Christian realism can aspire to do in respect of furthering the flourishing of the commonwealth by bringing to the surface and releasing the power of the virtual through valorising everyday objects and events, distributing new forms of knowledge and analysis, attracting performativities of postsecular caritas and reassembling the *ekklesia* as new expressions of the *Gestalten Christi*.

The Depth and Potentiality of Urban Materialities

As a coda to this chapter, it is important that we realign our more ecclesiological debates about the new reterrititorialisations of the urban church back into the philosophical purposes of this book. All three case studies in this chapter have to varying degrees attempted to draw a close interaction between the real, material ontologies of different objects, both human and non-human that lies at the heart of a Christian philosophy of materialism. In this regard they echo some clearer expressions of a liberative philosophy of materialism articulated within critical human geography, which has been applying post-Marxist social theory and Continental philosophy to urban change and development for some time. For example, the use of Deleuzian notions of assemblage in this tradition are highly relevant. Deleuze always hoped that the political Left might organise itself in assemblages or 'constellations of singularities' which expressed a political subjectivity orientated towards the actualisation of ideals and the realisation of potential: 'Deleuze envisaged the Left as a network of intersecting and conflicting assemblages ... a garden rather than a tree.'[53] Urban theorists like Colin McFarlane are keen to take these notions of assemblage as critical tools for thinking about 'a more socially just and ecologically sound

---

[51]   Ibid.: 31.

[52]   Ibid.: 44.

[53]   Nicholas Tampio, 'Assemblages and the multitude: Deleuze, Hardt, Negri and the postmodern left', *European Journal of Political Theory* 8 (2009): 385.

urbanism'.[54] McFarlane suggests that assemblage thinking can be a descriptor of socio-material transformation. For example, he advocates thinking about the city as a decentred object which is 'relentlessly being assembled at concrete sites of urban practice ... as a multiplicity of processes of becoming, affixing sociotechnical networks, hybrid collectivities and alternative topologies'.[55] This account of the energetic juxtaposition of objects and their role in the creation of material processes and practices has clear echoes with the work of Harman that we have already alluded to, and his references to what he calls the 'molten core' of objects, and the way they express their 'volcanic' essence.[56] But McFarlane is also convinced that the notion of assemblage places greater emphasis on what he calls the 'depth' and 'potentiality' of urban sites, processes and actors. By depth, he refers to 'the crucial role of multiple and over-lapping histories in producing habits of practice, ways of going on, and trajectories of policy and economy that shape urban inequality'.[57] By potentiality, he articulates 'both the intensity and excessiveness of the moment – the capacity of events to disrupt patterns, generate new encounters with people and objects and create new connections in ways of inhabiting everyday urban life'.[58] McFarlane's urban case study in support of this deployment of assemblage methodology is his research into informal settlements in Mumbai. He aims to show how the materiality of the home environment in these chaotic and rhizomatic urban configurations plays a central role in everyday lives and hardships in ways that both inhibit but also enhance the possibilities of individual and communal flourishing and political connectivity. For example, the use of mundane and everyday materials such as railway tickets and stones by housing activists in their demands for better provision of basic amenities and regulation of planning laws:

> We could keep organised and in touch with the phones ... because we discovered we could use the public phone for free by inserting a railway ticket into the receiver. This meant we could make our phone calls to all the members of parliament.[59]

The activists, on the other hand, could also block the phones of members of parliament in order to prevent strategic alliances being formed between legislators that would block their populist demands. In this case, all that was

---

54   Colin McFarlane, 'Assemblage and critical urbanism', *City* 15.2 (2011): 205.
55   Ibid.: 207.
56   See pp. 90 and 91 for earlier discussion.
57   Ibid.: 209.
58   Ibid.: 209.
59   Ibid.: 217.

involved was 'a simple wire and two stones. It made a sound as if the phone was permanently engaged'.[60] The following quote from McFarlane's work, describing the domestic environments of the urban settlements in Mumbai, demonstrates the human/non-human intensity of urban materiality.

> The lack of space that characterises most neighbourhoods means that materials often spill over into public space, from children's toys to rickshaws, bicycles, cooking materials and drying clothes. Washing laundry is often conducted outside the house in an alley where lighting and drainage conditions are better. This material overspill disrupts boundaries of public and private space, and facilitates particular forms of sociability, commonality, discussion and conflict.[61]

McFarlane's political deployment of the concepts of depth and potentiality with regard to urban assemblage theory sums up beautifully the philosophical and missional dimensions of this enquiry into a philosophy of Christian materialism.

---

[60] Ibid.: 217.
[61] Ibid.: 216.

Chapter 6
Education and Relational Christian Realism

Introduction

Having laid out the theoretical dimensions of a relational Christian realist approach it is time to examine the more practical implications of this way of working and how the description of entangled fidelities applies to the outcomes. In this chapter we will look at a highly institutionalised area of religious practice, that of the field of education in the UK, and, in the next, at a far less institutionalised domain, that of engagement with environmental issues. In both of these the intention is to show how key aspects of the new approach will work themselves out in practice. In particular the following areas will come under scrutiny: the contribution of other (non-theological) disciplines to the process; how it is clear that values are always already embedded in the public debates and policy decisions; the need to draw upon a different discourse to illuminate what is to be discovered, for instance ideas of the human and non-human; the process of reassembling and the assemblages that are constructed; the necessity of establishing a level of commitment that is not determined by supposedly autonomous individuals and which represents an entangled fidelity. Crucial questions about both material religious practice and also belief will then come to the fore.

The UK Context and the Academy Agenda

One of the major themes that has emerged from the examination of our philosophical sources is the movement that Deleuze identifies as deterritorialisation and reterritorialisation. Abstract as this may sound, one can begin to grasp what it means by reviewing the recent changes in the educational system in the UK. Up until the late 1990s state education has been in the hands of Local Authority Education bodies (LEAs), although the main funding has been centrally sourced. Even those many schools which are designated as either

Voluntary Aided and Voluntary Controlled, hence have a proportion of their governors appointed by religious institutions such as the Church of England, and receive some funding from those sources, have been essentially serviced and controlled by LEAs. So there have been three tiers of governance; the Department of Education (central government); Local Authorities (LEAs); and then local Governing Boards.

In the late 1990s the then New Labour government introduced the idea of Academies. The original purpose of this was to find a way of reviving the fortunes of failing Comprehensive schools – secondary level schools often operating in relatively deprived areas – by leveraging in external sources of funding, invariably from wealthy private donors. This allowed the appointment of high flying heads or principals whose task it was to turn these schools round both educationally and financially. In some cases it also meant new purpose-built facilities and the creation of flagship projects echoing Tony Blair's pre-election mantra of 'Education, education, education'. This policy was not developed as an overall strategy for education in the UK.

Since 2010 however, when the coalition took power, this policy has now been extended to the point where every school, both secondary and primary, is intended to become an Academy or part of an Academy Chain. Implementing this is far from easy and will take longer than first anticipated. What this means is that the Local Education Authority level of governance and support services is being dismantled and what one is seeing is effectively a privatisation of education in the UK. LEA services are being destroyed county by county; former employees are setting themselves up as consultants, and individual schools are left with the problem of how to access their services now they are only available on a more commercial basis. One could argue that this is indeed a deterritorialisation of publically funded state education with the removal of an intermediate level of governance, and its replacement or reterritorialisation by a plethora of relatively independent and financially driven Academy Chains who have different lines of accountability.

A classic example of entangled fidelity is how the Church of England is trying to respond to this new operating environment. Through its secondary and primary schools it is responsible for educating approximately 1 million children in the UK, so it has a massive statutory stake in the process. Having worked closely and often effectively with LEAs and their staff it now has to rethink its relationships and adapt to the Academy movement. This is complex and rapidly changing as the coalition government works out policies as it goes along in its haste to roll this programme out whilst it is still in power. In effect it is creating a 'one-way ticket' in this direction, as it would be so difficult and costly to recreate the structures it is dismantling that no future regime would envisage this as a viable option. As some have said 'academies are the only show in town'!

Some of the challenges facing the Church of England in this process are as follows. To be financially viable as a stand-alone Academy requires (although the exact figure varies from county to county) a minimum of 250 pupils. Hence it is only either secondary schools or larger primary schools that can take this route. Many larger secondary schools have already taken this route, leaving lots of small rural primary schools, many of which are Church Aided or Church Controlled, with no obvious way forward apart from becoming part of an Academy Chain or what are called Multi-Academy Trusts. Quite a number of Dioceses have taken the decision to establish their own Diocesan Multi-Academy Trusts (MATs) in order to provide a 'home' for the schools within what they call 'the church family'. This is proving challenging and difficult for both financial and educational reasons.

All of this is happening in an increasingly competitive environment within which far larger and better funded independent Academy Chains, some of them operating from outside the UK, are stepping in and sweeping up the larger and more successful schools.

The problems for Diocesan MATs are therefore the schools that are 'left behind' and that no one else will wish to swallow up both for financial and educational reasons, plus a distinct lack of resources. In effect, Dioceses are trying to recreate their own equivalent of Local Authority Education bodies, but without significant sources of funding or access to the personnel required. In strictly economic terms they need a critical mass of schools to create the economies of scale to make their MATs financially viable – and this is difficult to establish given the factors described – and without the appropriate finance they cannot afford to recruit the calibre of staff required to guarantee the educational and managerial skills needed for their individual schools. Many are currently using already over-stretched Diocesan employees to staff their developing MATs in a way that is simply not sustainable. It has been whispered at government level that such bodies are being 'set up to fail', at which point other Academy Chains without any faith commitment will presumably be invited in to pick up the pieces! But what is the Church of England supposed to do in order to carry out its responsibilities to all those schools and to maintain the values that it would argue are distinctive to faith schools?

The reterritorialisation of the education system in the UK is all about the encroachment of commercial values and the handing over of schools to bodies who care more about profit than about education. There have already been a number of scandals relating to Academies who have been spending public money on their own 'extra-curricular' activities, plus Free Schools which have been unable to meet satisfactory educational standards. How will all of this then be regulated and monitored when resources are being reduced from these spheres of central government activity? One could argue that the scope for corruption is bound to increase. So what are the values that are being promoted through the Academy process and how do these relate to what faith bodies might argue are their reasons for being involved in education? What might it mean in practice to be 'faithful' within this developing system of education, which, as is now clear, is the biggest revolution in the process since the 1944 Education Act?

What it Means to Be or Become Human

The key question which underlies the discussion about the role of the churches in the field of education is surely that of what it is to be or to become human. Any system will be based upon implicit or explicit assumptions on this issue. So, for instance, what is it possible to expect of humans and what is it worth trying to achieve through learning and education? In previous publications there are suggestions on this – that is, the unconscious; practical consciousness; critical consciousness; transpersonal consciousness;[1] and then pre-autonomy; autonomy; post-autonomy.[2] At a later stage this was linked to the work of Ken Wilber, which is far more complex and adds many other layers.[3] This draws upon sources such as the work of James Fowler in faith development, itself building upon the writings of Jung, Kohlberg, Habermas and the feminist critiques of this concept. Is learning a means of taking humans through some sort of developmental process with a clear objective in mind? Recent work with Caroline Baillie and Jens Kabo in 'Heterotopia' on the role of threshold concepts and liminality in the educational process would question whether there can be any predetermined objective, apart perhaps from working towards greater social justice.[4] This is also consistent with the theologeme developed in earlier chapters which questions whether a relational Christian realism leads inexorably to any one specific identifiable objective.

₁   John Reader, *Local Theology: Church and Community in Dialogue* (London, UK: SPCK Publishing 1994), 22.

₂   John Reader, *Blurred Encounters: A Reasoned Practice of Faith* (Vale of Glamorgan, UK: Aureus Publishing, 2005), 135.

₃   John Reader, *Reconstructing Practical Theology: The Impact of Globalization* (Aldershot, UK: Ashgate, 2008), 75–80.

₄   Caroline Baillie, Jens Kabo and John Reader, *Heterotopia: Alternative Pathways to Social Justice* (Alresford, UK: Zero Books, 2012).

The next task then is to examine some of the sources for this debate which include: philosophy; theology and the philosophy of religion; psychology; theories of child development; history; politics; economics; neuroscience; biology; sociology. The background to this is that, as we have seen, in the UK the Church of England through its faith schools is responsible for educating around 1 million children each year. Hence it has a massive institutional stake in the formal education process which also includes the fact that over 90 per cent of the funding which comes through the CofE is actually provided by the government anyway. This is a clear case of being entangled. Other denominations and other faiths run schools of their own, so this is a significant area of religious practice which all see as not only about educating their own constituencies but also as an important service to the wider community. Is there a rationale for this which goes beyond either of those objectives, and how do faith groups reconcile themselves to working with and within a system which appears to hold different, if not contradictory values? It needs to be discovered how the contribution of other disciplines might help to address these questions.

Philosophy

In a recent book Anna Strhan utilises the work of Levinas and Badiou to critique the current objectives of education as being too instrumental and economically driven.[5] So, as an example of this she draws upon Badiou to show that the politics of decision-making in education has been replaced by management as education policy comes to be defended by reference to economic necessity rather than any other criteria. Thus it is the rule of market forces which now determines a great deal of this. Questions of truth are not allowed to impinge into discussions about the organisation of formal education. Even within the sector of private education in the UK, the control exercised by OfSTED – the government appointed inspectorate for all schools – forces supposedly independent institutions down the route of financial viability and probity as evidenced by transparent processes of governance, sometimes at the real cost of closing down apparently effective schools. Both Badiou and Levinas, although from very different starting points, would argue for an understanding of responsibility that exceeds both particularist identitarian claims and the totalising logic of commodification of education:

---

[5]   Anna Strhan, *Levinas, Subjectivity, Education: Towards an Ethics of Radical Responsibility* (Oxford, UK: Wiley-Blackwell, 2012).

Both the Levinasian teaching of infinite responsibility and Badiou's idea of an education by truths are anti-instrumentalist at their core. Both pose a radical challenge to contemporary structures of education in inviting us to see them not as a site for preparing people for work and economic participation.[6]

Both would also question the notion that education can ever be presented as a completed product as a subject is always open to the demands of the other, nor is this to be understood in any developmental sense, but rather as a deepening awareness of what the demand of fidelity or responsibility requires. So this perhaps is closer to the suggestion that there is no end point or goal of the process beyond working for greater social justice.

But whilst this might appear to be a worthy and justifiable ideal for education, how are those directly involved to survive in the current system with any integrity, when all seems driven by economic imperatives? Whilst one can agree with her critique, Strhan offers no real alternative programme, but rather a strategy of resistance from within the teaching profession with the hope that one can only 'fail again and fail better'.[7] The influence of Simon Critchley is a feature, and but he is perhaps too negative about alternative options also coming as he does, from a more anarchist background. But it raises the debates from within the Philosophy of Education about the objectives of the process and ways in which these are currently viewed, so is a good starting point.

Theology

A recent book, *Christianity and the New Social Order*, proposes 'the commitment to education as lifelong learning for all' as one of seven objectives for creating a fairer society, along with 'the flourishing of every child'.[8] In *Reconstructing Practical Theology* there is a chapter, 'Families, Children and Globalization', which examines some of the pressures on families as a result of globalisation[9] and builds upon the work with the toddlers group in Worcestershire written up in *Blurred Encounters*.[10] None of these really go into detail on the schooling issue as such though, instead setting out concerns and broad principles. What is required is detail on how these should be operationalised and what the principles

---

6   Ibid., 111.

7   Ibid., 190.

8   John Atherton, Christopher Baker and John Reader, *Christianity and the New Social Order: A Manifesto for a Fairer Future* (London, UK: SPCK Publishing, 2011) 125.

9   John Reader, *Reconstructing Practical Theology*, Chapter 6.

10   John Reader, *Blurred Encounters*, Chapter 5.

might mean in terms of a critique of current educational practice and policy. They assume education through institutions run by the government rather than questioning this. One could also show that there is an implicit theology underlying recent Church of England reports on the future of church schools, that is, the Chadwick Report of March 2012 and the subsequent work on the future of rural church primary schools which is now underway.[11] Terminology such as 'flourishing' and 'well-being' is heavily used and assumes that this is as critical of institutional, government-led schooling as one needs to be. But one could question whether this is radical enough. The dilemma of course is that the Church of England has a massive stake in the current system, as we have already seen; therefore it has to find ways of dealing and doing business with the current regimes whilst supposedly offering and upholding a distinctive if not alternative approach. So it is forced to assume institutional education as a good, as it is deeply entangled, and played a significant early role in the development of schools in this country. One might suggest, however, that a more radical critique is required, one that is less collusive with current understandings and practice. Along with the contributions from other disciplines, a relational Christian realism can begin to construct just such a critique, but from a position of even greater entanglement.

Politics

So we move seamlessly into contemporary motivations for this form of schooling. 'Education, education, education' was Tony Blair's mantra when he came to power with New Labour in 1997.[12] Why? Because we needed to raise educational standards in order that the UK could compete more effectively in the global economy. Exactly the same motivation is clear now in the approach of the coalition government. Why the pressure for all schools to become Academies? In order to improve standards and make the UK more competitive – supposedly. Also it is a means of destroying local authority control over education and indeed – so it would seem – the teaching profession as a source of (left-leaning) political opposition. Privatisation in one form or another, the breaking of the power of teaching and related professionals over the process and the creation of an efficient and compliant workforce appear to be the true objectives of this policy. What has any of this

---

[11]   Church of England Archbishop's Council Board and Education Division and the National Society, *The Church School of the Future,* March 2012, 9.

[12]   See Andrew Adonis, *Education, Education, Education: Reforming England's Schools* (London, UK: Biteback Publishing Ltd, 2012).

to do with the growth, development and well-being of children and adults for its own sake? The enforcement through OfSTED and its offshoots in the examination system right down to four-year-olds attending school and being put through an increasingly draconian process is all part of the same picture – despite evidence from other more 'successful' countries that trying to educate children through this degree of formality at this age is counter-productive. What is the real objective here? Getting women back to work as soon as possible would seem to be the answer, as this will mean less dependence upon welfare spending and more economically active people within the economy.

One can argue on the basis of all we have seen so far, that for the churches to remain involved in statutory education is a compromise of major proportions, as the current system and the values that lie behind it are inimical to any concept of what it is to be or become human that a person of faith might feel comfortable with. Talking to teachers themselves who are struggling to maintain their integrity, let alone to keep faith with the vision of the profession that brought them into teaching in the first place, one learns that most of them now feel so constrained and controlled by the political agendas that dominate the educational world that any freedom to construct or operationalise real alternatives feels like an illusion. Yet more directives are passed down from above on a regular basis and this limits the time and capacity even to fulfil the basic tasks of teaching, leading to frustration and a steady exit of teachers from the profession. The feeling is that the system is now in a shambles, and that the impact of a series of political decisions has been to destroy both essential infrastructure and indeed morale, and that there will come a point where education will go full circle and have to recreate what has been dismantled over the last two decades. In the meantime though, the damage will have been done, and the true objective of the educational process, nurturing and developing the children, will have sunk without trace beneath a mountain of misguided political directives.

This then would appear to be a sphere of activity where hoping for a Deleuzian gradualist approach, where new possibilities are somehow contained within the system and will fight their way to the surface despite attempts to suppress them, is now unrealistic. It feels as though the process has gone too far for this to be a way forward. The alternative then would be to embrace the more radical approach of Badiou, which would mean being open to that which is not yet visible or identifiable breaking in from the outside, in order to bring about the scale and nature of the changes required to rehumanise or reassemble institutional education in the UK. In other words, it will be difficult to articulate or express exactly how this will happen, as it will be the consequence of faithfulness to an event – as yet unforeseen – that will create the conditions for change. In the meantime, all we have to work with are glimpses of alternatives described by thinkers who are well beyond the mainstream of current educational theory or practice.

So, one comes to the truly radical critiques of institutional education of Ivan Illich and Paulo Freire (*Deschooling Society* and *Pedagogy of the Oppressed* both published in the 1970s but highly contemporary in terms of their critique).[13] For Illich, real education and learning has never happened within the classroom anyway, the latter existing for the benefit of teachers and educational professionals rather than for the children. Education as institutional and government driven needs to be challenged along with other institutions which attempt to control and manipulate and often achieve the opposite of what they claim – others being the church and health care. Drawing upon Freire, Illich argues that people themselves possess both the motivation and the capacity to learn and that the role of a teacher is to work alongside them basing progress upon the encounter with the problems facing them in their daily lives:

> Freire trains his teachers to move into a village and to discover the words which designate current important issues … I have frequently witnessed how discussants grow in social awareness and how they are impelled to take political action as fast as they learn to read. They seem to take reality into their own hands as they write it down.[14]

Clearly the context for this type of learning seems a far cry from what is required in schools, but there just may be something of more general importance to be gleaned from this about the human capacity to learn, and which provides a further critique of current educational approaches. Certainly the contemporary corruption of the education system brought about through the single-minded focus on results and league tables (with which most parents sadly collude) is consistent with Illich's claims that teaching has become far too rigid and formulaic. The idea that anyone, child or adult, should 'take reality into their own hands' is far too subversive and challenging for the objectives of contemporary educational policy.

Freire of course was essentially an adult educator, arguing for a dialogical concept of education rather than the banking concept which sees 'teachers'

---

[13]   Ivan Illich, *Deschooling Society* (London, UK: Marion Boyars Publishers Ltd, 2002); Paulo Freire, *Pedagogy of the Oppressed* (London, UK: Penguin Books Ltd, 1972).

[14]   Ibid., 18.

depositing knowledge (which only they possess of course) into the minds of others, but this critique may still apply when dealing with younger age groups. There is a danger at the moment that knowledge becomes just another commodity to be purchased, and which will somehow equip its possessors to become productive and compliant citizens – those who cannot afford or benefit from the process of knowledge transferral are then the losers in the local or global economy. Both Illich and Freire offer alternatives and this is perhaps why they still demand attention, even though the growth of technology and globalisation have changed certain aspects of the environment significantly since their work was published. They remind us that the context of learning and the importance of placing what happens in a setting which is true to the external environment, rather than depending on a distanced and abstract concept of the world, is more likely to foster the thirst for knowledge that is the best motivator of growth and development.

A further radical alternative that is even less well known is that of the French philosopher Jacques Ranciere.[15] Following the story of the late eighteenth- and early nineteenth-century French schoolmaster, Joseph Jacotot, who discovered an unconventional teaching method that took hold for a while and spread panic throughout the learned community of Europe, Ranciere suggests that most education begins from an assumption that means it is doomed to perpetuate a system of inequality. Jacotot found that the normal process of explication was not required in order for people to learn, and that neither was knowledge a prerequisite for teaching. This led him to the conclusion that all people are equally intelligent and capable of learning for themselves. This resulted in what he called 'intellectual emancipation' which essentially set people free from any externally imposed educational process and enabled them to make their own progress:

> Emancipation is the consciousness of that equality, of that reciprocity that alone permits intelligence to be realized by verification. What stultifies the common people is not the lack of instruction, but the belief in the inferiority of their intelligence. And what stultifies the "inferiors" stultifies the "superiors" at the same time.[16]

---

[15]   Jacques Ranciere, *The Ignorant Schoolmaster: Five Lessons in Intelllectual Emancipation* (Stanford, CA: Stanford University Press, 1991).
[16]   Ibid., 39.

In other words, if this is correct, and each of us already has the capacity to learn for ourselves, without the supposed benefit of external guidance which only serves to place the learner in a position of inferiority and the teacher in that of superiority, what is the real purpose of schools and education more generally? One is back to the need to provide a compliant workforce destined to operate within very specific guidelines and to serve the needs of capitalism rather than those of the children or adults. To turn this into a statutory requirement and then to add to this the contribution of faith groups which take this starting point for granted seems like a case of becoming thoughtlessly entangled. What might serve us better is indeed the vision that becoming human requires us to take reality into our own hands and therefore carry the responsibility for shaping and reassembling ourselves and our world. This, however, must be tempered by the insight that our control and autonomy is strictly limited, and that it is only by being faithful and fully engaged with projects which go beyond the scope of any one individual or community that our entanglements stand a better chance of being life-enhancing and creative.

Early Years Foundation Stage Objectives and the Posthuman

An excellent practical example of the espoused values which underlie the current UK educational system emerges from recent policy documents relating to the objectives being promoted by central government for the development of Early Years and Foundation Stage children (EYFS), that is, four- to five-year-olds. This is now what is being passed down to individual schools as their mechanism for evaluating their effectiveness at teaching this age group. Seven areas of learning and development are identified: three of these are presented as prime areas and four others as specific areas for development. The three prime areas are: personal, social and emotional development – these include making relationships; self-confidence and self-awareness; managing feelings and behaviour – physical development; and communication and language – this involves listening and attention; understanding and speaking. Four specific areas are those of literacy; mathematics; understanding the world; and finally expressive arts and design. Just to highlight a couple of these: Understanding the world refers to history, geography, encounter with religions, plus science and technology. Right at the bottom of the list under expressive arts and design comes 'being imaginative'. So these are what it means, under the current system, to become a 'fully rounded human being' presumably fit and ready to become part of the global workforce and to function effectively and responsibly within an environment of global capitalism.

Two comments spring to mind immediately. First, just how many adults could honestly 'tick all these boxes' and claim they are proficient in all of these different areas? Second, one might challenge whether the elements of management and control that are so explicit in the prime areas are a realistic or acceptable objective for what it is to be or become human, as they seem to rest upon a concept of human autonomy that can and should be brought into question. Thus to demote 'being imaginative' to the bottom of the list when it should perhaps be the prime area of human development is surely a distortion of a faith-based values set and immediately relegates spiritual development to a minor and subsidiary role. This is what is now being presented as the framework for four–five-year-olds however, and, once again, raises the question of what it might mean for a person of faith to operate in what can be seen as a limited, if not hostile environment.

At this point it would be appropriate to introduce as a counter-argument some more of the ideas that are emerging from philosophical discussions on the themes of human development and learning. The first of these is derived from a Deleuzian approach to the subject but made in the light of more recent technological advances.[17] Rosi Braidotti advocates a much more fluid and open understanding which she terms the posthuman, and which allows for greater scope for acknowledging the extent to which we are not isolated, individual bodies unrelated to new technologies or indeed the wider physical world, but always already part of both as these are impacted by humans but also impact upon us in return. Without going into the details of this she covers discussion of anti-humanism, the postsecular, the posthuman, and comes up with what she terms 'post-anthropocentrism' or 'life beyond the species':[18]

> "Life", far from being codified as the exclusive property or the inalienable right of one species, the human, over all others, or being sacralized as a pre-established given, is posited as process, interactive and open-ended ... It is the transversal force that cuts across and reconnects previously segregated species, categories and domains ... it is a materialistic, secular, grounded and unsentimental response to the opportunistic trans-species commodification of Life that is the logic of advanced capitalism.[19]

---

[17]	Rosi Braidotti, *The Posthuman* (Cambridge, UK: Polity Press, 2013).
[18]	Ibid., 60.
[19]	Ibid., 60.

Whilst some of this might be a challenge to a faith-based position, it does illustrate the extent to which the encounters with technology and also other species need to be taken into account as we develop our understanding of what it might be to become 'human' in the years to come. Certainly a simplistic concept of human autonomy as both a means of self-control and also control of the rest of the planet does not do justice to the complexity of our own nature, let alone interrelatedness to others both human and non-human.

A further source of challenge to such a notion is to be found in the work of one of the forerunners of Deleuze whose ideas are only just becoming available in translation.[20] Without once again going into the complexity of this, Simondon develops the notions of metastability and pre-individuation which have some synergy with the ideas of the pre-autonomous mentioned earlier. In other words, there is a prior level of human development which comes before what we now think of as the autonomous, and which is perhaps a more fluid and permeable state in which it is easier to effect change and development. Along with the ideas of liminal spaces, thresholds and 'zones of entanglement', it is here that we see a greater flexibility for human development through direct experience, sensation and affect – the imaginative and creative aspects of human learning that cannot be contained or controlled by the purely autonomous or the exercise of what we understand as reason:

> ... the pre-individual is not static or inert but fundamentally dynamic. It generates forces which act upon each other, which generate tensions, points of excess, the development of a tipping point or point of emergence, forms of becoming that exist at best uneasily. These points of instability are the sites around which individuality may emerge.[21]

One might argue then that the current approaches to education which appear mechanical and manipulative, based on a linear and simplistic model of how humans grow and change and are geared simply to create effectively functioning cogs in the capitalist machine, demand to be challenged, especially from within a faith perspective. These brief forays back into the philosophical sources which have inspired this book offer some clues as to how a critical perspective on current educational models might be developed.

---

[20]   Arne De Boever, Alex Murray, Jon Roffe and Ashley Woodward, eds, *Gilbert Simondon: Being and Technology* (Edinburgh, UK: Edinburgh University Press, 2012).
[21]   Ibid., 39.

So, where do we go from here and who is in a position to both practise and theorise genuine alternatives to the current educational system? This can only be the beginning of the debate. Up to this point we have a glimpse of the need to take into account the contributions of other disciplines and have seen evidence that despite any claims to be neutral, the whole debate about education already contains and is based on certain values and judgements about matters economic and political. We need to examine in more detail how a reassembling of various components within a specific context raises the question of how the concept of entangled fidelities illuminates the process of discernment from a faith perspective.

Chapter 7
Entangled Fidelities and Environmental Issues

It would seem intuitively obvious that the central Christian doctrine to resource and inform a faith-based engagement with environmental issues should be the doctrine of Creation, so we need to refer back briefly to some of the ideas developed in Chapter 4. The conclusion there is that, given the assumption of God as inconsistent multiplicity, hyper-chaos and radical contingency, then creation itself is always under threat, or menaced in various ways. The hope is that through the emergence of creative responses, the worst threats and dangers can be alleviated. There are, however, no guarantees of a final and definitive 'happy ending', just as there is no guarantee of an imperialistic victory of what is life-enhancing over what is life-denying. Creation is always entangled between the possibilities of being good or corruptible, redeemed and fallible. Things could always 'go either way'. Just as God can be described as 'immanent virtual creativity at work', so humans are 'pilgrims across the plane of immanence, finding and losing our way as we seek to embody the virtual'. As will be seen shortly, the relationships between the human and the non-human are themselves fluid and negotiable, and any sense that humans have some ultimate control over what happens is misplaced and unjustified. This does not close down the future, but leaves it open to new possibilities, some more positive than others. What are the implications of this for the current concerns over environmental issues and our understanding of the relationship between humans and what we call nature?

It is the main argument of this book that the description 'entangled fidelities' captures our current experience of both religious practice and public ministry. This is because whichever direction one is drawn in, it feels as though one is involved in a constant process of reconfiguring or reassembling what already exists in encounters with the new and unexpected. Sometimes it is a matter of putting the pieces of the jigsaw back together in a different way, but, more often, it is the introduction of new elements which require that shifting of the kaleidoscope. None of this is neat, tidy, or easy to categorise, but one way of trying to make sense of this is to split the experiences as follows: a reassembling at the individual or internal level; a reassembling at the collective, social or political level; a reassembling of the human with the non-human; and finally, a reassembling of the human with the divine. Quite often, a particular example will cross into all four of those categories, hence the use of the terms 'blurring' and 'entanglement' to heighten the tension that is created by this process. Not only is much of this confusing, but much is also uncomfortable and sometimes disturbing. In the midst of this, the challenge is to remain, or work out, how to be faithful. What would constitute an 'entangled fidelity'?

To revert to theory for a moment, a major argument is that we currently lack an appropriate discourse for the articulation of alternative ethical values. Hence one of the objectives of this approach is to highlight the values that are always already embedded within supposedly neutral or value-free discourses, so for instance those on education as espoused by the coalition as in the previous chapter. Once this has been done it is easier to argue that this is only one value-laden stance and that alternatives are possible and justify being brought in at an early stage of the debate. Ethical values are not to be left until it is too late and then introduced as some sort of additional extra which merely support or collude with a position already adopted. This is one of the tasks of reassembling. Another is to show that any such debate requires attention to detail instead of a hasty retreat to bland generalisations. This must involve empirical research and the insights and contributions of a range of disciplines. Politically committed religious practice should resist the temptation to 'trump' this level of debate by bringing in grand doctrinal statements. Latour's replacing of 'matters of fact' with 'matters of concern' is a useful way of reminding us of this requirement. If this means that we have to become entangled or implicated in the lived complexity of such matters of concern then so be it. Reassembling means taking apart and then attempting to put back together, always accepting that such a reconstruction will be provisional and subject to further change. It will also benefit from the introduction of new and unfamiliar language which itself points to alternative possibilities.

In a major text on the environmental crisis written from a theological perspective, Michael Northcott also draws upon the work of Latour to support his arguments.[1] His particular focus is on the relationship between nature and culture and the ways in which this has been understood since the time of Descartes. A strict division is assumed between subject and object as well as

---

[1]   Michael S. Northcott, *A Political Theology of Climate Change* (Grand Rapids, MI: Wm. B. Eerdmans Publishing Co., 2013).

between matter and bodies, themselves perceived to be wholly separate from a transcendent and distant God:

> Science constructs the modern "cult of facts" in experiments and laboratories whose new objects enable engineers, industrialists and medics to create bridges, steam engines, and antibiotics, and so control and direct the energies of nature into the fabrications of an industrial society.[2]

So nature is turned into the realm of scientific facts, brought under the power of knowledge, while culture is the sphere of moral and political fabrication, presided over by lone individuals who are unable to re-establish connections with the non-human. When Latour talks about 'matters of concern' rather than 'matters of fact', he is arguing that this Enlightenment or modern division between nature and culture needs to be overcome, and the relationship between human and non-human restored to its rightful place in our understanding. To the extent that we are unable to do this we must expect the damaging impact of our 'modern' worldview to continue to cause dire consequences for the environment. Religion has a potential role to play in this proposed restoration if it too can recapture its sense of environment as creation:

> ... the challenge climate change raises is how, in the midst of the vast technological scale of human power over nature and the unintended enhancement of natural power over humans (rising oceans, strengthening storms, enduring droughts), the primitive sense of an interconnection between nature, society, and the sacred might be recovered.[3]

In parallel with Latour who argues for a Politics of Nature,[4] Northcott proposes that the appropriate Christian response to climate change is a form of political theology, and should therefore stand alongside more conventional versions of this discipline which deal with economics and welfare issues. Given the increased frequency of extreme weather events across the globe with its mixture of floods and droughts, and the possible consequences of these for migration and conflict as groups fight to retain access to vital resources such as water and food, I would agree with Northcott on this. I would also agree that this requires paying attention to thinkers such as Latour who offer a

---

[2]   Ibid., 44–5.

[3]   Ibid., 193.

[4]   Bruno Latour, *Politics of Nature: How to Bring the Sciences into Democracy* (Cambridge, MA: Harvard University Press, 2004).

new and challenging perspective on the relationship between the human and the non-human.

Another important point of connection is back to the work of the philosopher Whitehead, once only associated with Process Theology in religious circles, but whose thought is now receiving more attention for its philosophical imagination. Somewhat like Latour many years later, Whitehead challenged the division between nature and culture, and questioned how and why this bifurcation had come about. The traditional dualism between body and mind which is a central feature of modern rationality and hence the concept of autonomy which we have already had cause to question has to be overcome by the recognition that bodily endurance is event specific:

> Minds reside in bodies and mindful behaviours appear to constitute their flourishing. But bodies endure not because minds make them but because they are part of a larger body, "nature", that they are never truly separate from, neither in life nor in death.[5]

Behind this, in Whitehead's view, is what he calls the 'fallacy of misplaced concreteness', in which abstractions which are useful as heuristic devices are given a more substantial reality than is warranted, and the importance of our direct perceptions of and experiences of the world are relegated to a minor role. This is one of the dangers of the professionalisation of science (as of other areas of human activity), in which (as Latour might agree) an exclusive attention upon 'facts' detracts from those wider matters of concern which should be our real focus. As Whitehead says:

> When you understand all about the sun and all about the atmosphere and all about the rotation of the earth, you may still miss the radiance of the sunset. There is no substitute for the direct perception of the concrete achievement of a thing in its actuality. We want concrete fact with a high light thrown on what is relevant to its preciousness.[6]

In other words, the very discourse that we use is itself a barrier to an appropriate response to the environmental challenges that now face us, and we badly need to recover this understanding of our interrelatedness to each

---

5   Northcott, *A Political Theology*, 79.
6   Isabelle Stengers, *Thinking with Whitehead*, her own translation of this passage from *Science and the Modern World* (Cambridge, MA: Harvard University Press, 2011), 140.

other and the world, if we are to avoid the direst consequences of climate change and the threats of rising sea levels resulting from our own industrial and economic activities.

Moving to a practical example taken from the environmental debate, one can argue that to present the matters of concern in terms of the relationship between the human and the non-human may be an effective way of opening the discussion and beginning to see things differently. A particular local issue and one that has arisen in other parts of the UK is that of erecting wind farms as a contribution to renewable energy. It is instructive to see how the controversy was presented. The particular proposal was for a small wind farm on farmland between two villages, each of them in a different county, which itself created complications. Resistance within the locality was substantial and enough to add to the opposition from the two local authorities involved. Hence the scheme was turned down. The debate however centred around the obvious objections that the scheme was too close to human dwellings, but with the underlying theme that subsidies that would have been paid to landowners were simply a means of putting extra money into the pockets of the already wealthy who happened to have good political connections. There was also a question of just how much energy this would have produced and of how efficient such schemes are anyway. The frustration is that the real heart of the debate about the coming energy crisis and the need for renewables never really entered the discussion. Unfortunately then an opportunity for serious debate was missed as the whole issue got turned into a mixture of 'Not In My Backyard' and cynicism about the motives and profits of the specific energy company, its shareholders and then large landowners. In other words, it was all about humans in relation to other humans and neglected wider environmental concerns or those which might better be described as the non-human dimension.

Not being an expert in these matters – and this is where it becomes so difficult for ordinary members of the public to make a reasoned judgement and one has to rely on 'experts' – this was mentioned to a number of colleagues and contacts more heavily involved at a national level. It would seem that wind farms are becoming more efficient and that they will indeed make an important contribution to the generation of additional renewable energy, but one needs to examine each case on its merits and enter into practical detail when making a judgement. There is a recent book on the subject written from a Christian perspective, *No Oil in the Lamp: Fuel, Faith and the Energy Crisis*, by Andy

Mellon and Neil Hollow[7] which suggests a number of sensible approaches to this controversial topic. They mention the following criteria: the potential renewable resource should be carefully and honestly analysed to ensure that resources are not being wasted; developers should work closely with the communities most directly affected; there should be a strong element of community benefit rather than pure profit and this would include calculating distances from human dwellings. Now it seems that these are sensible and wise guidelines, that had they been followed in the local instance might at least have led to a reasoned debate on the wider issue. One knows that energy companies pay lip service to the idea of local consultation, but what is required is a much closer and more honest process where local communities are involved in proposed schemes from the very beginning rather than just receiving a standard letter from the Public Relations department or consultant being employed for these purposes. Thus there are examples of community-led wind farms which have proved effective as well as acceptable.

How does this represent a different relationship between the human and the non-human though? It takes into account the technology involved and the importance of non-human factors such as the land itself, let alone the wind which will generate the energy. Of course the direct benefit is for humans and their energy requirements, but the longer-term benefit is for the wider non-human creation as it cuts down the dependency on renewable energy which we know is a factor in human destruction of the environment. So all of the various factors, parties both human and non-human, should be part of the debate and decision-making process, so there is a reassembling of the human in relation to the non-human. One might suggest that most other environmental issues could be presented in a similar way and that this would lead to solutions that are closer to a faith-based approach as illustrated in the example above. The issues must not be reduced to the human or business profit motive or seen in purely economic terms.

One needs to register the fact that there are Christian organisations already operating in this area. One is the eco-congregation movement, but there are also A Rocha UK and A Rocha International plus the John Ray Initiative. Interestingly these are evangelically based, and it is this wing of the churches which has taken environmental issues on board, even though some of us pre-date their involvement and were working in this area trying to raise awareness through community projects earlier than this (see *Local Theology: Church and*

---

7   Andy Mellen and Neil Hollow, *No Oil in the Lamp: Fuel, Faith and the Energy Crisis* (London, UK: Darton, Longman and Todd, 2012).

Community in Dialogue, SPCK 1994 and the account of the local conservation project 'Friends of Hopesay Meadow'). There is also the Christian Rural and Environmental Studies Course based at Ripon College, Cuddesdon, Oxford, of which the aforementioned organisations are sponsoring partners. They would not claim to be mainstream, however, as the whole area is seen as the province of a small and specialised section of the wider Christian family, rather than as an essential expression of faith. It also needs to be said that the theology of these groups is biblically based and not yet, at least, open to the more radical reassembling of language that one could argue would make these movements more effective.

A dimension of this that has yet to receive adequate attention is how these faith-based environmental movements link or relate to other groups within society who share similar objectives but would express their motivation in a different way. There are already some Christians involved in the Transition Initiative movement – groups who prepare themselves to power down in the face of the impact of climate change and peak oil – but very little is heard of this outside the circles of the 'already converted' who are very often from within the evangelical networks. Why is this so and what research needs to be carried out before one can see how and why environmental concerns can be introduced to a wider faith audience? Is the language employed by this particular wing of the Church itself off-putting or a barrier to this? In which case the exploration of an alternative terminology becomes an imperative.

A further case study which is proving to be of national importance both in the US and the UK is that of fracking. The term refers to a process for extracting natural gas from deep shale beneath the water table. The process – also known as hydro-fracking – involves drilling down and then pumping a mixture of water, sand and various chemicals into the well at high pressure in order to create fissures in the shale through which the gas can escape. The gas is then processed, refined and shipped to market. 'Flowback water' or waste water returns to the surface once the process is completed and is then contained in steel tanks until it can be reused for other purposes. During the summer of 2013 encouraging words have been uttered by the UK government and the prime minister in particular, suggesting that this process offers a significant solution to the looming energy shortage and is therefore to be supported. Specific drilling sites have become a location for protest and the whole issue has become front page news. Where might someone of faith stand on this and why?

The Diocese of Blackburn, which covers part of the north-west UK (Lancashire), and where there has already been some drilling and concerns raised about its possible impact, has issued a press release and statement on the issue, produced by the Diocesan Rural and Environmental Project Officer. His response is to suggest that there are a number of problems that those of faith need to be aware of and should insist are addressed before any firm decision is made. These include: concerns about contamination of surface, ground and drinking water; pollution from lorry traffic and storage tanks; damage to valuable habitats and to other environmentally sensitive areas. After describing the process and then expressing these concerns he asks the question as to where faith communities should stand in the arguments between economists and environmentalists and presents the issue as one between economic gain and having a healthy environment. Until a proper impact study has taken place, he proposes that no further drilling be carried out. The theological rationale that he offers is that any solution must be rooted in scripture, employ our ability to reason, stem from listening to the experience of people who have direct contact with fracking, both positive and negative, and then to discern under God's guidance what is good and right. This, in itself, is a very interesting statement, and one might wonder whether what he proposes as a process is either viable or likely to take place. For one thing, it begs the question about the relationship between scripture and reason, which would include the issue of the role of scientific research and how this is to be squared with the interpretation of ancient biblical texts. So although this response is thoughtful and well-meaning, it does have its limitations when it comes to the reassembling that a relational Christian realism would require.

What makes this case study even more interesting is that the Central Church of England, through the Chair of the Board of Mission and Public Affairs, has issued a statement of its own which is in contrast to that from the Diocese of Blackburn. Amongst other things this says that the Church of England has no official policy either for or against fracking, and that there is a danger of viewing this through a single issue lens and ignoring wider considerations. This reads like a mild rebuke of the Blackburn statement and a steer that taking a narrowly environmentally committed stance is not acceptable. One wonders, however, whether this is another instance of the Church hierarchy, and its officers, being out of tune with the views of some its own constituents, and therefore taking a reasoned and balanced stance when others are more directly committed to the environmental cause. The arguments given for this are important though. Balancing considerations should be: the issue of fuel poverty and the impact of rising energy bills on the worst-off in society; the requirement for proper monitoring of the process which could minimise potential risks and harm to the environment; acknowledging that even though all carbon-based fuels contribute to global warming, yet gas is less environmentally damaging than coal. This alongside the possibility of job creation and greater energy self-sufficiency are factors that need to be weighed in the balance before making a commitment one way or the other.

It has to be said that despite the well-meaning and reasonable nature of this response, it does come across as the Central Church bending over backwards to 'sit on the fence' and to diffuse any involvement in the developing controversy. The statement also refers to the land holdings of the Central Church and the question of mineral rights, and makes it clear that this is not a factor in the equation as some might suggest. Perhaps, though, it represents a failure to grasp the depth of feeling of those of faith engaged in environmental concerns, and who see this as more of a priority than the leadership of the Church of England and its officers at General Synod level. It is Latour who suggests that those of faith might have something to teach environmentalists who struggle to understand why it is that strength of feeling cannot be translated into political policy or action as they are the ones who are capable of mobilising the emotional responses and not reducing everything to the level of 'sweet reason'. So who has got this right and how should religious practice engage with both fidelity and reason?

There is a third response to the fracking issue that raises the most serious issues and that neither the Diocese of Blackburn nor the Board of Mission and Public Affairs address. These should be at the centre of public debate. This is an online article written by Paul Ekins who is the Professor of Resources and Environmental Policy at University College, London (14th August 2013 from the site 'The Conversation'). Ekins is in charge of the UK Energy Research Centre's Energy Systems theme and has extensive knowledge of the fracking process itself. His view is that the 'dash to frack' is in complete contradiction to the espoused UK government policy on energy. The policy is based on the assumption of the decarbonisation of the energy sector in order to meet the emission reduction targets enshrined in law by the 2008 Climate Change Act, so encouraging fracking is inconsistent with this. It is also founded on the principle of reducing UK dependence on imported fossil fuels and their prices, as well as the aim of meeting both these objectives without effecting the competitiveness of UK business or driving low-income households into fuel poverty. Despite what the Central Church response says about these latter two, Ekins argues that in just two weeks this painstakingly crafted energy strategy has been torn up.

The problems with pursuing a fracking policy are that even if significant quantities of shale gas are accessed (and without consequent immediate environmental damage), then its use will increase carbon emissions and cause the UK to miss its targets. It will also dissuade possible low carbon investors, such as Siemens and Mitsubishi, from investing in the UK offshore wind industry. Why would they do this when the government appears intent on pursuing another source of energy? There is, however, outside government circles, doubt as to whether the best outcome of the production of significant amounts of shale gas becoming available will actually be achieved in any case. The geology of the US, where this appears a viable option, is different from that of the UK, and the latter has much fewer sparsely inhabited spaces. So what is the real agenda behind the 'dash to frack'? Ekins suggests that this might be a means of destroying the Climate Change Act by making its targets untenable, and this might represent the lobbying power of a fossil fuel industry that is determined to claw its way back into pole position as the primary energy provider. What are the future prospects then for a low carbon UK? This seems to me to be the real heart of the matter and something that neither church response acknowledges.

Where does this leave the contribution of a relational Christian realism? All of the above is an initial attempt to carry out the reassembling and examination in detail of the matters of concern that constitute this particular issue. It is complex, requires considerable unravelling and attention to the insights of a variety of viewpoints and experts. Those of faith who are deeply committed to the environmental cause may be correct in their instinctive opposition to fracking, but not effective at articulating, as yet at least, what are the real issues that need to be addressed. So they elicit a more supposedly balanced and considered response that also fails to get to the heart of the matter. Other factors and other views need to be brought into the process of discernment – a way of keeping the references circulating as Latour would suggest. The values of those supporting the fracking policy need to be brought to the surface and critically examined, and then other values introduced into the debate, not as an afterthought, but as central to the discussion. Presenting these in straightforward 'religious' or scriptural terms may well not be the most convincing or effective way of doing this, hence the discourse of the relationship between the human and the non-human might offer a better alternative. Which leaves the question of what it means to exercise fidelity in this situation.

Becoming a subject in the terms that Badiou describes means that there is an event into which one is then incorporated, often with others who are drawn into the same process. This is not a matter of rational choice or deliberate policy, but more of an encounter with a new and unexpected situation where one cannot not respond, even though this might entail a personal cost or sacrifice. This is where attempts to construct or devise balanced or reasonable solutions begin to break down. In order for real change and transformation to take place there may well have to be sacrifice – not all the hoped for objectives can be achieved and some may have to be abandoned as less important. If there has to be a trade-off between fuel poverty and creating a low carbon economy, for instance, then perhaps one of these has to be let go of in order to achieve the other. Or one might want to question a political system within which there is that type of injustice in the first place. There is no alternative to being entangled and caught up in the midst of often intractable problems as we have seen in the areas of both education and environment, but it would surely be wrong to rule out in advance the possibility of the radically new and unexpected breaking in and disrupting the settled dimensions of the established responses. These are not likely to be interventions that we could either foresee or welcome, but once they have occurred our collective calling may be to follow them through, to risk entering the liminal spaces, or 'the cloud of unknowing', in order to exercise that fidelity that is an essential component of the developing human and non-human assemblages. We are part of the process and that is not to be underestimated, but as individuals we are not in control or even the main determining factor. The crucial issue is that with which we began these two chapters – what does it mean to be or to become a human being?

Chapter 8

Christian Materialism and the Contours of a New Political Imagination

Thus far, this volume has sought to bring together in creative and critical dialogue three elements in the service of a new philosophy of Christian materialism (aka relational Christian realism), namely: contemporary themes in continental philosophy and their impact on constructing new political and material imaginaries for the twenty-first century; the construction of new theologemes which reformulate existing systematic Christian categories of thought in the light of these new political and material imaginaries; and finally we have looked at how Christian and faith-based interventions have influenced the relationships between different objects and materialities. This was done in order to ground some of the more abstract discussion of this volume within the lived practices of religion, as well as to analyse faith-based engagement in the public sphere in terms that are new and fresh. In this final chapter we briefly reflect on the more strategic and political implications of the performative dimensions of a relational Christian realism. We do this with reference to three elements; a reappraisal of human agency, the ongoing debates about the post-political following the 2008 financial crash and a reformulated theology of hope that addresses the deficits in a hopeful and progressive imaginary in ways that are simultaneously political, philosophical and theological.

Practicing Human Subjectivity

As we have outlined earlier, a relational Christian realism reformulates traditional Christian realism by reframing the anthropocentric and ontologically hierarchical basis of that school of thought into more pro-inclusive and ethical ends. We enact this reformulation by engaging with the work of the so-called Speculative realists and their predecessors and successors (such as Latour and Bryant). Characteristic of this new philosophical outlook is a flat or object-oriented ontology which places all beings on the same level and presents them as being entangled, enmeshed and to be encountered in a multiplicity of assemblages which can also be described as rhizomatic. It is our argument that this is not simply a matter of theory, but that such descriptions do justice to the realities of the life of faith, its complexities, entanglements and often discomfort as one struggles in the midst of this to be and to become faithful. To engage in the assemblages of contemporary ethics or politics is to feel oneself hemmed in from every side. As we saw in Chapter 6 regarding current attempts by faith-based education providers to humanise the market-driven and utilitarian priorities of the education framework in the UK, there is often little room for manoeuvre. And yet these providers hope that by trying to remain faithful to certain values and insights, this will, from time to time, yield an effective means of resisting the worst impacts of neoliberal capitalism in its various manifestations. Vital to this faithful resistance to all that seeks to minimise the conditions of human/non-human flourishing, therefore, is the development of new ways of understanding and practicing human subjectivity, and this is where we have drawn upon the ideas of Deleuze, Braidotti and Badiou as well as those already mentioned. Central to the thinking of these authors is the notion that one becomes a subject by being fully immersed in the activities to which one is called, rather than already being a subject who chooses to become involved. Thus we need to take into account those levels of human subjectivity which we have called pre-autonomous: the level of feeling, affect and sensation which are always already a part of what we are, but which receive little recognition within the reductionist and largely rationalistic understanding assumed by contemporary politics and culture. Yet these levels do not precede the autonomous in a chronological manner, but are ever present as the source of metastability, and hold open the prospect of change and development and themselves point towards the new and creative which can emerge if we are prepared to enter the liminal spaces and thresholds of different perspectives and practices. It is our argument that an engagement with material religious practices can be a vital source of contact with both the pre-autonomous and the critical creativity that can then follow the subsequent opening up of a narrow concept of human autonomy. As we explored in Chapter 5, our case studies in urban and community empowerment showed how faith-based actors felt compelled to inaugurate processes of greater facilitation and participation. There are some situations to which we cannot but respond. Having then responded we become part of the networks of relationships and assemblages which offer glimpses of the alternatives to the enclosures which form contemporary global politics and culture. From this baseline of performative materialist ethics flow other aspects of relational

Christian realism which also distinguish it from alternative Christian approaches which we believe are too deterministic and imperialistic. The two most obvious of these are Radical Orthodoxy and Post-Liberalism. In their different ways, we have argued, they hold to an unrealistic and somewhat hubristic notion of the Christian community as the vision of what life is to become, and to a certain extent already is. Within an increasingly diverse and postsecular public square this reversion to a Christendom-type model of engagement and apologetics can become disengaged and disconnected from the public sphere, This is because, if we are reading the signs of times correctly, increasing numbers of citizens (especially the younger ones) are deeply committed to a form of what Cloke defines as theo-ethics (see Chapter 5). If the secularising tendencies expressed in current sociological trends are correct, younger citizens have neither the inclination nor indeed necessary religious literacy to prop up hierarchical ecclesial superstructures and those forms of medieval metaphysics associated with it.[1] Part of what this book is expressing is the formulation of a post-Christendom philosophy and ecclesiology in which the desire for an ethical and performative freighting of Christian caritas in the public sphere is, if anything, growing more intense, but where the new structures and methodologies by which this caritas will burst through are far from clear (assuming that they ever will be). This is why a theology and philosophy of deep-interconnectedness (or entanglement), negotiated on a common and immanently transcendent plane rather than a separated and rarified one, may offer a more productive way forward. Of course, the role of institutional religion continues to have a place within the economy of the divine commonwealth, but as we said earlier, its place is not as a fixed point resisting change and evolution, but is part of the eternal and restless dynamic of deterritorialisation and reterritorialisation that maintains the health and balance of the system. By our analysis and in line with the new discourses and epistemologies of this book, the Christendom model of church continues to be radically and swiftly deterritorialised in favour of new expressions of collectivity, ethics and what is understood as truth. 'Truth', we are suggesting, is what emerges and changes from within a process rather than something we can be certain of or dictate in advance. This also demands that we work alongside and learn from both other disciplines and other practitioners with

---

[1]   For example, the growth of those who would define themselves as Spiritual But Not Religious (SBNR). Robert Fuller, *Spiritual but Not Religious* (Oxford, UK: Oxford University Press, 2001), and the Pew Research Center survey '"Nones" of the Rise' (2012) on-line report: http://www.pewforum.org/2012/10/09/nones-on-the-rise/ (retrieved 7 July 2014).

whom we share the matters of concern that motivate us to become and remain engaged. For instance, as we saw in Chapter 7, from the environmental groups, the contribution of the Transition Initiatives movement is one that Christians are beginning to value and get drawn into.[2] We, as people of faith, do not pretend to have all the answers, let alone a monopoly of insight, but ours is one contribution alongside others, albeit often one that requires less hubristic, but equally bold and creative forms of political leadership.

Reassembling the Public Square – Neoliberal Hegemonies and the Post-Political

Within this book then we have taken note of and drawn in the debates, the contributions of other disciplines and activists. We believe that the best way to construct the new discourses required to address the global challenges we face, and reassemble the public square into a more just and flourishing environment, is to take the best and most helpful ideas from other sources. These sources are often philosophical, but also sociological and political. One of the key lessons we learn from Latour, for instance, is that values are always already embedded in every debate and not simply to be introduced as an after-thought once the real decisions have been made on supposedly neutral or value-free grounds. So the process of reassembling should aim to draw to the surface whatever those values are in order that alternative ones can be there from the beginning. This requires careful analysis and judgement. In Chapter 6 we explored the debate about the ethical and developmental assumptions of the educational service in the UK and the current policy relating to Academies. Although the debate might claim to be simply about standards in education, it clearly enshrines certain other values and aims which might be perceived to be in conflict with what those of faith would propose as appropriate objectives for institutional learning. It is almost always financial and political objectives which drive such processes once one scratches the surface. We suggest that 'scratching the surface' is exactly what those of faith should be doing from the start, in order to reveal what is really going on. One might describe this as a commitment to some sort of discourse analysis as one attempts to identify where and how power is being exercised in any particular matter of concern. In unmasking sources and impacts of power, we acknowledge that there will always be a tension surrounding the decision as to whether one should become engaged at an institutional level, or simply operate in the interstices or spaces where there may be greater freedom for movement and

---

2   See for example, Timothy Gorringe and Rose Beckham, *Transition Movement for Churches – A Prophetic Imperative for Today* (London, UK: Canterbury Press, 2013).

creativity. There is no one answer to this dilemma, nor could there be, as judgement, discernment and reflexivity are always part of the process of being entangled. It may be that where one finds oneself in any particular process of reassembling will always shape the level at which one engages. On the UK education debate we noted there is already a high degree of institutional involvement from which faith groups could not easily disentangle themselves, and might even be wrong to do so. One works from where one finds oneself accepting the limitations of that, but still trying to exercise a faithful ministry. Environmental issues, as we saw in Chapter 7, are less institutionalised but then probably always more marginal to both political and faith mainstreams as a result. This leads to its own frustrations and limitations. Engaging with urban renewal and current debates about poverty and welfare reform is, if anything, even more complex and entangled. Faith practitioners are often invited to the table because of the resources they bring in terms of social and religious capital (that is, the physical and material resources they provide).[3] However, they then face the dilemma of colluding with policies and practices to which they might feel deeply opposed on the basis of their spiritual capital (that is, the beliefs, values and visions for change that emerge and are shaped by the worshipping, prayer and deep communality that are unique to religious groups). This is the classic 'blurred encounter' or entangled fidelity where one cannot do nothing, but whatever one does do feels inadequate and compromising. The challenge is the constant one of trying to be faithful subjects in this particular context. It could be argued that each of the case studies we have described represents a wider cultural malaise that people of faith should be resisting and addressing, one based on that inadequate and reductionist understanding of what it is to be and to become human referred to above. It may also be the case that recent social movements such as Occupy are a protest against this dis-ease, and that one needs to be examining whether and how there might be common cause between such movements and faith groups. At this point, the work of Castells and his analysis and description of recent social movements across the globe becomes vital.[4] In what is basically an optimistic interpretation of the scope for change represented by a variety of uprisings, including Tunisia, Iceland, the Arab uprisings, the Indignados in Spain and the various Occupy movements, Castells offers perhaps the most important perspective on these social movements. Whilst acknowledging that there are significant differences between them, he identifies

---

3   See Chris Baker and Hannah Skinner, *Faith in Action – The Dynamic Connection between Religious and Spiritual Capital* (Manchester, UK: William Temple Foundation, 2006).

4   Manuel Castells, *Networks of Outrage and Hope: Social Movements in the Internet Age* (Cambridge, UK: Polity Press, 2012).

certain common characteristics such as: a sense of togetherness based on community which helps individuals overcome their fear; the importance, both symbolic and psychological, of occupying public spaces; the subsequent creation of hybrid spaces where the physical and the virtual (using social networks for instance) can work together to construct spaces of autonomous communication.[5] Castells refers to these technologies and methodologies of resistance as 'a rhizomatic revolution'.[6] Although it seems that he is unaware of the philosophical derivation of this term (Deleuze and Guattari of course), he finds this an appropriate way of describing what happened. What mattered in the particular example of the Indignados was that the movement was self-reflexive; that process was more important than end product; that networks of relationships were the driving force, and that, finally, the roots of the process then spread out across society without there ever being any central plan, strategy or controlling centre.[7] Hence the spontaneity and growth of the process is best described by this alternative terminology which we have also found appropriate for talking about recent developments within faith communities (Messy Church was one example given earlier). Is this though a long-lasting and effective way of organising that carries the prospects of significant change, or simply an idealised view of the use of internet technology and the social media which confer certain advantages onto more well-established forms of protest? In a way Castells reserves judgement on this, most notably in his assessment of Occupy. He asks what the movement(s) have actually achieved and finds it difficult to measure in conventional terms. Were they simply expressions of frustration and anger towards the institutions, especially the financial ones, that seem to have been the root cause of the global financial crisis, and also an articulation of the lack of trust in politicians who appear to collude with these interests? After all, it is those who had least to do with the causes of the crisis who are bearing the brunt of the cutbacks in welfare and state funding which have been the consequence of those events in 2008, and have most cause for complaint. And many of those involved in the protests were not unanimously opposed to capitalism itself or aiming to overthrow it. So perhaps on the surface, not much has changed, and what has in fact happened since 2008 is more of a consolidation of the power of the wealthy.[8] In fact, counter evidence suggests that little has changed, and that, if anything, conditions have deteriorated for those at the sharp end of government policies and their practical implications. Why is this the case? In a detailed discussion of

---

5   Ibid., 10–11.
6   Ibid., 140.
7   Ibid., 144.
8   Ibid., 197.

how and why neoliberalism has tightened its grip on economy and politics, Colin Crouch argues that corporations and the private sector are strategically placed to benefit from the downturn.[9] The already well-established relationships between such businesses and government mean that the former are in a good position to retain their influence. But what is also at work is the dominance of market ideology when it comes to the decision-making process. The processes of this dominance; namely the interlocking relationships between key economists who advise the state, economics departments in prestigious universities and think tanks and lobby groups who receive prodigious amounts of funding from the wealthy elite, have also been well documented by Philip Mirowski.[10] As we have already stated, using Latour, values are always already embedded in the process and thus difficult to articulate let alone challenge. This, Crouch claims, undermines democracy in ways that are not normally recognised:

> But democracy does not operate like profit, providing a single measurable indicator. It constantly has to be interpreted by politicians, their advisors and other public opinion-makers. In the end therefore, the ethics of professions and public service are displaced, not by the market, but by the ethics of politicians and, increasingly, by their private sector management consultants.[11]

The impact of these dynamics generated by 'full-spectrum' neoliberalism[12] is that many public policies are supposedly placed beyond the range of conflict and debate, and beyond the reach of difficult ethical choices, as they are presented as simply issues of management and control. A disturbing example of the implications of the shift from government to governance is the evidence that Non-Governmental Organisations, charitable movements, and indeed protest itself, is now being corporatised and implicated (entangled?) within the neoliberal culture. On one level it is obvious how and why this should happen. Organisations need funding and permanent staffing if they are going to make a long-term difference and go some way to achieving their objectives. In order to obtain this they are tempted in to developing relationships with commercial businesses, who themselves have a vested interest in being seen to be friendly and supportive towards 'good causes'. This is nothing new, but the scale of this

---

9   Colin Crouch, *The Strange Non-death of Neoliberalism* (Cambridge, UK: Polity Press, 2011).
10   Philip Mirowski, *Never Let a Serious Crisis Go to Waste – How Neo-liberalism Survived the Financial Meltdown* (London, UK: Verso Press, 2013).
11   Crouch, *Strange Non-death*, 91.
12   Mirowski, *Never Let*, 140.

interaction has accelerated in recent decades as the marketisation of the general culture has taken more of a hold. As Badiou says, this is the model of the business world encroaching upon every area of life, including that of the charitable sector itself. Dauvergne and Lebaron look in detail at three dimensions of this: securitising dissent (following the events of 9/11 especially); the privatising of social life; and the institutionalising of activism – each of those worthy of greater examination at some point for faith groups. The conclusion they reach is somewhat depressing:

> As consumerism strengthens, as states suppress dissent, and as activism corporatizes and deradicalizes, we see little chance of a global grassroots uprising being able to transform the world order. This does not mean, however, that community activism is powerless – quite the contrary; but, even among grassroots activists, corporatization is causing much turbulence.[13]

If this is then the root of the more general cultural malaise, disillusion with what is presented to us as democracy, and the underlying cause of much contemporary protest and public dissent, how and where do faith groups concerned for issues of social justice and indeed environmental sustainability fit into and contribute to the process of protest and change? Are we too now also so subject to the consumerist and commercial culture, enfolded and enclosed within its grasp as we fight for 'market share' in a competitive religious environment and search for a brand identity that will hopefully sustain our existence, that integrity is compromised and all hope of real alternatives simply an illusion? How entangled are we and in what ways is it still possible to be faithful, or to work towards that faithful subjectivity? Are any of our material religious practices convincing avenues of dissent?

Toward a New Political Theology of Hope

In roughly the last third of the twentieth century, a powerful theological movement arose in response to the historical pessimism of mid-century theologies of crisis.[14] Perhaps it is needless to say, in an era characterised by the problems engendered by global capitalism we have identified in this volume,

---

13   Peter Dauvergne and Genevieve Lebaron, *Protest Inc: The Corporatization of Activism* (Cambridge, UK: Polity Press, 2014), 142.

14   For examples of the latter, see Karl Barth, *The Epistle to the Romans*, 6th ed., trans. Edwyn C. Hoskyns (London, UK: Oxford University Press, 1933), and Rudolph Bultmann,

that such pessimism is not without appeal today. In any case, the 'theology of hope', associated with figures like Jürgen Moltmann and Wolfhart Pannenberg sought to reconfigure Christian thought around the question of the future. At the conclusion of this book we might ask: is not such hope precisely what we need? Is not a quest for 'realism', even a 'relational' one, insufficient to sustain motivation for the kinds of difficult entanglements that are required of us today? In both Moltmann's and Pannenberg's theologies, hope was founded on an account of history as radically contingent and open.[15] In this way the theology of hope is suggestive of some themes we have emphasised here. The openness of history was not absolute, however, as reliable glimpses of the 'future of God' were seen in a 'proleptic' way through the historical events deemed revelatory of what would come to be.[16] For Pannenberg, the intelligibility of the idea of God itself depended upon the fulfilment of hope foreshadowed in the revelatory prolepses. God comes to fulfilment in the future, and faith in God is justified only eschatologically – only, that is, in terms of the end of history. Despite all of their talk about history being radically open, in the end these theologies of hope left little to chance, as it were. The revelatory prolepsis was seen as indicative of a single future – one which was as secure as the reality of God itself. Even though it was still a future that had not yet crossed over onto 'our' side of the temporal horizon, it is quite clear that Pannenberg's theology of hope would stand or fall on its arrival, an arrival necessitated by the very nature of God.

From our perspective, this is a hope that is insufficiently radical. First of all, the God of relational Christian realism is not tied so definitively to any particular future because God's primordial reality is virtual rather than actual – God is first of all the infinite stirring of the multiple, of difference itself. Therefore, on the one hand, God's reality is not subject to confirmation or disconfirmation on the basis of what happens in history that may benefit any particular collection of beings. As earlier theologians like Jonathan Edwards insisted, God will be God even if and when all of our projects and plans collapse into nothingness.[17] In a radically contingent universe, perhaps anything can happen, from millennia

---

History and Eschatology: The Presence of Eternity (New York, NY: Harper and Brothers, 1957).

[15] Seminal texts of the movement include Wolfhart Pannenberg, et al., *Revelation as History*, trans. David Granskou (London, UK: Macmillan, 1968), and Jürgen Moltmann, *Theology of Hope: On the Ground and the Implications of a Christian Eschatology*, trans. James W. Leitch (New York, NY: Harper and Row, 1967).

[16] Wolfhart Pannenberg, *Systematic Theology, Vol. I*, trans. Geoffrey W. Bromiley (Grand Rapids, MI: Eerdmanns, 1991), 49–58.

[17] See, for example, Edwards' *Dissertation on the End for which God Created the World*, in *The Works of Jonathan Edwards, Vol. I* (Carlisle, PA: Banner of Truth, 1834), 94–119. For

of routinised predictability to system-level change, to catastrophic destructions of whole biospheres, but none of these expresses the reality of God less than another. And, on the other hand, in our view the expressions of divine reality through historical actualities are necessarily fragile and subject to limitation, counter-action and even death. The virtual God is everlasting though incapable of identification.

Concrete actualisations of God, on the other hand, come and go. So, a theology of hope that embraces contingency in the most thoroughgoing way must affirm at least two things: first, actual history is not driven by or in any way controlled by a directionally oriented divine power, since the virtual is multiple and capable of coming to expression in many ways which are not governed by a predetermined principle. Thus the openness of history is radical. And, second, the divine comes to expression contingently in history and any such actualisation is itself limited and subject not only to affirmation and empowerment but also to destruction and dissolution. So, what are the grounds for a hope that can sustain motivation in the face of such grim possibilities?

Hope, in our view, has to do first of all with the ontological impossibility of mastery. Any God or other organising centre of power that may come on the scene of history is unable either to plumb the depths of or to exercise complete control over other objects that make up the fabric of the actual. A God, even a puppet-master type of divinity, is always reciprocally influenced, stubbornly resisted or perhaps co-opted by the actions of other actants who operate on the basis of their own volcanic identities. And this of course means also that any such centre of power is subject to the same forms of resistance. Even global systems are just relatively large objects, and so they also may be resisted, transformed and reconstructed. Another way to say this is that hope is grounded in confidence that the political process, cosmically as well as historically conceived, can go on, even in the face of realities that threaten hegemonic or even totalitarian restriction. In relational Christian realism, politics – even democracy – is ontologised: any object comes to be and persists precisely by its power to petition the commonwealth. Nothing can be overwhelmed, and nothing can come to dominate in an absolute way. And this of course means among many other things that the ways in which neoliberal governance tends toward the dominance and colonisation of both public and private realms of life faces inevitable resistance, and this resistance is a force to be leveraged toward political and economic transformation. There is a second

---

a more recent Edwardsian account, see James M. Gustafson, *An Examined Faith: the Grace of Self-Doubt* (Minneapolis, MN: Fortress Press, 2004), 106–10.

feature of hope that is also tied to the notion of radical contingency, and that is perhaps even more powerful than the impossibility of mastery. Radical change at all levels of reality is always possible. Indeed, we may go further and specify, adopting a point made by Quentin Meillassoux, that the primordial creativity of the divine virtual expresses itself most clearly during moments of radical change. Not every occurrence that comes to expression from the infinite play of creativity represents something that is new in relation to what has gone before. Most often, in fact, occurrences fail to rise to the level of what Badiou calls an 'event'. Rather than subtracting from local or global conditions, they simply rearrange or redeploy them. But, the radical contingency of the actual order of things makes it possible that, without adequate grounding in previous states of affairs, new configurations of value, meaning and power may emerge. This is what Meillassoux calls 'advent'. This utterly contingent eruption of novelty is conceivable in terms of any of the materialist ontologies surveyed in this book: it is the hopeful spectre that haunts the Deleuzian distinction between virtuality and actuality, the Badiouan distinction between mulitiplicity and the event, and Graham Harman's distinction between real and sensual objects. And what is more, we may affirm that for creativity to continue to actualise itself as creativity rather than an eternal return of the same, it is only as such novelties surface that God is expressed as God.

Therefore, though the emergence of novelty is absolutely contingent, there is in fact an ordering toward novelty that is intrinsic to creativity itself. And this means that it is not quite true that 'anything can happen', because much of what might happen wouldn't be a genuine 'happening', but only a kind of 'bare repetition' of the past. Systemic injustices and the hegemonies perpetuated by neoliberal governance continue to assert themselves, but there is an ontological if not ontic vector toward a kind of symmetry-breaking in which previous orders give way to the novel. Importantly, these breakthroughs may never occur – hope is and remains without guarantees. But we can hope in the continuing efficacy of creativity – that creativity will remain creative – and that means we can intelligibly hope for radical change. These two points are clearly in tension with each other: one suggests continuity and the other discontinuity. They reflect, respectively, the nomadic emphasis of the Deleuzian vector on which we have drawn throughout this book, and also the contrasting emphasis upon radical breaks we find in Badiou and Meillassoux. But this conceptual tension reflects the features of a posture of entangled fidelity: on the one hand, it is characterised by deep relations with a broad sweep of shifting, plural configurations of being and of power as it seeks to engage the world; on the other hand, it is oriented by a specific commitment and a particular hope for transformation. Both trajectories, therefore, are important for understanding a fidelity that is entangled.

From our perspective, there is no reason to suppose that this tension need be heightened to an outright contradiction: there is room for both, we believe, in a Latourian perspective that is characterised by contingent trials of strength between actants in an ever-evolving commonwealth. In the processes of taking into account and putting in order, there are stretches characterised by a high degree of continuity, others of nomadic experimentation on macro and micro levels; and there are also explosive moments of discontinuity, of breakthroughs to a new kind of order. But even these moments of symmetry-breaking never end the comparatively pedestrian process of collection itself: always, the commonwealth goes on by taking into account and putting in order. Thus a relational realist political theology of hope stresses the contingency of all our political, economic, social and ecclesiastical arrangements toward the end of pressing both quotidian practices and revolutionary breaks toward broader and fuller democratic participation for all actants, all constituents of the real. There is hope that our under-served and under-represented, both human and non-human, will find their voices and that their claims will be registered. The ongoing reconfiguration of the commonwealth is revolutionary, since it continually undermines static hegemonies and disrupts hierarchies. But such a politics is what both Leon Trotsky and H. Richard Niebuhr called a 'permanent revolution'.[18] Relational Christian realism veers toward a Niebuhrian deployment of this originally Marxist expression, specifying not so much a single, protracted step toward a communist end of historical struggle, as an unending series of transformations and realignments in which greater degrees of equality and democratic participation are always at hand as concrete possibilities. Revolution is permanent because the politics of the multitude is not simply a matter of overthrowing reactionary forces – rather, it is a matter of continual adjustment to new political claims being made across the whole commonwealth of being. It is about making and sustaining durable attachments between objects that present themselves and advance their claims. We all, proletarian and bourgeois, Eastern and Western, human and non-human, living and nonliving, find our way in face of the virtual – in other words, in face of the empowering as well as limiting reality of a God who may come. It is with such hope that we risk all of the chanciness and the complexity of entanglement.

---

[18]   Leon Trotsky, *The Permanent Revolution* (New York, NY: Pathfinder Press, 1969). Niebuhr's reappropriation of the term is in H. Richard Niebuhr, *The Meaning of Revelation* (New York, NY: Macmillan, 1941), 133ff.

Bibliography

Andrew Adonis, *Education, Education, Education: Reforming England's Schools*, Biteback Publishing Ltd, London, 2012.

John Atherton, Christopher Baker and John Reader, *Christianity and the New Social Order: A Manifesto for a Fairer Future*, SPCK, London, 2011.

Augustine, *The City of God against the Pagans*, ed. and trans. R.W. Dyson, Cambridge University Press, Cambridge, UK, 1998.

Augustine, *The Trinity*, trans. Edmund Hillk, O.P., ed., John E. Rotelle, O.S.A., New City Press, New York, NY, 1991.

Alain Badiou, *Being and Event*, trans. Oliver Feltham, Continuum Books, London, UK, 2005.

Alain Badiou, *Deleuze: The Clamor of Being*, University of Minnesota Press, London, UK, 2000.

Alain Badiou, *Philosophy for Militants*, Verso, London, UK, 2012.

Alain Badiou, *Second Manifesto for Philosophy*, Polity Press, Cambridge, UK, 2011.

Alain Badiou, *St Paul: The Foundation of Universalism*, Stanford University Press, Stanford, CA, 2003.

Alain Badiou, *The Century*, Polity Press, Cambridge, UK, 2007.

Alain Badiou, *Theory of the Subject*, Bloomsbury Academic, London, UK, 2013.

Caroline Baillie, Jens Kabo and John Reader, *Heterotopia: Alternative Pathways to Social Justice*, Zero Books, Alresford, UK, 2013.

Chris Baker and Hannah Skinner, *Faith in Action – The Dynamic Connection between Religious and Spiritual Capital*, William Temple Foundation, Manchester, UK, 2006.

Chris Baker, Entry to Enterprise: Constructing Local Political Economies in Manchester, in John Atherton and Hannah Skinner (eds), *Through the Eye of a Needle – Theological Conversations over Political Economy*, Epworth Press, Peterborough, UK, 2007.

Christopher Baker, *The Hybrid Church in the City – Third Space Thinking*, SCM Press, London, UK, 2009.

Chris Baker, John Reader and Daniel Whistler, Speculative Philosophies and Religious Practices – New Directions in the Philosophy of Religion and Post-secular Practical Theology, *Political Theology* 13.2, 2012.

Christopher Baker, Roots and shoots and the curious case of Schleiermacher's tree (aka 'Is rhizomatic truth seceding arborescent reality?'), *International Journal of Practical Theology* 17.2, 2013.

Karl Barth, *The Epistle to the Romans*, 6th ed., trans. Edwyn C. Hoskyns, Oxford University Press, London, UK, 1933.

Karl Barth, *The Word of God and the Word of Man*, trans. Douglas Horton, Harper and Row, New York, NY,1957.

John C. Bennett, *Christian Realism*, Student Christian Movement Press, London, UK, 1941.

Franco 'Bifo' Berardi, *The Uprising: On Poetry and Finance*, Semiotext(e), Los Angeles, CA, 2012.

Ian Bogost, *Alien Phenomenology: Or What It's Like to Be a Thing*, University of Minnesota Press, Minneapolis, MN, 2012.

Dietrich Bonhoeffer, *Ethics*, trans. Neville Horton Smith, Simon and Schuster, New York, NY, 1955.

Mark Bonti and John Protevi, *Deleuze and Geophilosophy: A Guide and Glossary*, Edinburgh University Press, Edinburgh, UK, 2006.

Rosi Braidotti, Nomadic Ethics, in Daniel W.Smith and Henry Somers-Hall (eds), *The Cambridge Companion to Deleuze*, Cambridge University Press, Cambridge, UK, 2012.

Rosi Braidotti, *Nomadic Theory: The Portable Rosi Braidotti*, Columbia University Press, New York USA, 2010.

Rosi Braidotti, *The Posthuman*, Polity Press, Cambridge, UK, 2013.

Ray Brassier, *Nihil Unbound: Enlightenment and Extinction*, Palgrave Macmillan, London, UK, 2007.

Levi Bryant, *The Democracy of Objects*, Open Humanities Press, Ann Arbor, MI, 2011.

Rudolph Bultmann, *History and Eschatology: The Presence of Eternity*, Harper and Brothers, New York, NY, 1957.

Alex Callinicos, *The Resources of Critique*, Polity Press, Cambridge, UK, 2006.

Helen Cameron, John Reader, Victoria Slater with Chris Rowland, *Theological Reflection for Human Flourishing*, SCM Press, London, UK, 2012.

Manuel Castells, *Networks of Outrage and Hope: Social Movements in the Internet Age*, Polity Press, Cambridge, UK, 2012.

Martin L. Cook, *The Open Circle: Confessional Method in Theology*, Fortress Press, Minneapolis, MN, 1991.

Simon Critchley, *The Faith of the Faithless: Experiments in Political Theology*, Verso, London, UK, 2012.

Clayton Crockett, *Deleuze Beyond Badiou: Ontology, Multiplicity and Event*, Columbia University Press, New York, NY, 2013.

Colin Crouch, *The Strange Non-death of Neoliberalism*, Polity Press, Cambridge, UK, 2011.

Antonio Damasio, *Descartes' Error: Emotion, Reason and the Human Brain*, Picador, London, UK, 1995.

Peter Dauvergne and Genevieve Lebaron, *Protest Inc: The Corporatization of Activism*, Polity Press, Cambridge, UK, 2014.

Miguel De Beistegui, The Deleuzian Reversal of Platonism, in Daniel W. Smith and Henry Somers-Hall (eds), *The Cambridge Companion to Deleuze*, Cambridge University Press, Cambridge, UK, 2012.

Arne De Boever, Alex Murray, Jon Roffe and Ashley Woodward (eds), *Gilbert Simondon: Being and Technology*, Edinburgh University Press, Edinburgh, UK, 2012.

Gilles Deleuze, *Difference and Repetition*, Continuum Books, London, UK, 1994.

Gilles Deleuze, Immanence: A Life in *Pure Immanence: Essays on A Life*, trans. Anne Boyman, Zone Books, New York, NY, 2001.

Gilles Deleuze and Félix Guattari, *Anti-Oedipus*, Continuum Books, London, UK, 2006.

Gilles Deleuze and Félix Guattari, *A Thousand Plateaus: Capitalism and Schizophrenia*, Continuum Books, London, UK, 2008.

Gilles Deleuze and Félix Guattari, *What is Philosophy?* Columbia University Press, USA, 1994.

Susan Nelson Dunfee, *Beyond Servanthood: Christianity and the Liberation of Women*, University Press of America, Lanham, MD, 1989.

Jonathan Edwards, Dissertation on the End for which God Created the World in *The Works of Jonathan Edwards*, Vol. 1, Banner of Truth, Edinburgh, UK, 1979.

Jonathan Edwards, The Nature of True Virtue in *The Works of Jonathan Edwards*, Vol. 1, rev. Edward Hickman, Banner of Truth, Edinburgh, UK, 1979.

Edward Farley, *Ecclesial Reflection: An Anatomy of Theological Method*, Fortress Press, Philadelphia, PA, 1982.

Richard Florida, *The Rise of the Creative Class, Basic Books*, New York, NY, 2002.

Paulo Freire, *Pedagogy of the Oppressed*, Penguin Books Ltd, London, UK, 1972.

Francis Gauthier and Tuomas Martikainen (eds), *Religion in Consumer Society*, Ashgate, Farnham, UK, 2013.

B.A. Gerrish, *Continuing the Reformation: Essays on Modern Religious Thought*, University of Chicago Press, Chicago, IL, 1993.

B.A. Gerrish, 'Theology Within the Limits of Piety Alone: Schleiermacher and Calvin's Doctrine of God' in *The Old Protestantism and the New: Essays on the Reformation Heritage*, University of Chicago Press, Chicago, IL, 1982.

Langdon Gilkey, *Naming the Whirlwind: The Renewal of God-Language*, Bobbs-Merrill, Indianapolis, IN, 1969.

David Goodhew (ed.), *Church Growth in Britain: 1980 to the Present*, Ashgate, Farnham, UK, 2012.

Timothy Gorringe and Rose Beckham, *Transition Movement for Churches – A Prophetic Imperative for Today*, Canterbury Press, London, UK, 2013.

Elaine Graham, *Between a Rock and a Hard Place: Public Theology in a Post-Secular Age*, SCM Press Ltd, London, UK, 2013.

James M. Gustafson, *Ethics from a Theocentric Perspective*, Vol. I: Theology and Ethics, University of Chicago Press, Chicago, IL, 1981.

James M. Gustafson, *An Examined Faith: the Grace of Self-Doubt*, Fortress Press, Minneapolis, MN, 2004.

Gustavo Gutierrez, *A Theology of Liberation: History, Politics, and Salvation*, rev. ed., trans. and ed. Sister Caridad Inda and John Eagleson, Orbis Books, Maryknoll, NY, 1988.

Jürgen Habermas, Equal treatment of culture and the limits of postmodern liberalism, *Journal of Political Philosophy* 14.1, 2005.

Peter Hallward, *Out of This World: Deleuze and the Philosophy of Creation*, Verso Books, London, UK, 2006.

Michael Hardt and Toni Negri, *Commonwealth*, Harvard University Press, London, UK, 2009.

Michael Hardt and Toni Negri, *Empire*, Harvard University Press, London, UK, 2000.

Michael Hardt and Toni Negri, *Multitude*, Penguin Books, London, UK, 2004.

Graham Harman, *The Quadruple Object*, Zero Books, Alresford, UK, 2010.

Graham Harman, *Quentin Meillassoux: Philosophy on the Making*, Edinburgh University Press, Edinburgh, UK, 2011.

Graham Harman, *Towards Speculative Realism: Essays and Lectures*, Zero Books, Alresford, UK, 2009.

Charles Hartshorne, *The Divine Relativity: A Social Conception of God*, Yale University Press, New Haven, CT, 1948.

Julian N. Hartt, Encounter and Inference in Our Awareness of God in Joseph P. Whalen (ed.), *The God Experience: Essays in Hope,,* SJ, Newman Press, New York, NY, 1971.

Katherine Hayles, *How We Became Posthuman: Virtual Bodies in Cybernetics, Literature, and Informatics*, University of Chicago Press, Chicago, IL, 1999.

Paul Heelas and Linda Woodhead, *The Spiritual Revolution: Why Religion is giving way to Spirituality*, Blackwell, Oxford, UK, 2005.

Ivan Illich, *Deschooling Society*, Marion Boyers Publishing Ltd, London, UK, 2002.

Tim Ingold, *Being Alive: Essays in Movement, Knowledge and Description*, Routledge, Abingdon, UK, 2011.

Thomas A. James, Responsibility Ethics and Postliberalism: Rereading H. Richard Niebuhr's The Meaning of Revelation, *Political Theology* 13.1, 2012: 40–49.

Immanuel Kant, *A Critique of Practical Reason*, trans. T.K. Abbott, Prometheus Books, Amherst, NY, 1996.

Immanuel Kant, *Religion Within the Limits of Reason Alone*, trans. Theodore M. Greene and Hoyt H. Hudson, Harper and Row, New York, NY, 1960.

Daniel Kahneman, *Thinking Fast and Slow*, Allen Lane, London, UK, 2011.

Gordon D. Kaufman, *In Face of Mystery: A Constructive Theology*, Harvard University Press, Cambridge, MA, 1993.

Gordon D. Kaufman, On Thinking of God as Serendipitous Creativity, *Journal of the American Academy of Religion* 69, 2001.

Søren Kierkegaard, *The Sickness Unto Death: A Christian Psychological Exposition for Edification and Awakening by Anti-Climacus*, trans. Alistair Hannay, Penguin Books, London, UK, 1989.

Christoph Koch, *Consciousness: Confessions of a Romantic Reductionist*, MIT Press, London and Cambridge, MA, 2012.

Joseph Ladue, *The Synaptic Self: How Our Brains Become Who We Are*, Penguin Books, New York, NY, 2002.

Bruno Latour, Its Development Stupid or How to Modernize Modernization, in Jim Proctor (ed.), *Postenvironmentalism*, MIT Press, Cambridge, MA, 2008.

Bruno Latour, *On the Modern Cult of the Factish Gods*, Duke University Press, Durham, NC, 2010.

Bruno Latour, *The Pasteurization of France*, trans. Alan Sheridan and John Law, Harvard University Press, Cambridge, MA, 1993.

Bruno Latour, *Pandora's Hope: Essays on the Reality of Science Studies*, Harvard University Press, Cambridge, MA, 1999.

Bruno Latour, *Politics of Nature: How to Bring the Sciences into Democracy*, Harvard University Press, Cambridge, MA, 2004.

Bruno Latour, *Reassembling the Social: An Introduction to Actor Network Theory*, Oxford University Press, Oxford, UK, 2005.

Bruno Latour, *Rejoicing: On the Torments of Religious Speech*, Polity Press, Cambridge, UK, 2013.

Bruno Latour, Will non-humans be saved? An Argument in Ecotheology, *Journal of the Royal Anthropological Institute* 15, 2009.

Bruno Latour, Why has Critique Run out of Steam? From Matters of Fact to Matters of Concern, *Critical Inquiry* 30, Winter 2004.

John Law and John Hassard, *Actor Network Theory and After*, Blackwell Publishing, Oxford, UK, 2005.

Immanuel Levinas, *Totality and Infinity*, trans. Alphonso Lingis, Duquesne University Press, Pittsburgh, PA, 1969.

John Macquarrie, *Principles of Christian Theology*, Second Edition, Charles Scribner's Sons, New York, NY, 1977.

Catherine Malabou, *Ontology of the Accident: An Essay on Destructive Plasticity*, trans. Carolyn Shread, Polity Press, Cambridge, UK, 2012.

Catherine Malabou, *Plasticity at the Dusk of Writing: Dialectic, Destruction, Deconstruction*, trans. Carolyn Shread, Columbia University Press, New York, NY, 2010.

Catherine Malabou, *What Should We Do with Our Brain?* trans. Sebastian Rand, Fordham University Press, New York, NY, 2008.

Jean-Luc Marion, *God Without Being, Hors Texte*, 2nd ed., trans. Thomas A. Carlson, University of Chicago Press, Chicago, IL, 2012.

Colin McFarlane, Assemblage and Critical Urbanism, *City*, 15.2, 2011.

Quentin Meillassoux, *After Finitude: An Essay on the Necessity of Contingency*, Continuum Books, London, UK, 2008.

Quentin Meillassoux, Spectral Dilemma, *Collapse* IV, May 2008.

Bernard Meland, *Fallible Forms and Symbols: Discourses on Method in a Theology of Culture*, Fortress, Philadelphia, PA, 1976.

Andy Mellon and Neil Hollow, *No Oil in the Lamp: Fuel, Faith and the Energy Crisis*, Darton, Longman and Todd, London, UK, 2012.

Mary Midgley, *Beast and Man: The Roots of Human Nature*, Routledge, London, UK, 1979.

John Milbank, *Being Reconciled: Ontology and Pardon*, Routledge, London, UK, 2003.

John Milbank, *The Future of Love: Essays in Political Theology*, Cascade Books, Eugene, OR, 2009.

John Milbank, *Theology and Social Theory: Beyond Secular Reason*, 2nd ed., Blackwell, Oxford, UK, 2006.

Adam S. Miller, *Speculative Grace: Bruno Latour and Object-Oriented Theology*, Fordham University Press, New York, NY, 2013.

Philip Mirowski, *Never Let a Serious Crisis Go to Waste – How Neo-liberalism Survived the Financial Meltdown*, Verso Press, London, UK, 2013.

Jürgen Moltmann, *The Coming of God: Christian Eschatology*, trans. Margaret Kohl, Fortress Press, Minneapolis, MN, 1996.

Jürgen Moltmann, *Theology of Hope: On the Ground and Implications of a Christian Eschatology*, trans. James W. Leitch, Harper and Row, New York, NY, 1967.

Timothy Morton, *The Ecological Thought*, Harvard University Press, Cambridge, MA, 2010.

Timothy Morton, *Realist Magic: Objects, Ontology, Causality*, Open Humanities Press, Ann Arbor, MI, 2013.

H. Richard Niebuhr, *Christ and Culture*, Harper and Row, New York, NY, 1951.

H. Richard Niebuhr, *Faith on Earth: An Inquiry into the Structure of Human Faith*, ed. Richard R. Niebuhr, Yale University Press, New Haven, CT, 1989.

H. Richard Niebuhr, *The Meaning of Revelation*, Macmillan, New York, NY, 1941.

H. Richard Niebuhr, *Radical Monotheism and Western Culture*, Westminster/John Knox Press, Louisville, KY, 1960.

Reinhold Niebuhr, *Faith and History: A Comparison of Christian and Modern Views of History*, Charles Scribners Sons, New York, NY, 1951.

Reinhold Niebuhr, *An Interpretation of Christian Ethics*, Harper and Brothers, New York, NY, 1935.

Reinhold Niebuhr, *The Nature and Destiny of Man: A Christian Interpretation*, Vols I and II, Charles Scribners Sons, New York, NY, 1941, 1943.

Reinhold Niebuhr, The Sickness of American Culture, *The Nation* 166/9, 6 March, 1948.

Michael S. Northcott, *A Political Theology of Climate Change*, Wm B. Eerdmans Publishing Co., Grand Rapids, Michigan, MI, 2013.

Wolfhart Pannenberg, *Systematic Theology*, Vol. I, trans. Geoffrey W. Bromiley, Wm B. Eerdmans Publishing Co., Grand Rapids, MI, 1991.

Wolfhart Pannenberg, *Systematic Theology*, Vol. 3, trans. Geoffrey Bromiley, Wm B. Eerdmans Publishing Co., Grand Rapids, MI, 1997.

Wolfhart Pannenberg, et al., *Revelation as History*, trans. David Granskou, Macmillan, London, UK, 1968.

Hollis Phelps, *Alain Badiou: Between Theology and Anti-Theology*, Acumen Publishing, Durham, UK, 2013.

Sarah Pink, *Situating Everyday Life: Practices and Places*, Sage, London, UK, 2012.

William C. Placher, *The Domestication of Transcendence: How Modern Thinking about God Went Wrong*, Westminster/John Knox Press, Louisville, KY, 1996.

John Protevi, Deleuze and Life, in Daniel W. Smith and Henry Somers-Hall (eds), *The Cambridge Companion to Deleuze*, Cambridge University Press, Cambridge, UK, 2012.

Jacques Ranciere, *The Ignorant Schoolmaster: Five Lessons in Intellectual Emancipation*, Stanford University Press, CA, 1991.

Larry L. Rasmussen, *Dietrich Bonhoeffer: Reality and Resistance*, Westminster/John Knox Press, Louisville, KY, 2005.

John Reader, *Blurred Encounters: A Reasoned Practice of Faith*, Aureus, Glamorgan, UK, 2005.

John Reader, *Local Theology: Church and Community in Dialogue*, SPCK, London, UK, 1994.

John Reader, *Reconstructing Practical Theology: The Impact of Globalization*, Ashgate, Aldershot, UK, 2008.

John Reader, Speculative Realism and Public Theology, *Special Edition of Political Theology* 13.2, April 2012.

John Reader, Truth in Science and Theology, in Christopher R. Baker and John Reader (eds), *Entering the New Theological Space: Blurred Encounters of Faith, Politics and Community*, Ashgate, Farnham, UK, 2009.

Lord Rogers of Riverside, *Towards a Strong Urban Renaissance*, HMSO, London, UK, 2005.

Friedrich Schleiermacher, *The Christian Faith*, trans. H.R. Mackintosh and J.S. Stewart, T and T Clark, Edinburgh, UK, 1999.

Laurel C. Schneider, *Beyond Monotheism: A Theology of Multiplicity*, Routledge, London, UK, 2008.

Laurel C. Schneider, Promiscuous Incarnation, in Margaret D. Kamitsuka (ed.), *The Embrace of Eros: Bodies, Desire, and Sexuality in Christianity*, Fortress Press, Minneapolis, MN, 2010.

Sergio Sismondo, *An Introduction to Science and Technology Studies*, Wiley-Blackwell, Oxford, UK, 2nd ed., 2010.

Baruch Spinoza, *Ethics*, trans. Samuel Shirley, Hackett Publishing, Indianapolis, IN, 1992.

Max Stackhouse, *Creeds, Society, and Human Rights: A Study in Three Cultures*, Wm B. Eerdmans Publishing Co., Grand Rapids, MI, 1984.

Isabelle Stengers, *Thinking with Whitehead*, Harvard University Press, Cambridge, MA, 2011.

Anna Strhan, *Levinas, Subjectivity, Education: Towards an Ethics of Radical Responsibility*, Wiley-Blackwell, Oxford, UK, 2012.

Nicholas Tampio, Assemblages and the multitude: Deleuze, Hardt, Negri and the postmodern left, *European Journal of Political Theory* 8, 2009.

Kathryn Tanner, Grace without Nature, in David Albertson and Cabell King (eds), *Without Nature? A New Condition for Theology*, Fordham University Press, New York, NY, 2010.

Charles Taylor, *A Secular Age*, Harvard University Press, Cambridge, MA, 2007.

Paul Tillich, *The Courage to Be*, Yale University Press, New Haven, CT, 1952.

Paul Tillich, *Systematic Theology*, three volumes, University of Chicago Press, Chicago, IL, 1951, 1957 1963.

Ernst Troeltsch, *The Christian Faith*, ed. Gertrud von le Fort, trans. Garrett E. Paul, Fortress Press, Minneapolis, MN,1991.

Leon Trotsky, *The Permanent Revolution*, Pathfinder Press, New York, NY, 1969.

Manuel Vasquez, *More Than Belief: A Materialist Theory of Religion*, Oxford University Press, Oxford, UK, 2011.

Francisco J. Verela, Evan Thompson and Eleanor Rosch, *The Embodied Mind: Cognitive Science and Human Experience*, MIT Press, Cambridge, MA, 1991.

Pete Ward (ed.), *Perspectives on Ecclesiology and Ethnography*, Wm B. Eerdmans Publishing Co., Grand Rapids, MI, 2012.

Derrick Watson, Critical acts of gathering: 'Old Men of Cathcart', green guerillas and new lines of desire. Unpublished paper for *Urban Shifts 2 – Desire Lines? Joining dots in local communities*, University of Chester, 2014.

Alfred North Whitehead, *Process and Reality: An Essay in Cosmology*, The Free Press, New York, NY, 1929.

Nathan Widder, *Political Theory After Deleuze*, Continuum Books, London, UK, 2012.

Andrew Williams, Postsecularism as Practice: theo-ethics and religion without religion in a Salvation Army Drug Programme. Unpublished paper given at the Compassion, Charity and Hope in the Postsecular City conference, University of Groningen, 2012.

James Williams, Difference and Repetition, in Daniel W Smith and Henry Somers-Hall (eds), *The Cambridge Companion to Deleuze*, Cambridge University Press, Cambridge, UK, 2012.

James Williams, *Gilles Deleuze's Logic of Sense: A Critical Introduction and Guide*, Edinburgh University Press, Edinburgh, UK, 2008.

Linda Woodhead and Rebecca Catto, *Religion and Change in Modern Britain*, Routledge, Abingdon, UK, 2012.

John Howard Yoder, *The Politics of Jesus: Vicit Agnus Noster*, 2nd ed., Wm B. Eerdmans Publishing Co., Grand Rapids, MI, 1994.

Index